Public Markets and Civic Culture in Nineteenth-Century America

PUBLISHING FOR THE WORLD
125 Years

THE JOHNS HOPKINS UNIVERSITY PRESS

CREATING THE NORTH AMERICAN LANDSCAPE

Gregory Conniff, Edward K. Muller, David Schuyler
CONSULTING EDITORS

George F. Thompson
SERIES FOUNDER AND DIRECTOR

Published in cooperation with the Center for American
Places, Santa Fe, New Mexico, and Harrisonburg, Virginia

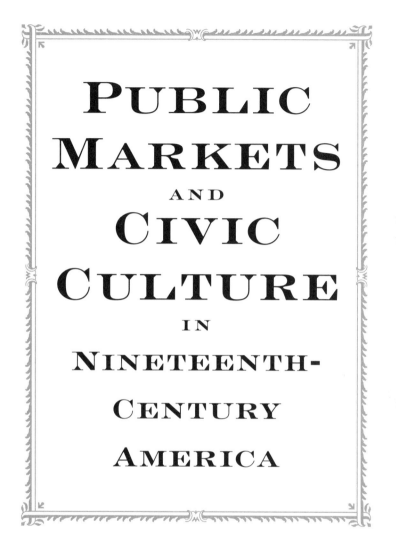

PUBLIC MARKETS

AND

CIVIC

CULTURE

IN

NINETEENTH-CENTURY AMERICA

HELEN TANGIRES

The Johns Hopkins University Press

BALTIMORE AND LONDON

2   4   6   8   9   7   5   3   1

The Johns Hopkins University Press
2715 North Charles Street
Baltimore, Maryland 21218-4363
www.press.jhu.edu

Library of Congress Cataloging-in-Publication Data

Tangires, Helen 1956–
Public markets and civic culture in nineteenth-century America /
Helen Tangires.
p.   cm. — (Creating the North American landscape)
Includes bibliographical references and index.
ISBN 0-8018-7133-6 (hardcover : alk paper)
1. Markets—United States—History—19th century. I. Title. II. Series.
HF5472.U6 T36 2003
381'.1'097309034—dc21   2002005381

A catalog record for this book is available from the British Library.

Frontispiece: John Ockershausen's condiment stand,
Center Market, Washington, D.C., 1917.

FOR DENNIS

CONTENTS

PREFACE

My interest in public markets, and in urban foodways more generally, began with my family's lunch wagon business in Baltimore. Although it was exciting to visit all corners of the city selling quick meals and snacks at construction sites, factories, and shipyards, I was always aware of the territorial nature of urban food retailing. Keeping us on guard were parking restrictions, unexpected competitors, random health inspections, and difficult weather. Despite the daily encounters on this urban battlefield, it was always reassuring to know that our business was part of a large network of social and economic relationships. Our suppliers of food, beverages, and paper goods were usually relatives or close friends, doing business in the city's wholesale districts and public markets.

The old Marsh Market, Baltimore's principal outlet for fresh produce, had been home to my grandfather's lunch stand, which he built from old crates under the rear sheds of the market about 1938. Curious to see a photograph of "Jim's Lunch," I found one in the records of the United States Department of Agriculture in the National Archives. This collection revealed a large and mostly hidden world of American public markets and inspired me to learn more about its buildings, people, and spaces.

Since I was starting on fresh ground, the history of public markets in nineteenth-century America offered me no canon to revise or texts to revisit. I am indebted, therefore, to three great teachers at George Washington University who helped me shape the theoretical framework for this book. Richard Longstreth persisted in ensuring that I articulate the architectural changes in the market house over time as well as the ways these buildings and spaces continued European precedents or diverged from them. His own work on the development of regional shopping malls and drive-in markets has been a model for exploring how the built environment contributes to a larger understanding of American culture. Howard Gillette Jr., now at Rutgers University–Camden, offered the viewpoint of a historian who looks critically at the way urban policy affects the quality of life in the American city. Reflecting his work, this book views the public market as an institution that has survived and adapted to new urban strategies and to social and economic imperatives to modernize. John Michael Vlach's work on the architecture of slavery seems a long way from market houses, but the unmeasured, unspoken, and unlegislated ways that folk created and appropriated space were relevant to the study of market butchers, farmers, and street vendors, who constantly pushed their mandated boundaries. Thanks to him, I have learned to look beyond the walls of the market house.

Other historians whose advice and criticism have been particularly helpful along the way include William Becker, Norma Evenson, James Henretta, Michael Lewis, Carl Lounsbury, Richard Stott, and Dell Upton. I also thank David Schuyler, of Franklin and Marshall College, and several anonymous readers who provided critical suggestions for strengthening the text.

My research was funded by a Robert H. Smith Fellowship from the National Gallery of Art, an Andrew W. Mellon Foundation Fellowship from the Library Company of Philadelphia, and the Scholar-in-Residence program of the Pennsylvania Historical and Museum Commission. Photographic support was provided in part by the Center for Advanced Study in the Visual Arts, National Gallery of Art.

Institutions whose staffs and resources were particularly helpful include the Library of Congress, National Agricultural Library, National Archives, National Gallery of Art, New-York Historical Society, New York Public Library, Pennsylvania State Archives, State Law Library of Pennsylvania, U.S. Department of Justice Library, and York County Heritage Trust, York County, Pennsylvania. David K. O'Neil, former manager of Reading Terminal Market, also deserves thanks for graciously letting me use his market archive and for sharing his firsthand knowledge and expertise in public market management. I also thank my colleagues at the Center for Advanced Study in the Visual Arts, National Gallery of Art, whose staff and fellows offer intellectual stimulation and an opportunity to share and exchange ideas, references, and visual materials. Special thanks go to Henry Millon and Therese O'Malley, whose encouragement over the years contributed significantly to the realization of this book, and to Elizabeth Cropper, who continues to make it possible for me to pursue scholarly work while at the Center.

I would also like to thank George F. Thompson at the Center for American Places for welcoming this book into the series and Randall Jones for helping me get the manuscript into shape. Alice Bennett deserves special thanks for her careful eye and suggestions at a critical moment in the book's process. Carol Zimmerman also deserves thanks for her editorial advice and for seeing production of the volume to its fruition.

Finally, my deepest appreciation goes to Dennis K. McDaniel for his indispensable observations, encouragement, and companionship. His acute political awareness, coupled with his appreciation for good food and travel, spiced this work in innumerable ways.

INTRODUCTION

I began this book as an exploration into the rise and decline of public markets, with the assumption that this form of urban food retailing had virtually disappeared from American cities, superseded by chain grocery stores and supermarkets. Moreover, in the late 1970s and early 1980s, the popularity of festival marketplaces such as Faneuil Hall in Boston and Baltimore's Harborplace only reinforced my assumption that real public markets were doomed to extinction, being slowly replaced by imitations designed primarily to attract tourists.

Subsequent events have changed my view that public markets are relics of the past. For at least three decades, people working in many disciplines and professions—economists, city planners, public policy analysts, historians, environmentalists, and others—have been seriously engaged in solving the problems of urban food distribution. They recognize the public market as an antidote to the serious breakdown in our contemporary food system, characterized by numerous product recalls and hygiene scandals and by the threat of global pandemics. The dangerous and immoral consequences of growing genetically engineered crops, of using bones and offal from diseased animals for feed, and of overcentralizing poultry, pork, and beef production have made us consider once again the benefits of local and regional markets. The public market will continue to be vital in sustaining agriculture, biodiversity, and a healthy relationship between urban and rural populations, economies, and production.

Public markets have also been valued as remedies for the social and economic deterioration of urban centers. When many urban supermarkets relocated to lower-rent suburban areas in the 1970s and 1980s, many of America's poorest urban residents were left without convenient, affordable fresh food. Since then, cities have taken an interest in developing public markets to revitalize neighborhoods and to provide healthy alternatives or supplements to supermarkets and other mass-market food outlets.

A strong social philosophy, combined with health concerns and recent food security disasters, continues to fuel the popularity of public markets as critical sources of the urban food supply. According to the National Farmers' Market Directory (2000), published by the United States Department of Agriculture, the number of farmers' markets grew by 63 percent in the last decade of the twentieth century, from 1,755 in 1994 to 2,863 in 2000. Coinciding with this boom has been an international public market conference sponsored by the Project for Public Spaces, held biannually since 1987 in various market-friendly cities in the United States and Canada. This conference draws participants ranging from individuals interested in starting an outdoor farmers' market in a downtown parking lot to managers of mammoth public markets such as Seattle's Pike Place. Being more than just agoraphiles, they share the belief that a public market is the key connecting point for food, land, and culture and that public markets stimulate local economies by forging links between consumers and producers.

The public market is a key piece in understanding the profoundly important shift from an agrarian to an industrial food system in nineteenth-century America. Public officials, farmers, butchers, commission merchants, consumers, and street vendors shaped public markets—the system and the buildings—in order to maintain their rights in a rapidly changing society. More than just public spaces for buying and selling food, public markets were civic spaces—the common ground where citizens and government struggled to define the shared values of the community. The public market is society's conscience—the place where we can evaluate our success or failure at organizing urban life.[1]

Anyone who consults a book on local urban history published in the nineteenth century is likely to find "markets" in the index. The establishment of the first market square, the building of a new market house, or the tearing down of an old market shed were all worthy of documenting in a town's early history. Yet rarely have contemporary urban historians acknowledged the persistent role that public markets continued to play in the evolving politics and urban landscape of the American city. Concentrating more on the development of new building types such as armories, libraries, parks, and schools, American urban history has ignored the way the public market persevered and adapted to a world changed by industrialization, technology, new patterns of consumption, and differing views on the role of government.

As a place where a wide variety of competing interests converged over issues of power and space, the public market is a compelling demonstration of the persistence of the moral economy despite the disruptive effects of a capitalist market economy in nineteenth-century America. The moral economy reflected local government's effort to maintain the social and political health of its community by regulating the ethics of trade in life's necessities. Since antiquity, cities have established market laws designed to limit profiteering and regulate built spaces devoted to the sale of basic foods, at times restricting individual liberty and property in order to guarantee citizens an adequate supply of healthful food at affordable prices. The city alone, however, did not manage the moral economy. The community helped to police and regulate the public market, the principal place where it could observe and respond to the successes and failures of its government.[2]

The public market in nineteenth-century America continued to reflect society's willingness to enforce the moral economy. Evidence can be found in the vast number of municipal ordinances, statutes, and legal cases that revealed the commitment of local government and the courts to protecting the common good through well-regulated public markets.[3] Evidence of the moral economy also can be found in the countryside, where behavior demonstrated that the welfare of the community often took precedence over individual gain and profit.[4]

Physical evidence that local government was expected to maintain the moral economy can be found in the market houses themselves, thousands of which dotted the American landscape in the nineteenth century. Whether a simple open-air shed or a major public building, the market house continued to reflect government's commitment to providing this basic public amenity. Because of its central location, access to roads and waterways, and open, flexible plan, the market house (and its environs) also was a focus of urban life and provided a place for public ceremony and display. The area might be used by street entertainers, public officials hosting a grand opening, or butchers parading prize cattle through the streets to the slaughterhouse. Like other public processions, ceremonies, and celebrations, those in and around the market house nurtured civic culture and pride.[5]

The public market system was still vital in nineteenth-century America, despite the proliferation of private meat shops and company-owned market houses. These individual privatization efforts did not go unchallenged, particularly where there was a long public market tradition, such as in New York and Pennsylvania. Thomas De Voe, a butcher in New York's Jefferson Market and superintendent of the city's public markets in the 1870s, understood the value of the public market tradition and fought relentlessly to save the system. He provides an important voice throughout this book. Other primary voices are the anonymous mayors who faced the privatization of public markets against their will, the judges who argued in favor of well-regulated markets, and the many vendors displaced by the transition from public markets to private meat shops and market houses.

I also draw on secondary sources on the history of public markets, which are vast but generally confined to specific disciplines. Analyses of central marketplaces and periodic markets (held cyclically on certain days of the week) have been the domain of economic anthropologists and ethnographers who study peasant societies and underdeveloped economies. In recent works these scholars have argued that markets in former peasant societies continue to integrate city and country, cut across class and ethnic lines, and promote social, political, and economic communications that are vital to regions dependent on both agriculture and industry.[6]

European urban historians have also contributed to the literature by considering the role of markets in city building. English scholars have been particularly prolific, proposing a well-developed market town thesis that has influenced the recent generation of local histories. Equally significant has been a new study of the grand age of market hall construction in Britain during the nineteenth century, when traditional open-air markets became mammoth multistory buildings.[7] Italian urban historians have focused on the architecture and civic culture of public markets in the early modern period—the very same buildings and spaces that are as much a part of civic life in Italy today as they were then.[8] In addition, they have taken the lead in developing a contemporary architectonics for understanding the structural dimensions of buildings and spaces devoted to food marketing.[9] Finally, no European public market has generated more scholarship than Les Halles, the central market in Paris. This institution has been the subject of an immense amount of study by architectural, urban, and social historians alike.[10]

Historiography in the United States has been equally varied. Architectural historian James Mayo identified some of the economic forces behind the transition from "street market houses" to "markets on the block"—a transition further demonstrated by Jay Barshinger's study of nineteenth-century market houses in southeastern Pennsylvania.[11] That the market house evolved into new architectural forms in the twentieth century—in response to the cultural and economic changes brought by the automobile—is best explained in Richard Longstreth's work on drive-in markets, chain grocery stores, and supermarkets in Los Angeles.[12]

Although one would expect to find an analysis of public markets in the literature on municipal history, oddly enough these studies treat markets as just one of many public services like roads, wharves, canals, bridges, water, sewerage, and lighting. As a result, they add little to our understanding of the market's contribution to political philosophy, civic culture, growth of cities, and the urban landscape. Likewise, historians of the late nineteenth-century city have overlooked the fact that public markets still dominated discussions in city council meetings during this time of rapidly expanding programs for the preservation of urban health, the construction of streets and waterworks, and the beautification of cities.[13]

This book moves chronologically, beginning in the aftermath of the American Revolution, when well-regulated public markets were intended to preserve the republican values of egalitarianism, good government, and citizenship. Part 1 establishes the context by presenting the basic components of a public market in the first three chapters: the laws and regulations, the buildings and spaces, and the market people—the street vendors, farmers, merchants, and consumers who together created a unique marketplace culture. All these features of the public market contributed to its reputation as a civic center.

Part 2 presents case studies of the most dramatic and well-documented examples of deregulation of public markets. Chapter 4 introduces the meat shop controversy that led to the legalization of private shops in New York City in 1843. Chapter 5 deals with the unparalleled construction of private market houses in Philadelphia after 1859, when the city removed the municipal market sheds from Market Street. Both movements—the meat shop controversy and the market house company mania—exposed the tensions that were paramount between government and business at midcentury.

The immediate consequences of deregulation are discussed in chapter 6, which describes the many changes that privatization brought to the urban landscape in Pennsylvania and New York City. New York was left with most of its market houses intact, though limping from neglect, but construction of new market houses was unsurpassed in the Commonwealth of Pennsylvania, which took the country's lead in incorporating market house companies. The private market houses in Pennsylvania were off the streets and claimed to be superior to public markets in service, atmosphere, and facilities. The alleged benefits of private market houses contributed to the overall culture of "laissez-faire" that dominated market politics at midcentury.[14]

Part 3 shows how local government devised strategies for maintaining, or in most cases regaining, control over urban food marketing and distribution. Chapter 7 begins with a broad look at the state of public markets in the United States after the Civil War, when the United States Department of Agriculture initiated cursory measures to improve them. More active, however, were the cities themselves, which took market reform into their own hands because they viewed the system as a viable alternative or complement to other systems of urban food retailing. Boston, for example, provides a colorful story of how a late nineteenth-century city came to recognize the disastrous consequences of deregulation. Chapter 8 describes the state of public markets at the end of the nineteenth century, when the desire for order, hygiene, and urbanity as well as cheap, affordable food for wage earners made public markets a solution—not a problem—in the industrialized city.

The alleged demise of public markets in the United States in the twentieth century is usually attributed to their having been "naturally" overtaken by chain grocery stores and then by supermarkets.[15] Although the public market did lose its dominant position in food marketing, I conclude that "market share" was not the most important factor in determining success or failure. Public markets survived and adapted—in tandem with other forms of urban food retailing—because of their inherent civic qualities and their ability to preserve a common ground for the public good. The history of public markets in nineteenth-century America also reminds us that for a long time we had a mechanism for monitoring the moral economy at the local level—where familiar people, in a familiar place, could see, hear, touch, taste, and smell whether government was doing its job.

PART I

Building the
Common Ground

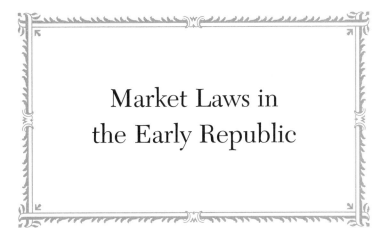

ONE

Market Laws in
the Early Republic

Your Honorable Board must no doubt see the propriety of
extending to the inhabitants of this district an equal facility of
procuring the necessities of life as their fellow-citizens enjoy in the
other wards. They beg leave to state that this vacant space remains
entirely unoccupied, and they can conceive no purpose to which it
can be applied with equal propriety as to that of a public market.

Inhabitants of the Fifth Ward,
New York City, 1805

W hen nearly two hundred inhabitants of New York's Fifth Ward petitioned the city council in 1805 for a market house at the foot of
Duane Street, they were continuing a long tradition. The public market was
a widespread urban institution in the early republic, as it had been since antiquity throughout the Western world. In addition to building wharves, docks,
bridges, and roads, local government was expected to provide facilities for
buying and selling food. These facilities were more than a mere convenience;
it was the duty of the state to ensure that the urban populace would have an
adequate, wholesome, and affordable supply of necessities. Regulated public
markets were critical to the survival of the town—without them unbridled
competition and unfair dealings could jeopardize the public welfare.[1]

Before the market house was ever built, laws and ordinances were in place to ensure equitable marketing at specified times and places. Although licenses, price controls, and regulations were not limited to food vendors, the sale of daily provisions under the careful guidance of the municipality was the overarching symbol of government's commitment to a well-ordered public economy. Deeply rooted in English and Continental common law, customs, and practices, market laws in the early Republic were intended to protect citizens from unfair commercial maneuvers such as buying products before they reached the market, monopolizing the market to drive up prices, and selling food that was spoiled or short in measure. They were also intended to encourage country producers to bring their goods into town and to stimulate employment in the food trades.[2]

In the aftermath of the American Revolution, citizens clung to the notion of regulated public markets, particularly after war disrupted normal trade patterns and created opportunities for hoarding, monopolizing, and creating artificial scarcity. Increased regulation and new market houses therefore were common features of postrevolutionary city government. But the scope of regulation went beyond enforcing ethical trade practices. Strengthened by postrevolutionary rhetoric, butchers clamored for more stalls, street vendors demanded the right to sell in the area around the marketplace, property owners insisted on new market houses to enhance the value of their holdings, and city officials searched for equitable methods of assigning stalls and spaces. All these pressures fueled the moral economy and prompted government to maintain its traditional role of providing a common ground for buying and selling food. Proponents of regulated public markets believed the system could foster the republican values of hard work, honesty, and good citizenship. It was in this spirit—the physical, moral, and sociophilosophical environment of the early Republic—that cities and towns in early nineteenth-century America embraced the public market tradition.[3]

The Municipal Corporation

Although some cities established markets on their own initiative, most were empowered to do so by colonial and subsequently state authority.[4] Once a state legislature authorized a newly incorporated town to establish and regulate markets, local officials quickly adopted existing state market laws or strengthened local ones. Such was the case in 1797, when the Maryland state legislature transferred responsibility for three markets to the city of Baltimore and granted authority to enact additional laws necessary to "suppress and prevent many inconveniences and abuses which have crept into the several markets of the said city." Likewise, the 1779 session of the Spanish colonial administration in New Orleans proposed construction of a market building to protect provisions from the elements. The council also hoped that a covered market "would result in untold good to the public."[5]

Local authorities collected taxes, tolls, stall rentals, licenses, and fines as payment for ensuring trustworthy weights and measures and for maintaining the market as a desirable place to buy and sell. Newly incorporated towns thus quickly established marketplaces, drafted regulations, and collected market revenues. Citizens expected an incorporated town to provide a public market. Traveler Anne Newport Royall understood this when she reported with astonishment that Staunton, Virginia, had "no market-house, nor has it either a watch or patrol, although it is an incorporated town."[6] Most incorporated towns had at least one market, depending on who was counting. According to John Melish, New York had five and Baltimore, Washington, and Philadelphia each had three. John Adams Paxton, however, reported nine markets in Philadelphia, counting separately the five sheds in High Street, two sheds at the South Second Street Market, and two sheds at the Northern Liberties Market.[7]

Unincorporated towns were usually too small to warrant a market house. Residents obtained fresh meat and vegetables through informal social networks such as trade or barter between farmers and neighbors, from itinerant peddlers or hawkers, from general stores, or from their own kitchen gardens. The absence of a public market in Hampton, Virginia, has been attributed not only to the availability of these alternatives but also to the town's proximity to the public markets of Norfolk and Williamsburg.[8]

Forestalling, Regrating, and Engrossing

Market laws reflected the universal need to curb unethical trade practices, particularly the trio of offenses known as forestalling, regrating, and engrossing. Forestalling, from the Old Saxon *fare*, to go, and *stall*, to hinder, meant buying goods privately before they had reached the open market, buying in the market before the accustomed hour, or spreading false rumors regarding available supplies. Violators were subject to a combination of fines, whipping,

In COUNCIL.

Philadelphia, July 8, 1779.

WHEREAS it is reprefented to this Board, that divers Irregularities and Abufes have lately happened in the public Markets, highly difcouraging and injurious to the good People of the Country, and tending to prevent the ufual and neceffary Supplies for the ufe of this City. AND WHEREAS it alfo appears, that notwithftanding the Clerk of the Market, divers Conftables, and many well-difpofed Private Citizens, have attempted to prevent the Abufes above-mentioned, yet the fame were continued on the laft Market-Day, from which there is great reafon to believe, that many difaffected and ill-defigning Perfons are endeavouring to diftrefs the City, and thereby excite Tumults and Infurrections. Therefore,

Refolved,

That the Juftices, High Sheriff, and Conftables, be directed to attend at the Market, for the Prefervation of the public Peace, and the protection of fuch Perfons as fhall expofe Commodities to Sale, and that they be directed to arreft and commit to Goal all Perfons without favour or affection, who fhall be found difturbing the Peace and good Order of the Market, in order that they may be dealt with according to Law. And that it be alfo recommended to the well-difpofed and faithful Citizens, not only to difcountenance fuch Practices, but to give all Aid and Affiftance to the Officers of Juftice, in the difcharge of their Duty on this Occafion. It being the determined Refolution of this Board, fully and effectually to protect and fupport the Inhabitants of the Country, in their intercourfe with the City. And that this Refolve be immediately publifhed in Hand-Bills, and that the Sheriff caufe it to be Proclaimed through the City on Friday next.

Extract from the Minutes,

T. MATLACK, *Secretary.*

PHILADELPHIA: Printed by FRANCIS BAILEY, in *Market-Street.*

FIGURE 1.1 Broadside warning citizens about forestalling in the public markets, Philadelphia, July 8, 1779. The Library Company of Philadelphia.

and confiscation of goods. An 1819 ordinance from St. Francisville, Louisiana, was typical: no one could sell meat, fish, wild game, poultry, eggs, cheese, butter, fruits, or vegetables "within market hours at any place within this town except at the market house and in open market and under the regulations for the government of the market." Similarly, the 1809 market regulations of Fredericksburg, Virginia, forbade the sale of provisions during market hours "in any part of the Corporation, or within the jurisdiction thereof except at the Public Market." While such laws against forestalling appear contrary to modern notions of free enterprise, there were practical reasons to forbid the sale of food beyond the legal boundaries of the public market. Consumers could procure their daily provisions from a single convenient location and could choose among several vendors; and by consolidating market activities the municipality could easily enforce health codes, police the market, and collect revenues.

Government maintained the right to restrict vendors' mobility because of the strong belief that selling food anywhere but in the public markets would threaten the survival of the Republic. Enforcement depended on informants, particularly in large cities like New York and Philadelphia, where it was difficult for a market clerk to discover private dealings in every neighborhood or along the docks (fig. 1.1). In 1786 the New York city council heard complaints that forestallers in the public markets committed "great abuses," and it ordered a committee to investigate the matter. Again in 1801, the council received a petition from nine of the city's most prominent butchers against Henry Astor, whom they accused of forestalling and of not personally attending his stall in Fly Market. Astor reportedly left his stall in the care of an unlicensed butcher while he rode into the countryside to intercept cattle drovers coming into New York. Astor, they claimed, purchased cattle privately not only for himself but also for other butchers. The petitioners complained that they were unable to do anything about Astor's "pernicious practices," which were "to the great detriment of the city." Forestalling was still a problem in 1811, since the council reported that the practice was constantly increasing.[9]

In 1797 a farmer complained to a Philadelphia newspaper that hucksters aggressively jumped onto farmers' boats before they had landed. "This is one of the many instances of these people's forestalling our markets by which means I believe they raise a tax upon us of one half and sometimes more than one half of the amount of our Market-house," the farmer wrote. He blamed the absence of market clerks, who had left the city during the yellow fever epidemic. Without law enforcement, the farmer argued, "the markets were, of course, consigned to [forestallers] who oppress the people as they will."[10]

Although laws against forestalling dealt with people who purchased goods from farmers en route to market, legislation was also necessary to prevent vendors from buying goods in the market with the intent of resale. Known as regrating, from the Old French *regrateor,* meaning peddler or huckster, this practice—like forestalling—was illegal, or closely circumscribed, to encourage people to buy directly from the producer and to encourage centralized competition. For example, a city of Washington ordinance of October 6, 1802, made it illegal to purchase provisions or food in Centre Market during market hours "for the purpose of selling the same again in the said market, or in any part of the city." Such antiregrating ordinances and restrictions on peddlers and hucksters were common.

Market laws also aimed to protect wage earners from engrossing—the illegal practice of hoarding in order to create artificial scarcity and drive up prices. In 1777 in New York, "monopolizing hucksters" purchased large quantities of potatoes and turnips, stored them in cellars near the dock, and "afterwards introduce[d] them into the market, and dispose[d] them at a very exorbitant price." The mayor ordered the vegetables seized and sent to the public almshouse. Although engrossing was a common offense during war, this unethical trade practice persisted in peacetime and extended to all kinds of provisions, necessitating regulation. No one in Trenton, New Jersey, for example, was allowed to buy more than twelve pounds of butter on any one market day; and to protect the supply of wild game, 1812 Philadelphia ordinances forbade killing certain species of fowl during specified months of the year, so as not "to deprive the market of that regular and wholesome supply." Social reformers in the early Republic, such as the New York surgeon Samuel Latham Mitchill, valued strict engrossing laws because a stable food supply would guarantee that the "poorest mechanic" could afford "the common necessaries of life."[11]

Weights and Measures

City dwellers also depended on local government to ensure that vendors used legal weights and measures. Market ordinances invariably contained a section that empowered the market clerk not only to examine and test privately owned scales and balances but also to check goods for proper weight using the official scales provided by the corporation. Goods suspected of being short in weight or measure were weighed in front of witnesses, which often caused a scene. In 1831 the market master of York allegedly caught a farmer named Herman selling light-weight butter. The market master seized Herman's basket, sold the butter, and delivered the proceeds to the borough coffers. Herman not only sustained an economic loss but also suffered the public humiliation of scowls and finger pointing from cheated customers and from other vendors angry because he had compromised the integrity of their market (fig. 1.2).

Local officials in Washington required vendors in the city markets to sell only goods that had been weighed on scales stamped by the sealer of weights and measures. The ordinance of March 29, 1806, required anyone guilty of using "steelyards, patent balances, or scales falsely balanced" to forfeit the equipment and pay a $5 fine—half going to the corporation and the other half to the informant. Although ordinances concerning weights and measures varied slightly from city to city, their principles were the same. They were intended to demonstrate government's duty and obligation to protect the public from even the slightest profiteering, fraud, and cheating. Market clerks confiscated provisions from forestallers or impounded goods weighing less than the standard measure and gave them over to the poorhouse, hospital, or asylum.

Protecting the Trades

Market laws also protected the trades by a strict allocation of vocational duties and opportunities. Only a licensed butcher in an official stall or place of standing could cut up meat in quarters, joints, or small pieces in the public markets. Violators, known as shinners, shirkers, or sharks, were vendors posing as country butchers, butchers who had lost their licenses but continued to practice the trade illegally, or agents who sold on commission for farmers. Left over from the medieval guild system, municipal laws against shinners were intended to protect legitimate butchers from those who practiced the craft without paying the fees for stall rent and licenses.[12]

Baltimore's 1805 ordinances protected local provisioners and manufacturers by requiring that meats and vegetables sold in the markets be raised by the farmer or producer. Similar ordinances specified that goods sold there be manufactured in the United States. These laws demonstrate an insistence on

FIGURE 1.2 Market master seizing light-weight butter from a farmer in the York
market. Watercolor by Lewis Miller, 1831. The York County Heritage Trust,
Pennsylvania.

the priority of local and regional markets—a fundamental feature of the moral economy. Without such restrictions, farmers could produce for more profitable distant markets while neglecting their own communities.

The Market Peace

Local government was also responsible for enforcing the market peace—a term used since the Middle Ages to describe a protected environment where buyers and sellers could effectively carry on trade. Maintaining the market peace included providing good roads for farmers going to market, protecting them against thieves, and keeping the marketplace in good order. In short, the peace referred to making the market safe both physically and economically.

Cities employed several techniques for maintaining order. Typical were provisions that forbade the sale of "wine, beer, or spiritous liquors of any kind" within the limits of the market. Furthermore, the constable was authorized to remove people who were disorderly, sitting, and sleeping. By 1835 a St. Louis ordinance was specific about the offenses that were grounds for arrest: being found to be "drunk, fighting, quarreling, reviling, threatening, swearing, blackguarding, pilfering, stealing, robbing, cheating, swindling or disturbing the good people, at or about, said market."

Order was maintained with strict parking ordinances for wagons, which established the times and places for unloading goods and restricted traffic through the market during business hours. Typically the city controlled traffic by temporarily hanging chains across the streets leading to the market. Philadelphia ordinances, for example, devoted pages to the exact times and places for "strong chains, well secured," to be stretched across the passages to keep people, carriages, and horses from entering. The ordinances also required market clerks to ring the courthouse bell ten minutes before fixing the chains, so that butchers had time to move their wagons. Other social welfare institutions in the nineteenth century, including prisons, asylums, almshouses, and schools, used similar techniques for controlling behavior and enforcing the strict allocation of space. In all its manifestations, the desire to maintain regularity, punctuality, and order was a common feature in the urban landscape of the new Republic.[13]

Judging from travelers' accounts, Philadelphia's High Street Market was a model of order (fig. 1.3). Attributing it to Quaker morality, J. P. Brissot de Warville wrote that "these people are composed and orderly in everything they do, even in the way the produce wagons and horses are lined up in the neighboring streets in order of their arrival. . . . Here is one of the most striking effects of habit, a habit inspired by the Quakers, who have implanted morality in this country, the habit of performing everything quietly, reasonably, and above all without injury to anyone and without the need for the intervention of a magistrate."[14] Similarly, Francis Baily commented on his visit to High Street Market that the city "is under an excellent police." In 1787 Rev. Manasseh Cutler observed that "every thing is adjusted in perfect order . . . , the marketers seemed to be all in and every thing arranged," and there was "no clamorous noise nor crying of wares of any kind." Josiah Quincy Jr. remarked that "the Philadelphians boast of their markets, and most of the southern gentlemen justify this vaunting: it is undoubtedly the best regulated on the continent." Concluding his remarks on High Street Market, Brissot de Warville claimed that "to maintain order in a market of this size in France you would need three or four police officers and a dozen soldiers. Here, law needs no muskets; education, morality, and habit do everything."[15]

Underpinning the apparent ability of Philadelphia Quakers to regulate themselves, of course, were elaborate and lengthy market ordinances that dictated, among other things, the placement of vendors. Two rows of fish vendors, five feet apart, facing each other with their baskets in front of them, were to line up on the south side of High Street. Produce from New Jersey could be sold only in the Jersey Market. A line of stands was devoted strictly to the sale of locally produced earthenware. And places were designated for the sale of fruit, garden seeds, meat, country produce, roots, herbs, vegetables, and meal.

Fixing Market Days and Hours

Another way the municipality ensured the integrity and success of the market was to fix days and hours of operation. The colonial practice was two days a week, usually Wednesday and Saturday, beginning at daylight and ending in late morning or early afternoon, depending on the season. Monday was the least common market day, because butchers would have to slaughter meat, and farmers gather produce, on the Sabbath. By the early Republic cities more typically held markets daily except Sunday, depending on local need. In places with multiple markets, local government set alternate days of operation. For example, when a second market house opened in Frederick, Mary-

FIGURE 1.3 High Street Market, Philadelphia. Drawn and engraved by William and Thomas Birch, 1798–1800. I. N. Phelps Stokes Collection, Miriam and Ira D. Wallach Division of Art, Prints and Photographs. The New York Public Library, Astor, Lenox and Tilden Foundations.

land, a new ordinance in 1835 declared that "markets shall be held in Frederick, every week, on Tuesday, Thursday and Saturday, at the market house on Market street, and on Wednesday and Friday at the market house on Patrick street." This traditional practice, known as the market cycle, was intended to keep multiple markets from interfering with each other.

The market clerk announced the hours with handbells or by ringing the bells in the courthouse or market house belfry, and no one was permitted to buy or sell outside those hours. In St. Louis, an ordinance of May 20, 1823, declared market hours "from daylight in the morning until twelve o'clock from the 1st of April until the 1st of September, and from daylight to 2 o'clock from the 1st of September until the 1st of April." "Daylight," of course, was subject to interpretation, and some cities had to be more specific. In 1835 the Frederick city council declared opening hours to begin "as soon as it is light enough to distinguish and count money."

In some cities, including New Orleans, certain provisions such as grain, fruit, and vegetables could be sold after market hours, probably because these products were less likely to spoil than meat or fish. Despite minor variations, limited market days and hours ensured simultaneous selling, minimized the length of time food was exposed to the elements, and allowed time to clear the market of trash and in some cases of ice and snow.

Limits of the Market

The municipalities designated spatial boundaries known as the "limits of the market." The 1805 ordinances of Baltimore, for example, defined the legal limits of Fells Point Market as beginning at the south side of Aliceanna Street and extending southward on the line of the curbs on each side of Market Street to a line drawn from the northeast corner of George Street to the northwest corner of Fells Street.

Municipalities also regulated the times and places for selling fish and livestock outside market houses. In port cities like Portsmouth, Virginia, fish and oysters could be sold directly from boats, according to an ordinance from March 2, 1811. In Wilmington, Delaware, an 1822 ordinance established separate markets for different kinds of provisions. Fish dealers could sell on Saturdays at the west end of the Fourth Street Market and on Wednesdays at the east end of the Second Street Market. Farmers from nearby New Jersey could sell on the south side of Second Street between Market and King. The cattle and horse market was on Second Street, between Market and Orange. Separating markets in time and space made it easier to enforce market laws and disperse traffic.

Duties of the Market Clerk

Municipal laws and ordinances prescribed the rules and boundaries of exchange, but ultimately the market's success depended on the clerk. Typically a mayoral appointee, the clerk assigned stalls, collected rent and fines, inspected food for quality and for proper weight and measure, and kept the market policed and swept. Duties varied in scope in different cities, with larger cities appointing a clerk for each market. Market revenues supported the clerk's salary, which could be fixed, a commission based on fees collected, or a combination. Salaries depended on the size of the market. In 1797 in Baltimore, for example, the clerk's annual salary was $150 at Center Market; $100 at Fells Point Market; and $80 at Hanover Market. In contrast, the clerk of Philadelphia's vast High Street Market commanded an annual salary of $700.

An important responsibility of the position was collecting fees, so market clerks were often bonded and sworn to loyalty. Cities wanted clerks who were trustworthy and honest, but they had varying success in finding candidates with such qualities. When James Culbertson and Rinier Skaats, the clerks of New York's Fly Market, collected more market fees than usual in 1790, city authorities rewarded them with a bonus and authorized a commission of 10 percent on future fees collected. They also praised the clerks for being model public servants and exclaimed, "What a pity we had not a *few* Culbertsons and Skaatses now-a-days to handle the public moneys, as well as to fill many of the public offices!" In 1792 Culbertson issued fifty fines: seventeen for light-weight butter, ten for spoiled meat and poultry, nine for forestalling, and the rest for selling meat through an agent and for selling goods forbidden in the public markets.[16]

The City of Norfolk was less successful in finding trustworthy clerks: it appointed thirteen between 1784 and 1797, evidently because of numerous scandals involving conduct and the pocketing of rent. In 1785 the council appointed a committee to investigate clerk Nathaniel Murphy. The committee removed Murphy and replaced him with James Boushell, who likewise was dismissed the next year with an injunction to pay debt, probably rent from stalls that he had withheld.[17]

Since market revenues were important to city coffers, some ordinances explicitly forbade clerks to accept bribes. Anyone who found a clerk behaving in an illegal, defiant, or negligent manner was encouraged to report the act—and would be rewarded with half the fine. Where there was no time to notify the clerk of offenses, self-policing was expected. In 1819, when John All-bricht, a wagon maker, was caught stealing beef from a market stall in York, Pennsylvania, no one waited to find the clerk. Several butchers took the law into their own hands by pelting the thief with raw meat (fig. 1.4).

Public Health

The most controversial aspect of the clerk's position was inspecting meat for spoilage, and for this job he relied on witnesses. In New York the clerk or his deputy, and any two butchers of his choice, could attest to "unwholesome"

FIGURE 1.4 Butchers apprehending a thief at York Market. Watercolor by Lewis Miller, 1831. The York County Heritage Trust, Pennsylvania.

meat. In Fredericksburg, Virginia, the clerk could fine sellers of spoiled meat, but condemnation required a magistrate. The clerk's authority may have differed from city to city, but enforcement was consistent: spoiled meat and poultry, as well as unclean furnishings, were thrown into the river or publicly burned. Violators were also charged a heavy fine, and part went to buy firewood for the conflagration. Wholesome meat was critical to the health and well-being of the community: failure to enforce inspection laws could create a public health hazard, not to mention embarrassing local officials.[18]

Related to laws against unwholesome food were those that dictated procedures for sanitary food handling and garbage disposal. Local ordinances forbade vendors to throw offal, dead fish, or rotten produce into the streets. New Orleans police codes extended sanitation laws to meat being transported to market. They required a covered cart "specially kept for that purpose," which was to be clean and free of persons "sitting on the meat" in transit. St. Louis market laws also protected the public health by forbidding anyone "afflicted with any infectious or contagious disease or malady" to enter the market square or market house during public hours.

A city could expect praise for a noticeably clean market, and Philadelphia, without a doubt, received more praise than any other city in the country. Francisco Miranda remarked that "the beef market is the best, cleanest, and most abundant I have ever seen. . . . Such is the propriety and cleanliness with which everything is regulated!" Travelers attributed the cleanliness of Philadelphia's High Street Market not only to good government but, once again, to the perceived ability of its vendors to regulate themselves. Brissot de Warville remarked that "here, cleanliness is everything. Even meat, which looks so disgusting in all other markets, has an attractive appearance, and the spectator is not revolted by the sight of streams of blood that infect the atmosphere and befoul the streets. The women who bring in produce from the country are all dressed modestly, and their fruits and vegetables are displayed with the greatest care in handsomely woven baskets."[19]

Street Vending

The subtlest municipal market laws were those that defined street vending as an instrument of social welfare. They frequently limited peddlers' licenses to the elderly, widowed, handicapped, and indigent. Street vending was an important safety net for those who had few options for supporting themselves and their families, particularly widows and African American women newly freed in the wave of postrevolutionary emancipations. In their straitened circumstances, female street vendors did not hesitate to petition local government to maintain their right to sell in the streets around the public markets. These petitions were powerful expressions of their entrepreneurial spirit, their desire to be part of the economic life of the city, and their longing for an equal opportunity to earn a living. Moreover, female hucksters understood that economic survival depended on equal access to public space—be it the street or the public market—and they looked for government protection.[20]

In 1805 a group of female hawkers petitioned the Philadelphia city council to keep their licenses because they were "rendered helpless by the infirmities of age,—enfeebled by sickness—or oppressed by the cases of widowhood—hav[ing], for some years past, endeavored to gain a livelihood for themselves and their children, by vending in the market place fruit, nuts, and other small articles, more in demand for the tables of the rich, than those in the middle walks of life." They asked the city council to reconsider the law against hucksters rather than increasing the burden on public and private charity. The women hucksters also complained that the city did nothing about engrossers—people wealthy enough to rent cellars in the immediate neighborhood of the market to hoard food and affect prices.[21]

In Pittsburgh, Robert Watson petitioned the borough council in 1805 to allow his wife Rachel to sell baked goods at a stall in the marketplace. Watson had a large family, and he encouraged his wife and daughter to supplement the family income by selling cakes. The huckster ordinance the council had recently passed prevented his family "from pursuing this honest mode of making an honest livelihood" and reduced them to "more than indigence." Evidently his petition was ignored, for a few months later the market clerk reported that Rachel Watson continued to practice her trade in defiance of the huckster ordinance.[22] Pittsburgh's revived huckster ordinances of 1816 prompted petitions from Bridget Eddy, Isabella Kilgor, and Margaret Ray, who claimed that they deprived them of earning a livelihood by selling cakes, fruit, beer, and cider at stands in the market house.[23]

The Baltimore ordinances of 1797 granted the poor licenses to sell fruit, cakes, nuts, and "such other articles as [have] heretofore been customary for persons of that description to sell" from tables or baskets on public sidewalks and curbs. Licenses were granted only with the consent of adjacent property owners, whose primary concern was noise and disturbance by vendors late at night.

The public's attitude toward street vendors ranged from disgust to admiration. Benjamin Davies, in his account of the markets of Philadelphia, complained of the "evil" and "growing nuisance" of "sturdy young females, who besiege almost every cart, wagon, and boat, that brings fruit to market." These vendors have, "by their increase in numbers and capital, made it difficult for all others to procure good fruit, except through their hands. These girls, by being employed in families, might become useful members of society; whereas, by the present system of their education, they are growing up in habits of prophaneness, effrontery, and idleness." Davies argued for more rigorous municipal market laws to suppress this "certain class of dealers."[24]

Being poor or needy did not, of course, exempt one from obeying public market laws. In 1797 the New York city council forbade hucksters to sell fruit at Fly Market because they had violated engrossing laws. The sudden and unexpected ordinance prompted twenty female hucksters to petition the council for return of their rights. They argued that "the support of our needy, destitute families depends in a great measure upon the privilege of exposing for sale fruit in the public markets." The city rejected their plea, however, because the hucksters were found with a large surplus of produce—a sign that they had been engaged in engrossing.[25]

In spite of the usual complaints from property owners and disgruntled merchants, local government generally tolerated street vendors, particularly in the growing urban centers of Philadelphia and New York.[26] Street vending offered the poor an honest trade and provided wage earners with quick, cheap meals or snacks. These favorable aspects were celebrated in several children's books from the period. *Cries of New-York* (1808) and *Cries of Philadelphia* (1810) depict street vendors in an encyclopedic format, describing their songs, clothing, food, and wares.[27]

Cries of Philadelphia was intended to instill in youth a regard for hard, honest work. Rather than complaining about the noise and disturbance of street vendors, the author took comfort in their songs, noting particularly "how rejoiced should we be to hear the sound of the little match girl" on a cold, dark night when we need to kindle a fire. The author continued to inform readers that "we therefore recommend to all good children, to consider that every comfort we enjoy is produced in part by the labor of the poor who are entitled to much humanity and no ill-nature."

Readers were also encouraged to patronize street vendors merely to reward their industriousness. They might buy radishes, for example, even if they did not need any. Furthermore, it was "more desirable and reputable, to be like the little girl in the picture, doing good, by being engaged in some useful employment, than like the gentleman-hog, only live to eat, drink, and sleep." The baked-pear vendor, "a little black girl," was also engaged in "an honest way to procure a living." Readers ought to consider it shameful "that any person, white or black, should be willing to live by any means that are not honourable and honest."

Honesty of the trade and service to the hungry were the moral messages that *Cries of Philadelphia* conveyed in the vignette of the pepperpot vendor, a familiar sight in the city's markets. Pepperpot was a soup made chiefly from tripe, ox feet, and other inexpensive cuts heavily seasoned and spiced. Vendors, typically African American females, supplemented family incomes by selling the soup from vacant stalls when the market was closed (fig. 1.5). Considered to be doing a public service, the pepperpot vendor was praised for selling soup "very cheap, so that a hungry man may get a hearty meal for a few cents." Just as pepperpot vending was a significant occupation for Philadelphia's free black females, so too was oyster and clam selling for free black males, who had a virtual monopoly on the business.[28]

To encourage the poor to earn at least a modest living, the New York city council granted licenses to coffee vendors in the streets near the markets. Beginning in the late 1790s, Susanna Dally, Thomas Hutchins, and Andrew Ross, among others, applied for stands to sell coffee in the streets near Fly Market. By 1810 the city had issued so many licenses that a committee concluded that if all licensed coffee vendors showed up at the same time "there would be pandemonium." The committee also found that there were many coffee shops nearby where "the early stirring and often chilled market man can here quaff his ambrosial coffee at as cheap a rate and with infinitely more comfort" than on the streets. Within days after the committee concluded that licensing of coffee vendors should be discontinued, the city council began to receive petitions. Hannah Perkins, a widow who had supported herself and three children for twelve years by selling coffee in the market, petitioned the city council to keep her license, and permission was granted.[29]

After experimenting with restrictions on street vending, New York City officials finally discovered that "stands for the sale of coffee, cakes, and other eatables, appear to be one of the fixtures of every well governed public

FIGURE 1.5 *Pepper-Pot: A Scene in the Philadelphia Market*, 1811. Oil on canvas by John Lewis Krimmel. Sumpter Priddy III, Inc.

market."[30] The service provided by street vendors who circulated not only in the markets but also through the vast network of streets and neighborhoods was proudly displayed on a scarf from 1814 featuring the New York city hall surrounded by vignettes of hawkers and their associated cries. The

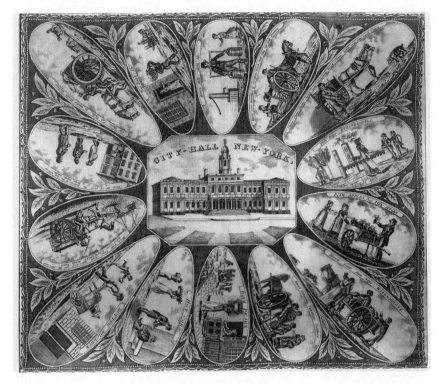

FIGURE 1.6 Printed scarf depicting the New York city hall surrounded by vignettes
of street vendors, about 1814. J. Clarence Davies Collection, Museum of the
City of New York.

scarf celebrated street vendors who sold not only delicacies and treats such
as oysters and hot corn but also bulky or heavy items that were too difficult
for the average person to carry home, such as cattails for bedding and sand
for construction (fig. 1.6).

Cities in the early Republic frequently repealed the colonial market laws
that forbade slaves to vend in the streets. These repeals were intended to benefit masters who sent slaves into town to sell goods on their behalf. Charleston
ordinances, for example, let slaves sell for their masters if they carried a ticket
listing the items for sale. Any white person could apprehend the slave and
seize articles that were not on the ticket. In general, cities took into account
the particular institution of slavery by permitting slaves to sell goods in the
marketplace but subjecting them to more severe penalties, such as extra
lashes and fines, if they disobeyed market laws.

In rare instances slaves could earn enough cash by street vending to purchase their freedom. In 1791 Sophia Browning, a slave who tended her own market garden, saved $400 from the sale of vegetables at the Alexandria Market. She secured the freedom of her husband, George Bell, then bought her own freedom after an illness lowered her purchase price to a mere five pounds in Maryland currency. Browning subsequently bought the freedom of two of her children. Her sister, Alethia Tanner, bought her own freedom for $1,400 in 1810. By the time of her death in 1864, Mrs. Tanner had bought and liberated twenty-two friends and relatives.[31]

Throughout the North and South, street vendors remained highly visible components of the urban landscape in the early Republic. Municipal toleration encouraged them to earn a living while satisfying those in need of a quick hot meal. Philadelphia painter John Lewis Krimmel captured the moral benefits of street vending in an aspiring republican society in his sympathetic depiction of a cherry seller (fig. 1.7). The epitome of hard work, the cherry seller sits on a bench purveying her fruit, wearing a bonnet to protect her from the sun. Her honesty is symbolized by the scales, and her sympathy toward others in need is captured as she looks at the crying boy who cannot afford to buy cherries. The young girl compassionately offers to share, while the kneeling boy selfishly devours his own. Such were the expectations of regulated public markets in the early Republic—a moral economy that aimed to protect the public welfare and promote good citizenship.[32]

The laws of the marketplace permeated not only art and literature but the cityscape itself, as market ordinances published in broadsides, handbills, and newspapers constantly demanded a well-ordered public economy. Disseminating market laws was in itself regulated by law, as cities and towns established ordinances that required the printing and posting of market regulations and penalties. That government was accountable for dissemination is evident in ordinances specifying that market regulations and penalties be printed in both German and English where necessary. In some cases local government established detailed standards for the quality and exact location of posted ordinances. In 1835 St. Louis required that they be exhibited "in a short and condensed form, which rules shall be printed in good paper (a single sheet) in plain type, and shall be smoothly pasted upon boards or canvas of sufficient size set in frames at least two of which shall during market hours be constantly

FIGURE 1.7 German-born artist John Lewis Krimmel captured the moralizing aspects of street vending in his genre scenes of Philadelphia. *Cherry Seller,* 1814 or 1815. Courtesy of the Reading Public Museum, Reading, Pennsylvania.

hung up in some conspicuous part of the market house, one in each end, and in the center, and elsewhere if need be." Although the market laws were part of the moral landscape—dictating the ethics of exchange and defining good social and economic behavior—ultimately the market house itself was the most visible proof of government's commitment to the well-being of the community. Built on consensus, it embodied everyone's desire for a fair place—a common ground—to earn a decent living and to procure life's daily necessities.

TWO

The Market House

The convenience of a market-house is, to have it long, narrow, and
open on all sides, so that the articles may be spread abroad, and
the people may have both room and light.

ANNE ROYALL, 1826

A lthough street vendors offered pedestrians convenient, economical
meals or snacks, the main business of the market house was as the primary source of the city's daily supply of fresh food. Local government made
an effort to ensure its success not only with regulations but by carefully considering site, financing, public support, simplicity and flexibility in design, and
a location convenient to buyers and sellers. These calculations were intended
to reduce risk and speculation, an important factor in the construction of
other public buildings like the courthouse or city hall. But no other public
building or space demanded such broad consensus and collective action. In
this single structure government's pride and reputation were at stake. Local
businesses and nearby property owners depended on its success, as did country producers and street vendors. And it required the approval of the neighborhood. More than any other public building, the market house stood as material evidence of complex decision making that involved many kinds of
participants who had reached common ground.[1]

The Site

Before being built, a market house had to fulfill conditions of accessibility and public support. Local authorities chose publicly owned sites with access to marshes, rivers, roads, and densely populated neighborhoods. The most persistent location of the principal market was the town square or the main thoroughfare, because these were convenient for city dwellers, vendors bringing goods by road or water, and officials responsible for enforcing market laws.[2]

In some cases the town plan determined the site, as in Charleston, South Carolina, where a 1796 ordinance established a public market on the site "laid out for a market in the original plan of the city, and commonly known by the name of the Beef market."[3] Likewise in Washington, William Thornton and Tristram Dalton, commissioners of public buildings and grounds for the District of Columbia, asked President Jefferson in 1801 for permission to establish a central market on the public reservation designated as market squares on the 1792 L'Enfant Plan. The public reservation was "originally intended for a market [and] is thought to embrace so many advantages, and is so central, that were a market established there, it would be a great accommodation to the City." Tiber Creek ran through the market squares, giving the area the nickname Marsh Market (fig. 2.1).[4]

Marshy, low-lying ground was ideal for open-air marketing, since it was likely to be already publicly owned and was of little value to investors and developers. Marshes were also popular dumping grounds before the existence of sewers and incinerators, and local government preferred to locate public markets where nature could do the cleansing. Moreover, farmers and fisherman with small boats could bring their goods directly to the market's wharves and landings. New York's Fly Market was near a long, low saltwater marsh along the East River, from Wall Street to Beekman Street. The market got its name from the Dutch word *vlie,* or *vley,* meaning marsh. Farmers from Long Island traveled to Fly Market in wagons and oxcarts that crossed the sound by ferry. Those who lived in New Jersey or neighboring counties along the North and East Rivers brought their goods in skiffs, rowing them with the tides to the market's riverbanks.[5]

The New Orleans meat market, built on the natural levee along the Mississippi River in 1813, took advantage of the benefits offered by both streets and water. The French had used the site for open-air marketing, as had the Spanish during the colonial period. The Creole-dominated city government

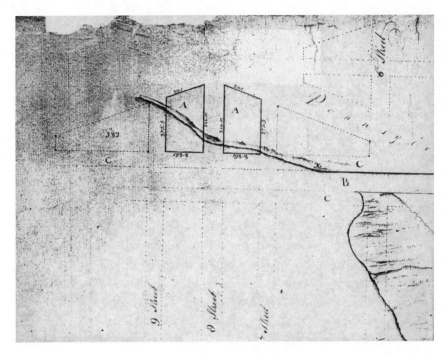

FIGURE 2.1 Public markets, such as the one in Washington, D.C., were often along creeks and marshes, where land was unsuitable for development. Detail, "A map of the market squares, and that part of the Canal, and Mall which is north of the Tiber-Creek," by Thomas Freeman, 1794. National Archives.

continued the tradition of using the levee for public purposes, including markets, since the land was publicly owned and near the Place d'Armes, the city's main square. The market was accessible by boat, and its waterfront location kept the noise, filth, and stench away from the residential area.[6]

Some sites were determined by individuals who donated land to the city in perpetuity provided it be used only for a market. In Frederick, Maryland, in 1785, William Murdoch Beall, Henry McCleary, John Gebhart, and Henry Zealer donated a lot 61 by 80 feet, as well as an alley 12 by 150 feet, to the trustees of the town for a public market. Their gift stipulated that the ground "be used for the purposes of the market, and no other . . . and shall forever remain, free and open for public use."[7] The terms of these "gifts" varied, as in Baltimore, where legend held that John Eager Howard, a Revolutionary War hero, generously donated land for Lexington Market to the citizens of Baltimore in 1804. In reality, Howard leased the land to the city for ninety-nine years; annual rent to Howard and his heirs was $228 in gold or silver; and in 1818 the City paid Howard $3,000 for additional parcels of land to extend the market.[8]

Wealthy landowners near growing towns were often beyond the reach of local market laws and held informal markets on their own farms, plantations, and orchards. Local officials tolerated these private endeavors unless they needed more space for public markets. This may have been the case not only in Baltimore but also in St. Louis, where authorities needed more market space and claimed a portion of private property that had evolved informally into an unauthorized marketplace. An ensuing court battle with the wealthy landowner, Antoine Soulard, began in 1804 and was not settled until after his death in 1825. In 1836 the city issued a quit claim deed to Soulard's widow, Julia Cerre Soulard, and in 1838 she deeded to the city the tract of land containing the marketplace. She stipulated, however, that if the city did not erect a market house on the land within ten years, the land would revert to her and her heirs "forever."[9]

The most popular site was the middle of a street wide enough to handle a market house as well as traffic on both sides. A street location let city officials economize by providing this basic amenity on property that was already publicly owned. Usually the street chosen was not only wide but also oriented along a prominent north-south or east-west axis of a grid plan, for the convenience of farmers bringing goods to market.[10]

High Street in Philadelphia was the quintessential market street, with its series of longitudinal sheds commencing at the Delaware River (fig. 2.2). Public reaction to sheds in the middle of the city's busiest street was mixed. In 1777 Jacob Duché, a Frenchman living in Philadelphia, remarked that "the principal street, which is an hundred feet wide, would have a noble appearance, were it not for an ill-conditioned court-house, and a long range of shambles, which they have stuck in the very middle of it."[11] When the city proposed to extend High Street Market from Third Street to Fourth Street in 1785, nearby property owners complained that the extension would deprive them "of the Air the Prospect and other Advantages of the largest Street of the City." They were "alarmed by divers Petitions of Inhabitants of the City and Country, pretending it would be much for the good or Convenience of the Public if Shambles should be erected before the Door of Your Petitioners." Inspired by the "Declaration of Rights, the whole Spirit thereof, and the 46th Section of the Constitution [of the Commonwealth of Pennsylvania]," the petitioners

FIGURE 2.2 High Street Market, Market Street from Front Street, Philadelphia, 1838. Lithograph by J. C. Wild. The Library Company of Philadelphia.

claimed their right and "all Men's Right to High Street and all other Streets of the City so as they were first laid out in the City Plan."[12] The property rights of the forty-one petitioners, including prominent attorney Jared Ingersoll, did not prevent the city from defending its role as principal provider of food retailing facilities for the more than a thousand people living around High Street between Third and Fourth Streets. The issue was settled when a 1786 act of assembly empowered the city wardens to extend the market.[13]

Street markets in other cities elicited negative remarks from the occasional resident or traveler. A gentlemen complained in the *Mobile Commercial Register* on November 12, 1828, that Government Street "had been shorn of more than half of its dignity, by building three market houses, plump in the middle of it—much to the annoyance of one gentleman of the long robe, who lived hard by, and who, in consequence, has disposed of his dwelling for less than half its value." Equally snobbish about the appearance of street markets was Benjamin Henry Latrobe, who described the one in Norfolk as having an "irregular position [that] is in harmoney with its filth and deformity."[14]

Despite random complaints from a minority of property owners and travelers, the street remained the most consistent and popular choice for a market site throughout the first half of the nineteenth century. Anticipating the eventual need for a market house, new towns also made provisions in their plans for an extra wide street for the purpose. The original 1828 plat of Logansport, Indiana, for example, declared that Market Street would be sixty-six feet wide, except between Walnut and Bridge Streets, where it would widen to ninety-nine feet for a marketplace. Early nineteenth-century plans for other towns in the Midwest, such as Detroit (1807), Indianapolis (1821), and Louisville (1836), indicate that locating a market house in the middle of a major thoroughfare was common practice and not confined to eastern cities (fig. 2.3).[15]

Financing

After selecting a site, cities financed market house construction in a number of ways. Lotteries stimulated public interest, avoided tax increases, and were popular fundraisers for market houses and other public buildings and services. They were susceptible to fraud, however, and were generally prohibited by the early nineteenth century (fig. 2.4). More common was fundraising by subscription. In Philadelphia, the Norwich Market superintendents offered 6 percent annually to those subscribing to loans for a new neighborhood market. They subsequently protected business in the new market by forbidding door-to-door hawkers and peddlers. The township printed the peddler ordinance in local English and German newspapers and on one hundred handbills. Other cities quickly passed ordinances protecting their investment in a new market house. In 1823 the city of Mobile, Alabama, restricted food retailing to its new market house on Government Street "and no where else" until it could pay builders John Ward and Turner Stark with revenues generated from stall rentals.[16]

Private individuals sometimes financed the construction of a new market house or the repair of an old one. Examples of such philanthropy, or perhaps economic necessity, were common after the Revolution. New York's Bear Market was in such a state of decay that several inhabitants, wanting to lure back the farmers, contributed to its repair without expecting the city corporation to reimburse them. The butchers of High Street Market in Philadelphia, equally eager to resume business after the British evacuated the city in

FIGURE 2.3 Plan of the central portion of Detroit, 1807. The market house is noted at the intersection of Jefferson and Woodward Avenues, *bottom center*, just a few blocks from the river. Courtesy of Cornell University Library.

1778, repaired the market in exchange for rent-free stalls. Not only war but also natural disasters prompted concerned citizens to act on their own. After a fire destroyed Savannah's old market on Ellis Square in 1820, "a large number of respectable inhabitants" petitioned the General Assembly to let them

LIST OF PRIZES
DRAWN IN THE
PRECINCTS MARKET-HOUSE LOTTERY.

☞ *Those Numbers to which no sums are annexed, are Prizes of Six Dollars.*

No.	Pr.	No.	Pr.	No.	Pr.	No.	Pr.	No.	Pr.	No.	Pr.	No.	Pr.	No.	Pr.
2		198		428		649		909		1153		1400		1611	
9		204		31		31		12		55		1		22	
12		9		33		34		15		60		2		23	
13		10		35		38		22		61		6		24	
15		11		36		39		23		62		7		25	
16		16		41		41	10	25		63		9		27	
17		19		42		44		26		64		13		29	
19	10	21		47		45		27		65		14		31	
27		26		50		48		34		66		15		34	
28		28		51		52		36		73		16		44	
34		31		52		54	20	37	100	74	25	18		46	
36		32	10	53		58		47		75	25	19		48	10
37		33		54		67		48		77	10	20		50	
42		40		58		69		52		79		21		53	
45		41		62		75		58		80		30		56	
47		43		64		79		66		85		31		59	10
50		45		68		81		76		88	100	34		60	
51		46		75		82		85		91		33		62	
54		52		76	20	85		87		92		35		67	
55		54		77		88		89		1202		38		69	
56		56		80		93		98		7	50	39		71	
57		57		83		95		99		9		44		74	
61		58		85		98		1000		13		46		77	
64		63		88		701		2		16		48		78	
67		66		90		4		8		17		50		79	
68		68		93		5		10		21		54		81	
69		70	10	94		13		11		23		55		85	
70		74		96		16		15		24		58		86	
71	10	76		500		17	50	17		30		61		88	20
76		77		1		18		20		33		70		89	
78		79		3	10	29		22		40		71		92	
79		80		6		31	10	23		43		87		93	
85		81		11	100	34		28		44		88		96	
86		83		14		39		30		45		89		97	25
88		84		16		41		31		50		90		1701	
89		86	10	25		42		35		52		91		4	
90		88		29		49		46		53		92		9	
91		89	20	32		55		48		58		95		11	
92		93	100	34		60		49		65		96		15	
93		93		44		64		58		69		97		18	
97		94	10	45		66		60		71		1502		19	
99		97		46		72		61		72	10	4		20	
104		98		47		74		62	100	75		8		21	
5		99		48		77		63		78		12		23	
6		308		49		84		66		80		16		27	
9		9	10	50		92		68		82		18		29	
10		11		53		99	20	69		83		19		30	
12		13		60		801		70		92		21		36	
14		14		62	50	2		80		98		26		37	
16	25	15		70	20	6		81		1304		37		41	
17		25		72		13		82		16		38		42	
18		36	10	73		15		85		18		40		46	
20		39		74		18		86		19	10	43		48	10
21		41	10	77		19		90		27		45		49	
23		46		78		26		91		42	10	47		59	
25		47		80		29		93	10	45		48		62	
29		50		83		32		94		49		54	10	63	
36		51		84	10	38		95		50		55		66	
38		56		85		40		99		56	10	63	25	69	
39		69		86		41		1104		59		64		70	
40		70		88		42		7		63		69		71	
43		72		90		43		10	10	64		71		73	
46		73		92	50	44		11		66		72		75	
47		79		93		49		16		67		77		78	
51		84		94		51		18		68		85		80	
56		87		95		54		22		70		86		81	
58		97		97		55		24		72		88		84	
65		99	10	98		63		26		73		91		85	
68		403		99		64	10	27		75		92		92	
70		8		604		74		29		81		1600		95	
75		10		6		78		34		84		1		99	
79		11		13		85		39		89		10		1804	
80		13		14		89		44		90		13		6	
81		17		19		98		45		95		14		8	
83		19		22	10	99		47		97		17		9	
85		22		23		903		49				20	10		

FIGURE 2.4 List of prizes drawn in the Precincts Market-House
Lottery, Baltimore, 1804–1809. The Maryland Historical
Society, Baltimore.

erect a public market on the square at their own expense, vesting all rents and profits in the city corporation.[17]

Local government often allocated the Freemasons space in the market house free of charge in exchange for their building, extending, or repairing it. In 1797 the town of Providence permitted St. John's Lodge of Masons to build a third story over the market for its use and at its expense. In 1798 the need for more market space (and perhaps a new roof) prompted the burgesses of Lancaster, Pennsylvania, to contract with Free Masons Lodge 43 to add a floor above the market that they could use in perpetuity. In 1817 Colonel Timothy Mountford dedicated the entire upper floor of the market house in Alexandria, Virginia, to a museum of the local Masonic lodge.[18]

In addition to collaborating with the Freemasons, towns exchanged free space in the market house for labor with a variety of other organizations and individuals. The trustees of Portsmouth, Virginia, let Edward Newman use the market hall for one year if he would glaze and repair the windows, install an interior staircase, repair the plaster, and whitewash the walls. The trustees, however, expected Newman to let them use the market on public occasions. Two years later they granted the Baptist Society permission to use the market hall if the members would put a new sill under the door, mend the plaster, and glaze all the windows.[19]

Complex social and economic relationships lay behind the construction of the market house in Charles Town, Virginia (now in West Virginia), where the building was financed by a combination of donated land, labor exchanged for use of the market, and profit from the sale of the builder's slaves. In 1801 Samuel and Dorothea Washington deeded the land to the town. In 1806 the town's trustees, eager to complete a market house, authorized Ferdinando Fairfax to finish it in exchange for use of the upper floor. Fairfax then sold his slave Charlotte and her sons Nicholas, Obadiah, and George to James Anderson for $650; in payment, Anderson gave Fairfax $200 in cash and completed the brickwork on the market house.[20]

Market House Typology

Cities and towns throughout the country considered several factors before building a market house. They looked at not only topography, shape of the site, financing, and construction costs, but also local building traditions, current trends in the style of public buildings, and projected number of tenants.

This multitude of considerations resulted in designs that can be found in any region of the country, at any time during the century, and in some cases within the same city. Basically, market houses were variations on two types: the shed and the mixed-use market house. Neither type is an American invention.

The simple, freestanding shed was the most prolific type of market house, lending itself well to a street location. It had been a standard form in colonial America, as it was throughout England and the Continent. Open or closed, it consisted of arches of stout timber or brick pillars supporting a low-pitched gable roof. Builders occasionally added wide projecting eaves to increase the space for marketing.[21] Sheds provided minimal protection from the elements for the least cost, did not require an architect, and were quick to build. Sometimes they were built over time as a string of separate structures that allowed for cross traffic and separated the buildings by food type. In part the shed was popular because builders were familiar with using a modular bay system to achieve the desired length for structures like barns and churches. In addition, the shed's multiple entrances made the market attractive and accessible to patrons coming from any direction; its openness promoted air circulation and helped in unloading goods; and it was easy to wash down at the end of a market day. Likewise, cities that were seats of local or regional government found it economical and convenient to append the market shed to the courthouse or town hall, as in York, Pennsylvania (fig. 2.5). In these locations builders had to adapt the size and plan of the sheds to existing public buildings and sites. Sheds could also be extended or added to as business demanded. By the 1850s, for example, the Pittsburgh courthouse was surrounded by covered market stalls, walkways, and a spacious semicircular market shed in the square across the street for selling bulky items and parking wagons (fig. 2.6).[22]

Its horizontal plan and low elevation made the shed an obvious market type for a street location. In general it provided the greatest flexibility for the least cost, and its widespread use attests to its popularity throughout the first half of the nineteenth century. The shed in the middle of Market Street in Albany, New York, was typical. Depicted by artist James Eights as it may have looked in 1805, the two- by eight-bay market house had sufficient clearance for traffic, was low enough not to overpower the residences and other public buildings, and was level and slightly raised for drainage (fig. 2.7).[23]

One of the longest markets was High Street Market in Philadelphia, which by 1807 consisted of three structures that extended from Water Street to Fourth Street (see fig. 2.2). Charles William Janson paced off the market and

FIGURE 2.5 Centre Square, York, about 1830. Watercolor by William Wagner. The York County Heritage Trust, Pennsylvania.

FIGURE 2.6 Courthouse and market, Pittsburgh, about 1840. Lithograph (1859) by Otto Krebs after a sketch by J. P. Robitser. Carnegie Library of Pittsburgh.

FIGURE 2.7 East side Market Street from Maiden Lane South, Albany, 1805.
Watercolor by James Eights (1798–1882), about 1850. Albany Institute of History and
Art Bequest of Ledyard Cogswell Jr.

determined that it was 420 steps long, excluding street intersections. High
Street Market's impressive length made it the standard for all others. When
Luigi Castiglioni described Baltimore's Fells Point Market, he referred to it
as being "built on the model of the one in Philadelphia." In describing New
York's Fly Market, a gentleman wrote that it was "perhaps as long as one of
the ranges of the Philadelphia 'High Street Market.'"[24]

High Street Market was praised not only for its length, but also for the symmetry and simplicity of its sheds. One admirer hoped that "no pragmatical architect will destroy this symmetry, by adopting new dimensions as to height
or breadth, and taking a different curve for his arch." The design needed "no
alteration," as "the piers are square, massive, simple in their mouldings," and
the "roof could not be higher without deforming the street, and incommod-
ing the inhabitants, and the arch below and pediment above are pleasing and
graceful." The architectural critic recommended that for the piers and roof
the city consider materials more durable than brick and wood, such as stone,
since it would be more cost effective in the long run for such an important
utilitarian structure.[25]

FIGURE 2.8 Old Market House, St. Louis, 1812. From Frederick L. Billon, *Annals of St. Louis in Its Territorial Days*, from 1804 to 1821 (St. Louis, 1888), 25.

Nineteenth-century local histories attest to the widespread use of market sheds in the Midwest. The "Old Market House" in St. Louis, for example, consisted of a simple shingled roof resting on stone pillars (fig. 2.8).[26] Similarly, the first market house in Logansport, Indiana, was described as "simply a roof resting on brick pillars ten to twelve feet apart." When a storm carried the roof away in 1845, the town built a second market house in the 1850s—this time in the middle of Market Street where it widened to form what was then known as the marketplace. The new structure, 150 by 30 feet, was still basically a shed, but its durability was improved with brick arches (fig. 2.9).[27]

Market sheds in the South were usually long one-story frame buildings with whitewashed walls and low-pitched roofs. The earliest known image of the principal market house in Houston, Texas, depicts such a structure adjacent to the city hall (fig. 2.10). Built for the city in 1840 by Thomas Stansbury and Sons, the Houston market house featured lattice sides to protect the interior from the sun while providing ventilation. A long one-story frame structure also served as the principal market house in Washington, D.C., throughout the antebellum period until it (like the market house in Houston) was replaced by a more substantial brick structure in the 1870s.[28]

The second type of market house—the mixed-use market—had an open, arcaded ground floor for marketing, surmounted by one or more stories devoted to other public purposes. In this type of structure marketing was secondary to the main purpose of the building, whether a town hall or a courthouse, and was primarily a source of revenue. Throughout the nineteenth

FIGURE 2.9 Market House, Logansport, Indiana, about 1851. Watercolor by Wils Berry. Cass County Historical Society, Indiana.

FIGURE 2.10 City market house and city hall, Houston, 1852. Watercolor by Thomas Flintoff. Courtesy Houston Metropolitan Research Center, Houston Public Library.

FIGURE 2.11 Portrait of Josiah
Quincy, 1824. Oil on canvas by
Gilbert Stuart. Quincy holds the ar-
chitectural plans of Faneuil Hall Mar-
ket, which appears in the background.
Gift of Miss Eliza Susan Quincy.
Courtesy Museum of Fine Arts,
Boston. Reproduced with permission.
© 2000 Museum of Fine Arts, Boston.
All rights reserved.

century, the mixed-use market house remained fairly constant in form, though the function of the upper stories changed based on local need. Town council minutes record dozens of uses for the upper stories of such market houses, including but not limited to city council chambers, clerk's offices, fire houses, prisons, watch houses, police headquarters, drill rooms, museums, libraries, schools, Masonic halls, opera houses, and theaters.[29]

By locating a market on the ground floor of another public building—to finance the building—cities could afford to indulge in new architectural refinements. When the Albany common council considered erecting "a new market & offices" in 1828, architect Philip Hooker proposed ten market stalls on the open, arcaded ground floor and a second story for a public justice room, courtroom, city surveyor's office, city superintendent's office, and two conference rooms. The Doric colonnade, simple entablature, and shallow-domed cupola reflected the current taste for Greek Revival in major public buildings. At the same time, Hooker's choice of a one-story shed for two other market houses in Albany demonstrated that the shed still remained a viable type, especially for smaller, less central sites.[30]

The most famous Greek Revival market house in the country was Boston's Faneuil Hall Market, built from 1823 to 1826 under the direction of Mayor Josiah Quincy (fig. 2.11). Unprecedented in the United States in size, cost, and

FIGURE 2.12 East view of Faneuil Hall Market, Boston, 1827. Lithograph by John Andrews. Courtesy of the Bostonian Society.

scope, the new market—designed by Alexander Parris and built with $1 million in public funds—provided more space for merchants and customers, who had outgrown the ground floor of the adjacent Faneuil Hall. An early example of urban renewal, the project involved closing narrow streets and demolishing dilapidated buildings on land obtained by eminent domain. The city constructed the domed section in the center of the market house and auctioned the surrounding lots to investors, who then built the wings in accordance with Parris's plans.[31] Observers hailed the granite market house (fig. 2.12), approximately 500 by 36 feet, as the largest and most elegant in the country and perhaps even "in the world"—a market house that "exceeded them all in boldness of design, in promise of public benefit, and in energy of execution."[32]

Anne Royall was less laudatory than the press concerning the promise of Faneuil Hall Market as a model. As she observed construction nearly finished in 1826, she noted the beauty of the smooth masonry walls but could not help commenting on the building's absurd size relative to High Street Market in Philadelphia. Royall wrote skeptically that "it is laughable (I mean for those who are not contra disposed,) to see the pains and cost they are at to construct a building the least calculated for the purpose intended of any thing else. . . . I mean the convenience of a market-house is, to have it long, narrow, and open on all sides, so that the articles may be spread abroad, and the people may have both room and light. The same money they are spending on this, would have built a complete market-house, three times as long, and ten fold more to the purpose."[33] Although Quincy's achievement boasted the architectural refinements usually accorded to the mixed-use market house, critics like Royall believed that construction costs did not justify its sole use as a market and that a long, low market house would have sufficed. Nonetheless, the debates surrounding Faneuil Hall Market revealed contemporary attitudes about the need to balance the functional and aesthetic aspects of market houses.

Construction

Regardless of simplicity in design, builders and architects were still accountable to local committees that dictated every detail of the market house—in some cases down to the size of the nails. The 1819 ordinance of St. Francisville, Louisiana, was typical, providing for the erection of a market house

53 feet long, 20 feet wide, and 12 feet from the floor to the plates, and built in the following manner, viz: There shall be raised on each side 5 brick pillars 3 feet wide and 18 inches thick of equal distance on which shall be laid the plates for the roof, the roof to be firmly framed in a manner to support its own weight, . . . and finished with an arched ceiling or otherwise at the discretion of the commissioners; the shingles for said roof shall be at least 20 inches long, ¾ inch thick, not to shew to the weather more than 6 inch and nailed through the middle with a 6d cut nail, and in every other respect laid in a workman like manner, all the timber in said roof to be of the best cypress, there shall be run parallel with and 5 feet from each wall of said house a fence of posts and one rail, and at each end of said house there shall be 2 turn stiles of suitable size as pass ways thro' the fence, said fence all to be made of good cypress timber and the turnstiles hung with iron bolts and ring. The floor of said house together with the whole space within the fence shall be a good brick pavement, all the brick work to be made of good & suitable materials.[34]

The ordinance established not only the right of the market commissioners to alter the design at their discretion, but also the right of city trustees to give final approval of the building and its site.

The 1806 ordinance for the erection of the market house in Charles Town stressed the features city officials most desired for public buildings—quality and speed of construction and simplicity in design. The ordinance authorized Ferdinando Fairfax to build a foundation of "earth well rammed inside, and outside, ready to be received a good pavement of hard brick . . . upon a good bed of sand." The ordinance also instructed Fairfax to provide the market house with "a strong neat roof," "plain cornice," rafters "strengthened either with studs, or collar-beams," "two tiers of strong joists," and "a good floor through-out." The three doorways were to be finished with "plain single architraves, the doors to be made plain and strong," and each large room on the upper floor was to be finished with "plain washboards and chair boards, a plain single mantle piece, and two coats of strong brown mortar plaistering all round."[35]

Subscribers and city officials were the final judges of quality. Although William Earl agreed to complete a new market house for the Borough of Pittsburgh in a "good and workman like manner," subscribers of the new market measured the dimensions against those in the contract and found the piers to be incorrect (fig. 2.13). The affidavit demonstrated that building standards were important, even for the simplest market house.[36]

A final statement of pride in even the most modest market was assigning a popular name. Crown Market in New York, for example, originally took its name from royalty, but in 1797 the city renamed it Liberty Market "to suit an emblem of our Republic." Likewise, in 1822 the New York city council named the new market house at the Old Slip Market after Benjamin Franklin. New York continued naming market houses after national heroes into the 1830s, when it established the Jefferson Market and Lafayette Market. It renamed the latter the Monroe Market shortly after the fifth president died in 1831.[37]

Floor Plans and Furnishings

The simplest market sheds had unobstructed floor plans without stalls, though vendors still were required to "take their stands" at specified locations under the roof. The 1805 ordinances of Baltimore required butchers to stay within a line "drawn six inches from the inner edge of one pillar, to six inches from the inner edge of another, and no butcher shall hang any meat or other thing, or place any fixture in the outside of said line." Moreover, though butchers could erect boxes or closets in their stands, furnishings had to remain under the shambles and be raised high enough off the floor for a broom to pass under them. Butchers who sold from unfurnished stands, such as New York butcher John Aimes, brought their own tables to market each day.[38]

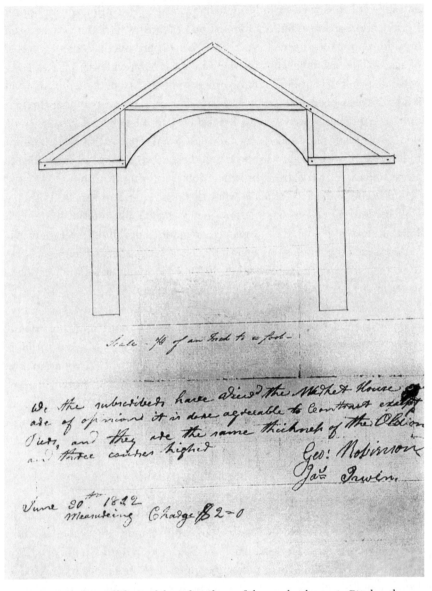

FIGURE 2.13 Affidavit of the subscribers of the market house in Pittsburgh, Pennsylvania, June 30, 1802. Pennsylvania State Archives, RG 48, LR 102, microfilm of Pittsburgh Borough and Council Papers, 1789–1917.

The Market House

More typically, market houses were repetitive-celled structures with built-in wooden stalls or benches as provided for in the plan. New York's Fly Market, for example, was 224 feet long and 20 feet wide, with one stall at the head of the market and eighteen stalls on the sides (thirty-seven stands). The back of each stall was placed in line with the inner side of the market posts, and an eleven-foot passageway ran down the center.[39]

Municipal ordinances specified stall dimensions to the inch, and no deviations were permitted without prior permission of the clerk. Specifications for a market house in West Chester, Pennsylvania, provide a detailed account of butcher stalls made of high-quality white oak. Benches were framed with posts four inches square, enclosed at the sides to form a box with a door at one end. A plank an inch and a half thick formed the countertop. Each bench was secured to the market house by an upright post, four inches square, framed into the end of the bench and the ceiling above. Meat rails consisted of three planks per stall, four inches by one and a half, secured horizontally into the upright post at one end of the bench and the mortise in the pillars at the other end. Each meat rail was supplied with eight iron hooks and could be taken down every night—implying that butchers were required to clean their meat rails daily and to secure them overnight in the box beneath the bench. Stall features evolved according to the needs of the trade and were probably fairly standard from city to city (fig. 2.14).[40]

Once the market house was completed, the responsibility of civic authorities for providing the community with food retailing facilities had just begun. The greatest challenge was to determine the "most just and equitable" method of assigning stalls, which was usually by lot.[41] Elaborating on the lot system was the borough council of Harrisburg, which managed construction of a new market house in 1815. On July 21 the council hoped to accommodate the increased population and "the necessity of raising a more efficient revenue" by renting the first fourteen stalls, beginning with the most expensive corner ones and ending with the cheapest. If the city found occupants for the first fourteen stalls, the clerk of the market would begin to auction off the next fourteen in the same manner, until all were spoken for.[42] Concentrating rented stalls at one end of the market had several advantages. It maximized city revenues by ensuring that the most expensive stalls were occupied first; the clerk could more easily supervise the market; the conditions were right for symbiosis, where vendors benefit from their proximity; and the vacant end of the market house could be used to store fire-fighting equipment. Until the fire station developed

FIGURE 2.14 Charles Brown's stall no. 10, probably Centre Market, New York. *The Butcher*, about 1840–1844. Watercolor by Nicolino Calyo. Gift of Mrs. Francis P. Garvan in memory of Francis P. Garvan, Museum of the City of New York.

into its own building type, fire companies typically stored their equipment in market houses or other utilitarian buildings and sheds.[43]

Once the stalls were assigned, the clerk maintained a record of occupants and in some cities, such as New York and Trenton, placed a sign over each stall with the name of the occupant "in large letters." Clearly marked stalls helped the public to recognize legitimate vendors as well as stalls that were available for rent.[44]

Despite its apparent disorder, the market house was a highly rational structure that allowed local authorities to satisfy both the functional and the aesthetic objectives of urban food retailing. It stood at the civic and commercial core of the city, forging relationships between farmers, small businesses, and local financial institutions, whose success was entwined with the prosperity of the market. The area around the market house attracted other businesses, such as a newspaper office, hotel, tavern, bank, bookseller, printer, dry goods establishment, clothier, shoe store, saddler and harness maker, blacksmith, and makers of stoves, tinware, and hardware—to name just a few. The economic power of the market as a magnet for commerce has been a long-standing urban pattern, with the livelihood of artisans and shopkeepers depending on their nearness to the marketplace. The area immediately around the market house was the most prized; after that came the major streets that led to the countryside. The market was thus a town's most precious asset.[45] It was given priority for a host of public services, including running water, lighting, fire hydrants, sidewalks, drainage, and other amenities. As a social and economic priority, the public market had a special atmosphere that no other place in the city could claim—an atmosphere that combined the pragmatic benefits of comfort and convenience with the added touch of excitement and entertainment. It is not surprising that in 1797, when the town council of Frederick, Maryland, authorized street repairs and improvements to Market Street, it declared the space "the most public street in said town."[46]

THREE

Marketplace Culture

The place where no distinctions are,
All sects and colors mingle there . . . ,
Nothing more clear, I'll tell you why,
All kinds of folks must eat or die.
Objects of honor or disgrace,
Are all seen at the market-place.

THEOPHILUS EATON, 1814

A consistent, fundamental function of the public market was as a civic center where people gathered to discuss politics, exchange news, celebrate, and socialize. This aspect of the marketplace derived in part from the ancient custom of reserving a place for country folk to sell their produce, since trading from shops was the privilege of the city's freemen. Freemen were not allowed to encroach on the space of the country vendors. Cultural historians of medieval and early modern Europe have recognized that this daily interaction and mutual respect between town and country at the marketplace promoted an unofficial folk culture. This second world within the official world offered a unique atmosphere of freedom and frankness and fostered a universal language and behavior that differed from that found in institutions such as the church or court. The continual aggregation of people for social interaction and commodity exchange created a special environment in which class representation found a public platform. The countless petitions between buyers and sellers, stall holders and itinerant vendors, and import merchants and local artisans produced an urban "laboratory" where members of the community attempted to reconcile their differences.[1]

Marketplace culture has also been defined by the periodic spectacles of fairs, festivals, and carnivals, when groups found an opportunity and a place for collective public expression.[2] The city's victuallers were particularly active in this regard and used the marketplace to celebrate their success and to advertise their skill by sponsoring elaborate parades. Likewise, town officials took advantage of the conspicuous location of the market house to gain favor with the public, to legitimize their power over trade, and to cultivate loyalty from the farmers and victuallers.

Marketplace culture would not exist without the patrons, whose presence gave rise to the expression teatro del mondo, "theater of the world," which chroniclers have used over the centuries to describe the marketplace as an urban microcosm or a city in miniature (fig. 3.1). Here one could judge the city's political alliances, social and economic health, and quality of life.[3] Granted, people might gather in other public places to discuss politics, exchange news, celebrate, and socialize, but only the market could claim so many virtues in one place. It supplied life's material necessities, employment opportunities, revenue for the town, a forum for debate about government regulation of trade, and incentives for commercial and urban development.

Merchants and colonists carried the public market tradition—its laws, architecture, and culture—to the North American colonies, with the hope that regulated public markets would protect the colonists, induce settlement, encourage trade and agriculture, and provide a locus for civic life. As a result, marketplace culture was as thriving in nineteenth-century America as it was in Europe.

Bringing Goods to Market

To understand marketplace culture in early nineteenth-century America one must understand the daily routine of urban food provisioning. Preparation began long before any customers arrived, when farmers slowly made their way by night from the countryside to the city. When Emily Burke visited Savannah in the late 1840s, she saw country women who had come eighty

FIGURE 3.1 *Yearly Market, or Publick Fare.* Watercolor by Lewis Miller, 1831. The York County Heritage Trust, Pennsylvania.

to one hundred miles from the interior to sell their produce. They made their journey from the back country in covered carts filled with goods and live animals and cooked their meals along the way. In town, Burke saw them sleeping on the cold, damp bricks of the market house before opening hours.[4]

Early morning traffic to Washington's Center Market began in adjacent Prince Georges County, Maryland, the city's principal source of fruits and vegetables. Farmers typically brought their goods in carts drawn by one, two, or three yokes of oxen. On arrival, they stocked their stalls or stands with produce, then moved their empty wagons to a designated parking area before the market opened. Farmers also took advantage of being in town to make their own purchases, particularly bulky items such as wood, hay, or coal. They also patronized the local banks, taverns, inns, and stores. Samuel Bacon's grocery store opposite Center Market was a popular stop for farmers, who bought coffee, sugar, flour, and dry goods, presumably more cheaply than at their local country stores.[5]

Fish typically arrived by boat wherever possible. The Washington firm of Knight and Gibson kept a stand in Center Market, which was stocked from its nearby fisheries along the Potomac River. The firm rented the Long Bridge Fishery for $2,000 a year and another fishery near Mathias Point, about seventy miles down the Potomac, for $6,000 a year. Knight and Gibson, as well as other fish merchants, floated the fish in "live boxes" to the canal, twenty-five feet south of the market, from which vendors could replenish their stalls with fresh fish as needed.[6]

Meat, too, had its own special itinerary. Cattle, sheep, and swine walked to the market prodded by a drover (fig. 3.2). Graphic accounts portray the drama of these markets on the move; it was estimated that in autumn 1810 forty thousand swine were driven from Ohio to the markets in Philadelphia, Baltimore, and other eastern cities.[7] Equally dramatic must have been the sight of a young man from Petersburg, Ohio, who drove a thousand turkeys to Pittsburgh in 1828. Reports of turkey drives in New England testify that the long walk was less of a problem for the drover than for the turkeys. Drovers had to walk the birds through warm asphalt to coat their feet for the long journey, but this did not prevent turkeys from flying into trees along the way to roost at night.[8]

Butchers and drovers transported live animals on steamboats or flatboats, but they preferred roads, "bad as they were." Likewise, the full advantages of transporting live animals to market by railroad were not realized until after the Civil War. Until then the question remained in the minds of some, including a writer for the *Frankfort (Kentucky) Commentator* in 1830: "Is there any way of transporting live animals so cheap, safe, and convenient as upon their own feet, followed by drivers?"[9]

Drovers arrived throughout the week and probably stalled their animals near livestock markets such as Brighton, about six miles from the center of

FIGURE 3.2 Butcher's weather vane, 1835. Index of American Design. Photograph © 2001 Board of Trustees, National Gallery of Art, Washington, about 1939.

Boston, where butchers and farmers went to make their purchases. Cattle season began the last week in August and was finished by Christmas; peak season for sheep was July through October; and there was a year-round business in barreled beef and pork, as well as dressed birds such as ducks, geese, chickens, and turkeys.[10]

Occupational mapping of early nineteenth-century cities shows that butchers tended to settle in neighborhoods one or two miles from the market house. Butchers Hill, in southeast Baltimore, got its name from butchers of German descent who had stalls at the nearby Broadway Market in Fell's Point. These butchers, like most, preferred to slaughter the animals themselves in back of their houses. The hill's 125-foot elevation not only dissipated the stench of slaughter but made it easier to transport heavy carcasses down to the market.[11]

With the help of apprentices, butchers brought their meat to market before daylight. After unloading, an apprentice took the cart home for the day and returned with the master butcher's breakfast. In New York, "small-meat butchers" like Andrew Paff, occupant of stall no. 3 in Catharine Market, had no apprentices, so they brought their meat to market in wheelbarrows. Mrs. Paff brought her husband breakfast and tended the stand while he ate. Afterward she chose something for dinner, put it in the wheelbarrow with the breakfast kettle, and trundled it home.[12]

Patrons

For centuries the bustle of market day was a popular subject for artists, writers, and travelers, and the markets of nineteenth-century America were no exception (fig. 3.3). The throngs had a particular meaning in the early Republic, when artists and writers were eager to depict the egalitarian features of the marketplace. Describing market day at Philadelphia's High Street Market, the Revolutionary War poet Philip Freneau was impressed that

> the market house, like the grave, is a place of perfect equality. None think themselves too mighty to be seen here—nor are there any so mean as to be excluded. Here you may see (at the proper hour) the whig and the tory—the Churchman and the Quaker—the Methodist and the Presbyterian—the moderate man and the violent—the timorous and the brave—the modest and the impudent—the chaste and the lewd, the philosopher and the simpleton—the blooming lass of fifteen, and the withered matron of sixty, the man worth two pence, and he of a hundred thousand pounds.[13]

Accounts from shoppers confirm the variety of buyers who frequented the market. Samuel Latham Mitchill returned home almost daily from New York's Washington Market with a market basket in one hand and sometimes a large fish, or something else for balance, in the other. Mitchill said that "the man who was ashamed to carry home his dinner from market, did not deserve any." In general a man was "not too proud to carry home a well-filled market basket, containing his morning purchase, which his purse or taste prompted him to select."[14]

Travelers noted that men were the principal shoppers at the Boston markets. C. D. Arfwedson was not convinced that food shopping was a man's occupation, especially in Europe, where men would consider shopping for a variety of dishes rather "troublesome." However, he was willing to tolerate the task of shopping "in a country where the manner of living is unostentatious" and where "one solid joint . . . forms alone the whole repast."[15]

FIGURE 3.3 Market day, York, about 1830. Watercolor by William Wagner.
The York County Heritage Trust, Pennsylvania.

One observer at New York's Fly Market reported in *American Farmer* in
1819 that 50 percent of the shoppers were servants sent by their masters. This
statistic alarmed the writer, who believed that a master should not entrust "a
careless servant to cater for him, who without system or economy, expended
ten dollars, when five would have been more sufficient." The writer also advised ladies not to go marketing unless they had no choice, as in the case of
widowed mothers. Popular journals encouraged respectable women to stay
home to wash and dress their children while the man of the house went shopping. Only a man, they argued, would "have the strength and courage to push
his way thro' crowds of rude servants, waggoners, and fish women."[16]

But public opinion on ladies' going to market was mixed. A writer for a
Philadelphia newspaper admired the practice of women's patronizing the
public markets and saw "no difference in a Lady's purchasing a nice pound of
butter, a basket of fruit, or a pair of pheasants" and purchasing a pair of shoes,
gloves, or a hat.[17] This was not to say that all women were comfortable amid
the chaos and the questionable characters around the market house. On October 20, 1775, Susanna Trapes of Philadelphia reported "a most misfortunate
disaster" that she encountered while passing through the marketplace to visit
her cousin one foggy, drizzly day. In her letter to the *Pennsylvania Magazine*,

FIGURE 3.4 East Market, Indianapolis, about 1850. Drawing by Christian Schrader. Indiana State Library, Lilly Negative.

Trapes wrote that the market wagons blocked the street. To avoid them she descended a steep hill and fell on the slippery stone pavement. She soiled her calico gown, broke her umbrella, spattered her cotton stockings, and lost the heel of a new shoe. Worse yet, she complained, "grate haw-buks set up a hoss-laf at me; and then hollud out, *take care, yung woman or youl sho your ankels; cum here sweet-hart and weel help you up again:* and such loe-life sayings. . . . Now isn't it a most monstrus thing that them filthy wagons shud be stuck rite akros the Street every markit-day, so that fokes can't pass?"[18]

Apart from a fragile few, unless they were wealthy enough to afford servants, women still frequented the markets and tolerated the predictable louts and swearing cartmen. Likewise they tolerated loose animals such as pigs and dogs, mischievous boys, the dangers of unloading heavy goods like bulk hay and lumber, and frequent encounters with obnoxious "others" (fig. 3.4).

Vendors

Equally diverse were the vendors. When Benjamin Henry Latrobe arrived in New Orleans in 1819, he was immediately impressed by the different "market folks" (fig. 3.5):

Along the Levee, as far as the eye could reach to the West, and to the Market house to the East were ranged two rows of Market people, some having stalls or tables with a Tilt or awning of Canvass, but the Majority having their wares

FIGURE 3.5 *Market Folks*, New Orleans, 1815. Watercolor by Benjamin Henry Latrobe. The Maryland Historical Society, Baltimore.

lying on the ground, perhaps on a piece of canvas, or a parcel of Palmetto leaves. The articles to be sold were not more numerous than the sellers. White men and women, and of all hues of brown, and of all Classes of faces, from round Yankees, to grisly and lean Spaniards, black Negroes and negresses and filthy Indians half naked, Mulattoes, curly and straight haired, Quarteroons of all shades long haired and frizzled, the women dressed in the most flaring yellow, and scarlet gowns, the men capped and hatted.[19]

Latrobe also marveled at the variety of food and wares, as well as the five hundred or so sellers and buyers, "all of whom appeared to strain their voices, to exceed each other in their loudness." The following year Latrobe's wife, Mary, visited New Orleans, and she too was astonished by the sights and sounds of the market, particularly the uproar, which she likened to Babel. The Babel metaphor was used often by nineteenth-century writers to describe the cacophony of public markets—one of the most universal features of the aural landscape of cities.[20]

Female Hucksters

The most colorful participants in the market were the female street vendors, a familiar sight in the urban landscape from New York to New Orleans and cherished figures in urban folklore. Mrs. Jeroleman, for example, who sold coffee and doughnuts from a table in New York's Oswego Market, was noted for her strong character and physique. She reportedly weighed 225 pounds, earning her the nickname "large dough-nut" from the butcher boys. Equally large and "well-formed" was Mrs. Fanny Watson, or "Aunt Fanny," a huckster in Centre Market.[21]

Nineteenth-century literature characterized the female huckster as not only large but also tough, as the result of an active outdoor life (fig. 3.6). This trait was useful in defense against "rowdies or robbers," who were known to attack women in the early, dark hours of the market. Another persistent characteristic of the female huckster was her ability to amass savings over years of hard, honest work. Mrs. Barbary Wiseburn, for example, was "a good, motherly, honest woman, who had no doubt seen a good deal of trouble, as well as hardships, in her early days." Her husband, Daniel, worked as a tailor and tended their market garden while she sold vegetables at Bear Market. After Daniel died in 1799, Mrs. Wiseburn continued to support the family from a vegetable stand at Washington Market, where she remained until her death in 1837. When "Aunt Fanny," the coffee and doughnut vendor in Centre Market, died in 1841, she too "left a snug property and a good name for industry, intelligence, and honesty."[22]

Street Entertainers

The public market was an excellent place to get the attention of large crowds and thus was an attractive arena for preachers, practical jokers, and entertainers. The Philadelphia preacher Joseph Pilmore took his stand every evening at the end of the market house, where he "found great freedom of mind to publish glad tidings to sinners."[23] Likewise, Johnny Edwards preached outside New York's Essex Market, where he got on his "favorite rock" and entertained crowds weekly with his "singular and sometimes pointed remarks." Down along the East River at Fly Market, a countryman stood on a butcher's block and ate fifty boiled eggs, "shells and all," in fifteen minutes for a small wager. Such stuntmen earned spare cash by performing

FIGURE 3.6 Fly Market, New York, 1816. From *Old New York; Views by S. Hollyer* (New York, 1905), pl. 26.

their feats at the crowded marketplaces.[24] In 1804 "some wicked boys" played a practical joke on a farmer in York, Pennsylvania: they dismantled a wagon and reassembled it on top of the market house just for fun (fig. 3.7).

Entertainers also used the marketplace for their performances. The first appearance of public "negro dancing" in New York occurred at Catharine Market (fig. 3.8). Most dancers were Long Island slaves on leave for holidays. They gathered roots, berries, herbs, birds, fish, clams, and oysters and took them to market in their skiffs. A "joking butcher" or other individual would hire them to perform a jig or breakdown for "pocket money." Spectators threw money to the dancers, who earned extra by dancing on a springy board or shingle. The dancer's partner kept time by beating his hands on the sides of his legs or tapping his heels. The most famous dancers were Francis ("Ned"), belonging to Martin Ryerson, Bob Rowley ("Bobolink Bob"), belonging to William Bennett, and "Jack," belonging to Frederick De Voo. Slaves from New Jersey also went to Catharine Market for dance competitions with the Long Island slaves. First they sold their masters' produce at Bear Market, then they would "shin it" for the Catharine Market. If no one contributed money to the collection, the winning dancer would accept eels or small fish.[25]

FIGURE 3.7 *Some Wicked Boys at the Market House*, 1804. Watercolor by Lewis Miller. The York County Heritage Trust, Pennsylvania.

Parades and Processions

The market's central location, unostentatious design, and multiple functions made it a frequent site for public celebrations. Its projecting eaves offered protection from the elements even when the market house was closed. These features were primarily meant to draw patrons and make loading and unloading goods easier, but they also made the market house attractive for parades, processions, and other civic pageantry. When the Washington Free School Society held a parade in Alexandria, Virginia, participants proceeded to the market, where they fired seventeen rounds. When the cabinetmakers of Baltimore decided to plan a Fourth of July celebration, they notified members to meet at the

DANCING FOR EELS, 1820 CATHARINE MARKET.

FIGURE 3.8 Dancing for eels, Catharine Market, New York City, 1820.
Photograph courtesy of Sotheby's, Inc. © 2002.

FIGURE 3.9 *High Street, from the Country Market-Place, Philadelphia: With the Procession in Commemoration of the Death of General George Washington, December 26th. 1799.* Drawn and engraved by William and Thomas Birch. I. N. Phelps Stokes Collection, Miriam and Ira D. Wallach Division of Art, Prints and Photographs, the New York Public Library, Astor, Lenox, and Tilden Foundations.

market. And when the several military corps in Georgetown, South Carolina, gathered for musters, they too assembled at the market house.[26]

An engraving of the procession in Philadelphia on December 26, 1799, held to commemorate the death of George Washington illustrates the market's role in civic pageantry (fig. 3.9). Although the market was closed for the occasion, the sheds protected those watching the procession and offered privacy to a weeping soldier. High Street Market's central location, open, shed-like plan with multiple entrances, street access on all sides, and projecting eaves contributed to its popularity as a stage for public events.

Butchers

Of all the vendors in the public markets, none were more organized, politicized, patriotic, and flamboyant than the butchers. This was due in part to the history and nature of their trade. Since market laws forbade butchers to sell anywhere but in the public markets, the mandatory centralization of meat retailing promoted trade solidarity; and municipal authorities issued licenses only to butchers who had completed an apprenticeship. The success of the city's meat retailing therefore rested on cooperation between local government and licensed butchers, who enjoyed a virtual monopoly.

Butchers in the public markets were wealthier, had better stalls, and fancied themselves more sophisticated and urbane than their country cousins— the "country butchers" from nearby farms who sold meat in the public markets under short-term licenses but were not permanent occupants of the market house. By contrast, the "regular butchers" rented market stalls year-round and depended on a steady, trusting, and reliable clientele. Cleanliness was their pride. *The Boston Patriot* reported on September 18, 1826, that "the new market does honor to Boston . . . but . . . the butchers are not dressed in duck clean long frocks, covering the person from neck to ankles, as in the case in Leaden Hall, London, and in Philadelphia. There are in the latter strict rules and orders respecting clean frocks, like those of soldiers on parade. In this Boston is behind Philadelphia." Although clean attire may seem rather obvious, the public image of butchers was clearly as important to civic pride as the market house itself, and Faneuil Hall Market evidently had nothing to boast about.

The butchers' trade was inconceivable without a market house. Describing the profession in 1837, Edward Hazen wrote, "In large cities and towns, the meat is chiefly sold in the market-house, where each butcher has a stall rented from the corporation."[27] Butchers always cited their stall number in advertisements and directories to remind customers of their exact location. They also projected an image of superiority and respectability, in part by wearing gentlemen's attire, complete with top hat, protected by a white apron or frock. Because the market house was theirs, butchers more than any other food vendors exerted their influence over its operation.

Butchers were also noted for their excellent physical condition, resulting from an active outdoor life, ample diet, and lack of stress. According to C. Turner Thackrah, butchers rode on horseback to neighboring markets and into the countryside to buy cattle; they ate fresh-cooked meat at least twice a day; they were "plump and rosy"; and they were "cheerful and good-natured" because they were "not subject to such anxieties as the fluctuations of other trades produce; for meat is always in request." Thackrah also noted that butchers, although they suffered from fewer ailments than other tradesmen, did not live long because of their excessive eating, drinking, and brawling.[28]

In addition to Thackrah's plump and happy stereotype, urban folklore promoted the butcher as a man of great strength and strong character. It was reputed, for example, that Thomas Collister, a hog butcher in Washington Market, "could lift a hog up by his bristles." Butchers were also noted for leadership, and they sometimes went into public service. Thomas Jeremiah, a butcher in New York's Washington Market for twenty-two years, served as county clerk, alderman of several wards, and finally representative to the state legislature in 1844.[29]

Grocers

Grocers located in shops and specialized in the sale of nonperishables such as coffee, tea, spices, rice, flour, dry goods, and liquor, and occasionally sold fresh meat (though only in small quantities). Their reputation in the early national period could not have been more different from the reputation of butchers, who were "too honest to defraud or cheat." Grocers "live[d] upon the poor" by buying goods cheap at wholesale, then selling them at exorbitant prices. Worse yet were the character of the grocer and the atmosphere of his store:

> Now look within a grocery,
> And mark what virtue there you see;
> . . . An now a jolly set of tars,
> Just in from sea, come hopping in,
> And order each a glass of gin;
> Then seat them by the counter's side,
> Regardless what effects betide,
> And swear so awfully and vile,
> (The grocer laughing all the while,)[30]

Eaton regarded grocery stores with such disgust that despite their convenience he advised readers to take a few more minutes to go out of their way to avoid them. The reputation of New York grocers for attracting the lower sorts and for promoting antisocial behavior persisted until the second quarter of the nineteenth century, when grocers began to locate in the middle-class neighborhoods.[31] Until then, grocers were associated more with disreputable neighborhoods like the infamous Five Points on the Lower East Side than with the public markets. Often likened to the proprietors of bawdy houses and grog shops, they were considered so disruptive that in an effort to maintain the market peace, New York City market ordinances periodically forbade grocers to rent stalls or cellars in the public markets.[32]

Butchers' Parades

The greatest promoters of the notion that butchers were superior to all other food dealers were the butchers themselves. Although numerous trade associations and militia units used the public market for celebrations, the butchers were the most conspicuous, treating the market house and the surrounding streets as a platform for proclaiming their political views, alliances, solidarity as a trade, and service to the public.[33]

The first significant public gathering of butchers in the young nation took place in New York on July 23, 1788. "The Great Federal Procession," in celebration of the Constitution, brought the city's butchers out in large numbers. Jotham Post, Alexander Fink, John Lovel, and Jacob J. Arden led the procession carrying a flag with the butchers' coat of arms and the motto "Skin Me Well, Dress Me Neat, and Send Me Aboard the Federal Fleet." Behind them were horse-drawn floats carrying a miniature ship, slaughterhouse, and partially built market house labeled Federal Market. Another float carried a model of a market stall in which two butchers and two boys were at work splitting lambs and cutting up and arranging meats. Then came one hundred butchers on horseback, wearing clean white aprons and carrying sharpening steels at their sides, followed by a band playing music.[34]

Butchers expressed their patriotism and solidarity in a number of other ways. In 1806 at least eleven New York butchers volunteered for Francisco de Miranda's filibuster to Venezuela—one of the earliest struggles for independence in Latin America. They joined the expedition with the justification that their principal duty was to guard the United States president during travel, and at other times to guard the mail at New Orleans. Lured by the supposed act of patriotism, as well as the promise of pay, butchers desperate to make a living after the yellow fever epidemic of 1805 embarked on the *Leander* on February 2, 1806. The Spanish captured the ship and imprisoned about sixty people, including butcher John Parsells, who spent over three years in prison in South America before returning to New York. Butchers who survived the Miranda expedition became heroes in the markets, and their adventures survived in the local lore.[35]

Daniel Burtnett, a butcher in New York's Washington Market, recalled the "spunky national feeling" that pervaded the ranks of apprentice butchers during the War of 1812. They decided to aid the government, as their masters had done, in constructing fortifications at Brooklyn Heights. After completing a lengthy breastwork, the young butchers cheered as they raised a flag with the inscription, "Free Trade and Butchers' Rights, from Brooklyn's Fields to Harlem Heights." Butchers served themselves as well as their country by these patriotic acts, for they reported their military service in the War of 1812, as well as in the American Revolution, in their petitions for stalls in the market houses.[36]

The butchers continued their penchant for extravaganzas with "fat-beef" exhibitions—the English practice of parading exceptionally large cattle (nearly two thousand pounds from one animal) to the market house before slaughter (fig. 3.10). In the 1790s, fat-beef exhibitions were cooperative ventures between a butcher and the farmer who fattened the steer. To encourage the quick sale of large quantities of beef, the butcher advertised in local newspapers—inviting the public to the sale at the market house. Accompanied by music, he paraded the steer, decorated with garlands and ribbons, through the streets to the slaughterhouse. Such displays of individual achievement were frequent in New York and Philadelphia, where fat-beef exhibitions "were got up in the most imposing, as well as the expensive manner."[37]

The first notice of fat-beef sales in New York's Bear Market was in 1794, when Samuel Winship, stall no. 1, invited the city's connoisseurs "to attend and partake of the purchase, and please their tastes."[38] By 1821, however, fat-beef exhibitions had evolved from displays of individual achievement into major publicity events for butchers' societies and agriculturists. March was a particularly active month in the rival cities of New York and Philadelphia. On March 15 Thomas Gibbons, a butcher in New York's Fly Market, advertised the sale of twenty first-prize, or "premium," cattle, in "hopes that his efforts to promote the agricultural interest of this State will meet the approbation and support of a magnanimous and generous public." The procession consisted of forty decorated butchers' carts carrying the beef through the principal streets to Fly Market. The leading cart carried the silver pitchers awarded at the New York Agricultural Show. When Philip Fink, of Orange County, sent his prizewinning cattle to Washington Market, the press claimed that this lot

FIGURE 3.10 Fat-beef parade at New Market, in South Second Street, Philadelphia, 1799. Drawn and engraved by William Birch. Free Library of Philadelphia.

of cattle "was finer than any collection of the like number that have ever been seen in this country, and it may safely be said that Philadelphia cannot furnish this season 64 head of fat cattle superior to those now offered at our fair."[39]

Not to be outdone by their New York rivals, the butchers of Philadelphia produced "one of the most brilliant spectacles ever exhibited since the celebrated Federal Procession" (fig. 3.11). On March 15, 1821, a crowd of thirty thousand gathered to view "the Procession of Victuallers," held to advertise meat from prize cattle. The publicity claimed that meat of such quality, beauty, variety, and quantity had never been slaughtered at any one time "in this, or probably in any other country." Leading the two-mile parade was a flag bearer carrying the butchers' standard and the motto "We Feed the Hungry." Following were two hundred boys in white frocks drawing carts of meat to the market, where all of it was sold within twenty-four hours. The procession celebrated the self-sufficiency and progress of a country no longer at war.[40]

Reflecting on the utility of fat-beef exhibitions, Dr. James Mease, vice president of the Philadelphia Society for Promoting Agriculture, believed that "zeal and spirit" were misapplied. He argued that the continued overfeeding of cattle at the end of their life in order "to clothe their bodies and line their interiors with loads of fat . . . was . . . absurd." Animal rights were not the issue; Mease went on to say that the bad effects of the processions were "the loss of work among every class of mechanics, the interruption to the education of the poor, and the temptation to useless expense for strong drink which they excite, at a time, too, when the means of employment are so greatly circumscribed as at present." The negative effects of the procession went beyond the confines of the city, for Mease believed that "the money expended, and even lost, by feeding heavy show beef cattle, impoverish more or less a country, by diminishing the means which the feeders would have had without such expenditure, of bringing to market a greater number of cattle in the future."[41]

Although Mease understood the delicate balance between city and countryside in matters of agriculture and husbandry, his paper had little effect, for fat-beef exhibitions were still advertised in the Quaker City as late as 1845.[42] They also persisted in New York City, particularly after the opening of the Erie Canal in 1825 once again sparked a public spirit among the butchers. To celebrate the occasion on November 4, the New York butchers joined farm-

FIGURE 3.11 *Procession of Victuallers*, 1821. Aquatint and etching, with watercolor, by Joseph Yeager. Gift of the Estate of Charles M. B. Cadwalader, Philadelphia Museum of Art.

ers for a parade of floats that represented the process of grazing and feeding
until the animal was slaughtered for market. Hand-held banners, such as one
with an image of an ox inscribed "Liberty Is Our Head" and another with an
image of a steak inscribed "To All We Divide a Part," attest to the butchers'
strong self-identity and perceived importance in a democratic society.[43] A few
years later they sought to establish a national reputation for the sale of choice
meats by purchasing the "President"—an extraordinarily heavy steer. On February 6, they paraded it through the streets to Centre Market carrying banners with their "modest" claim: "Centre Market against the World." "President" was offered for sale the next day, except for a choice piece of meat that
the butchers sent to President Andrew Jackson with a letter of thanks for his
public service and "private virtues." Jackson acknowledged their gift as a
token of their respect for his character and informed them that he anticipated
eating the meat the next day.[44]

United in their desire for representation, market butchers persisted in de-
manding a respectable, profitable, and permanent place in society, especially
in cities where the diversity of classes, conditions, occupations, and economic
interests strengthened the democratic impulse. Just as civic culture began to
flourish in Jacksonian America, the marketplace was disrupted in the 1830s
when certain butchers, in defiance of the law, began to sell in their own shops.
The trouble started in New York City.[45]

"Shop butchers," as opposed to "market butchers," set off on their own to
break up the "monopoly" in the public markets. They were the same class of
workingmen who challenged government protection of the carter trade, arguing that the system of awarding market stalls through auction and license
"was injurious to the spirit of free trade, was a denial of the right of free Americans to enter the trade of their choice and kept the occupation in perpetual
bondage to unscrupulous politicians." In an 1830 memorial to the New York
common council, the workingmen cited numerous politicians who had
awarded licenses based on patronage and corruption and argued that the licensing system was a remnant of the repressive laws of the English era.[46] The
workingmen's appeal did not have an immediate effect, for New York officials
still fined those breaking the law that forbade selling meat outside the public
markets. By the late 1830s, however, enforcement was erratic and meat shops
operated "in almost every part of the city with perfect impunity."[47]

PART II

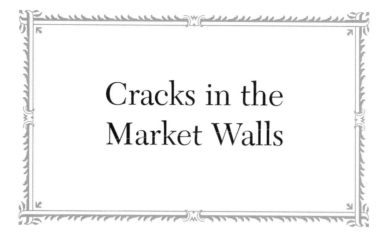

Cracks in the Market Walls

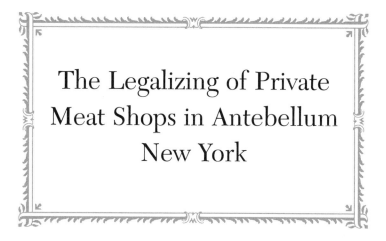

FOUR

The Legalizing of Private Meat Shops in Antebellum New York

Now that the Whigs are likely to manage the city as they please, we take leave to ask them if they intend to do anything with regard to the present odious, unjust, and oppressive laws, prohibiting the sale of fresh meats, except in stalls in the public markets?

New World, June 25, 1842

Although butchers never used the term "moral economy," they clearly understood its principles. They knew that market laws, no matter how stifling, benefited the common good, and that without public faith and government protection, their ancient trade would fall into the hands of novices and cheats. The New York butchers who had left the public markets to open their own shops did so not because they were "free traders" but because they considered unfair the city's practice of selling market stalls at auction to the highest bidder. They were also angry that the city failed to invest in new market houses yet channeled funds to other public projects such as the Croton Water Works. Egging on the angry butchers were young uptown residents, armed with "free trade" rhetoric and disillusioned with city government, who preferred the convenience of neighborhood shops to the public markets, which were all south of Tenth Street. Had the city kept pace with urban growth by distributing public markets throughout the city, the agitation for

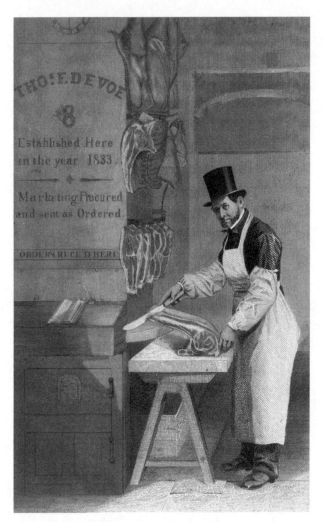

FIGURE 4.1 Thomas F. De Voe, butcher, stall no. 8,
Jefferson Market, New York, after a self-portrait. From
Thomas F. De Voe, *The Market Assistant: Containing a Brief
Description of Every Article of Human Food Sold in the
Public Markets of the Cities of New York, Boston,
Philadelphia, and Brooklyn* (New York: Riverside Press,
1867), frontispiece.

meat shops might never have materialized. The meat shop controversy was the first significant challenge to the primacy of public markets.

During the months when his butcher business was slow, Thomas De Voe spent time in the library of the New-York Historical Society, working on his partially published history of the public markets of New York, Boston, Philadelphia, and Brooklyn (fig. 4.1). De Voe knew the public market system in several capacities. He had been a butcher in Jefferson Market since 1833, and his years in the trade spanned the most turbulent time for public markets in New York City—during the meat shop controversy of the 1830s and 1840s and through the campaign against public markets of the 1850s. He knew exactly how space was negotiated in the markets, understood the elements of their success and failure, and fought relentlessly to keep overall control of urban food retailing in public hands. His firsthand knowledge of the butcher trade, as well as his insight into the history of public markets, make him an important source of information on the New York meat shop controversy.

The Auction System

De Voe made it clear that the butchers' anxiety began over the issue of auctioning stalls in Fly Market—one of the city's oldest markets, situated along the East River near Wall Street. In the colonial period, the city earned revenue for providing the public amenity of a market house by taxing according to the amount of meat sold. As Fly Market became crowded over the years, it was difficult for the market clerk to observe transactions, so butchers found it tempting to underrepresent their sales, making the honor system ineffective and dependent on informants. In 1810, for example, Charles Conlin's license was revoked after an informant reported him for paying tax on the sale of only ten sheep when he had actually sold eighteen. Other butchers were bolder than Conlin, leaving the market before the clerk even had time to collect any taxes. As a result, the city decided to abandon the tax system in favor of collecting rent for the privilege of occupying a stall. In 1795, in addition to annual rent, butchers who wanted to occupy stalls in the new Fly Market had to bid for them at public auction rather than obtaining them by lot as had been customary.[1]

Within a few years the corporation regretted the auction system because it led to favoritism and injustice. Young butchers who had just completed the apprenticeship could not afford to bid, nor could they find any vacant stalls for rent. Moreover, auctions created resentment because some butchers obtained the more desirable corner stalls by paying a premium price instead of the old way—by luck of the draw.

To remedy the situation, the corporation decided to buy back the butcher stalls at Fly Market and resume the practice of assigning them annually by lot. To the corporation's chagrin, the butchers refused the cash offer because "they found themselves independent with their stands, and they viewed them as estates for their children." As butcher Daniel Winship explained on their behalf, "We view [the stands] as our own property, and the property of our heirs." In 1824, when the city removed Fly Market, the butchers took their case to court and won a settlement of $10,272.46 in premium reimbursements.[2]

The city continued to foster resentment among the butchers; in 1816 it resumed auctioning premium stalls at Washington Market. This time, however, the city council tried to appease the butchers with a promise to give them occupancy rights for a specified number of years. More than forty petitioners argued that the new measure would cause them "great inconvenience and distress," since they would probably have to quit at the end of their term, not being able to afford to bid again for the same stand after they had just built up the business. They also feared that stands would "be purchased by some adventurer, who will receive the benefits arising from the industry of the former holder of said stand." In a final plea, the petitioners argued that "as persons of capital can alone bid for the stands, those butchers who are poor will not be able, during their lives, to procure a stand to follow their business at; and further, persons who are not butchers may hire persons who are butchers to hire such stands, and share the profits of the same, to which they ought not to be entitled; by which means many regular well-bred butchers will be deprived of the means of getting a living for their families."[3] The city accepted their case and returned to the lottery system for assigning stalls.

Not six years had passed before the common council yet again proposed a public auction for the sale of vacant stands at Washington Market. On April 15, 1822, petitioners asked the city to consider another system of assigning stalls "which would be equally productive to the revenue of the city, [and] more consistent with that equity which should exist in every department of society which has been attached to public markets." Market revenues would be more predictable if based on a collection system that was "consistent with justice, and equal to the value of the privileges enjoyed." Otherwise "industry is paralyzed." Furthermore, auctioning stands would attract purchasers whose character "had not been tested." In time, argued the butchers, "no permanency, society, nor character will ever attach itself to the profession." In defense of the consumer, the petitioners asked, "Can [consumers], if [we are] defeated in purchasing stands in a public market, buy elsewhere, and of whom they please? No—for the law confines them to public markets, and they must act agreeable to that law." The council accepted their arguments, and the contemplated measure was temporarily abandoned. But it was an endless fight. In 1835, when a new city council resolved to auction four new stalls at Centre Market, "this was more than the butchers could bear." With legal counsel they obtained a restraining order on the comptroller and prevented the sale.[4]

These events point to the germ of a new idea—one shared by the butchers and the civic authorities—that a market house was not a public amenity but rather an important piece of real estate. Butchers believed they owned their stalls in perpetuity, as did widows of butchers who suddenly found themselves in charge of the business. Although some widows petitioned the city to transfer their husbands' stalls to a relative or close friend, others wanted to keep the business for themselves. In 1812, for example, the city finally passed a law that automatically granted widows of butchers the right to their husbands' stalls for one year, as well as a license to practice the butcher's trade.[5] Similarly, by the 1830s the municipal corporation also had come to view markets primarily as real estate. It jealously guarded its holdings and kept count of its market buildings and grounds—preferring to maximize revenues rather than to provide satisfactory and economical public facilities.

Proposal for a Wholesale Market

In addition to persisting with the auction system, the New York city commissioners added to the butchers' resentment by proposing a new wholesale market north of the settled city. The Commissioners' Map of 1811 noted a future market site bounded north and south by Tenth and Seventh Streets and east and west by the East River and First Avenue (fig. 4.2). Motivated by practical concerns, the commissioners intended the new market to function as a "general mart," where retailers would purchase supplies and provisions for

FIGURE 4.2 Detail, map of the city of New York, 1811, with the proposed
marketplace at *bottom right,* along the East River. Library of Congress.

their stores. They believed a large wholesale market would accommodate the
city's projected growth over the next half century, alleviate congestion downtown, and stabilize prices throughout the city.[6]

According to the map's explanatory remarks, the proposed wholesale market was also intended to encourage neighborhood food retailing, thus saving
consumers' shopping time. Referring to public markets, the commissioners
argued that "to a person engaged in profitable business, one hour spent in
market is frequently worth more than the whole of what he purchases, and he
is sometimes obliged to purchase a larger quantity than he has occasion to use,
so that the surplus is wasted." They considered the public markets not only
inconvenient and costly to the average shopper but also disruptive to traffic

in the already congested downtown. The proposed suburban wholesale market, in combination with a network of retail stores, would improve food distribution and promote "cleanliness and health."

Not surprisingly, the notion of private shops was not popular either with the public market butchers or with the city's wage earners, cartmen, and New Jersey farmers, who remained loyal to their provisioners and customers at the city's familiar marketplaces in lower Manhattan. As a result of their opposition, plans for the new wholesale market never materialized. Although the city eventually built a market house on the site, it reduced the grounds substantially in response to an 1815 petition for the city to return part of the land to its original owners.[7]

By blocking the proposed wholesale market, butchers unknowingly failed to act in their best interest, for the proposed market would still have been publicly owned and protected by municipal law even though it would have operated in tandem with private shops. Although the proposal encouraged some private retailing, the city did not intend to forfeit its control over the larger wholesale food trade. As De Voe opined, the city deprived New Yorkers of what would have been a valuable marketplace "if it had been carried out as originally intended."[8]

The "Municipal Monopoly"

The city's greatest mistake, however, lay not in abandoning the proposed wholesale market but rather in holding butchers hostage to the public markets while failing to fulfill its municipal mandate of providing adequate and economical retail facilities. Particularly destructive to the public market system was the city's practice of luring butchers into buying premium stands with the promise of protecting their businesses. This was the case in 1827, when Alderman John Y. Cebra, chairman of the Market Committee, promised the butchers who were relocated from Spring Street Market to the new Clinton Market "that they need have no fear in bidding liberally, as no meat was hereafter to be sold south of Fourteenth Street, except in public markets." The corporation told the butchers that if they wanted stands in the new market, they must compete for them. Certain butchers had no choice but to establish shops, because they had lost out on their bids for market stalls. The city also alienated the butchers who bid successfully on stalls, because it soon broke its promise and ignored the meat shops that operated south of the mandated boundary.[9]

Happily for city coffers, the auction system was paying off, despite a few butchers who fled to shops. In February 1834 the Joint Committee on Markets reported that "there is no property held by the Corporation netting so large an amount on its cost as that derived from the rents and fees of the markets." Gross income in 1834 consisted of:

Premiums on butchers' stands	$10,857.28
Interest on premium stands	1,951.83
Market fees	19,484.17
Market rents	30,218.65
TOTAL	$62,511.93

The committee calculated that based on an estimated cost of $640,000, the city's thirteen public markets had yielded a net return of almost 10 percent on capital invested.[10]

By reducing the public markets to a source of revenue, city officials abused their mandate of maintaining the "moral economy" by channeling market revenues to other public works such as water, streets, and sewers. As the city's neighborhoods grew faster than the rate of new market house construction, and as the workingmen demanded an end to the system of awarding market stalls through auction and license, private meat shops opened in defiance of the law, and city officials looked the other way.

Sounding the "Moral Economy" Horn

Their patience having run out, the market butchers petitioned city hall using the old "moral economy" rhetoric.[11] In an 1837 petition, butchers from Clinton Market reminded the city council that they had obeyed municipal market laws under the threat of heavy fines and forfeiture of their stands and licenses. The butchers had never complained over the years because they knew that market laws "intended to promote the interests of the public and to secure the citizens an abundant and reasonable supply of sound and wholesome provisions." Most important, they also understood that the law forbidding the sale of meat at any place in the city except the public markets was the law the whole public market system depended on.

Addressing their concern for public health, the butchers persisted in arguing that meat shops would "become the vehicles of vending bad and unwholesome provisions, and the flesh of animals which have died from accident or disease, and which could not be exhibited in the public markets and exposed to experienced observers without detection." Shop butchers, they argued, "prefer their illicit trade to an open and fair competition in the public markets, where the quality of their meats and the fairness of their dealings would be subject to inspection, and be brought into comparison with others." Appealing to the city's financial interests, the butchers also claimed that if it suppressed meat shops, the stands in the public markets "could be filled without injury to your petitioners, and with increased benefit to the public." After all, rent from market stands, which ranged from $10 to $100, went back into the public coffers, whereas shop rent, ranging from $100 to $400, went into private hands, with the exorbitant cost passed on to the consumer.

In a final plea for upholding the ancient principles of the moral economy and the public market tradition, the butchers concluded that while "engaged in the lawful exercise of their business, and submitting to those regulations which the Fathers of our City have seen fit to establish for the public good, [they have] been assailed with obloquy and abuse by those who have grown bold enough in their impunity to claim as a right what they first practiced by stealth, and who stigmatize as aristocrats and monopolists those citizens who respect the laws which they are daily violating." They rejected as absurd the charge of monopoly, for if they were monopolists, then "so are all our citizens whose occupations are the subject of regulations for the benefit of the whole community."

In an attempt to appease the market butchers, the common council authorized $150,000 to refund their stall premiums. At the same time, it insisted on licensing meat shops in order to legalize those shops already in operation. This proposal met with strong objection from the Select Committee, which reported in March 1840 that the city's public markets, now valued at $1 million, produced a net annual income of $42,000. The committee believed that legalizing shops would have the effect of "greatly diminishing, and perhaps entirely destroying that branch of the public revenue," which was badly needed, since the city was in debt from building the Croton Water Works. Furthermore, the cost of refunding premiums to butchers would have to be paid by loan or taxation, because the city's market laws did not permit using market revenues for such purposes.

The Select Committee also believed that "had markets been erected of a less size, and at less expense than those now in existence; had they been increased in number and more equally distributed throughout the city, the public convenience would have been greatly advanced." The committee concluded that existing market laws did not violate the city charter or the state constitution and that they should be upheld until other arrangements could be made to repay outstanding premiums to butchers.

Reporting on the issue in January 1841, the Market Committee of the Board of Aldermen again advocated preserving the old market laws. Peter Cooper, one of the more articulate and influential members of the committee, along with Freeman Campbell, admitted to the Special Committee on the New York City Market Laws that "the restrictive features of the present market system, it appears, are disapproved by a large portion of our citizens, who regard those features as unconstitutional, oppressive, and unjust."[12] However, the committee did not recommend repealing the market laws, because "there are many advantages obtained by having several stalls together, both as to the variety furnished, and the security from imposition, by the competition between the Butchers and the contrast between their meats. There are other advantages from having meat sold in public markets, such as bringing together a proper variety of vegetables, and enabling the inspector of markets to see that nuisances are not created, and improper meat suffered to be sold."[13] As a remedy to the market problem, the committee proposed a series of small market houses with no more than twelve stalls and no fewer than four. It suggested converting some of the city's obsolete market houses into stores and tenements and using the rental revenue to construct new market houses in neighborhoods that needed them. Committee member Cooper was a renowned reformer of city government, but he may also have been personally motivated to recommend neighborhood market houses because his home and glue factory were at Fourth Avenue and Twenty-eighth Street—eighteen blocks from the closest public market. Nonetheless, the Market Committee's position was telling. It implied that some city officials believed a system of small, widely dispersed market houses was preferable to fewer large ones, *and* that markets should remain publicly owned.[14]

In the wake of the meat shop controversy, public support for the Market Committee's proposal was highly unlikely, especially since the city had just enlarged Centre Market at great expense, despite neighborhood opposition.[15] Situated on the block bound by Grand, Rynders (Centre), Orange, and Broome Streets, the new market, designed by architect Thomas Thomas, opened on January 17, 1839. The newspapers hailed it as "the first in this country which may be deemed a complete building. Faneuil Hall, Boston, is something like it, but the London markets of the first class come nearer to it." The city's largest (over 380 feet long) and most valuable ($43,000, plus $63,000 for the grounds) market house was a far cry from the utilitarian sheds that had once served the city so well.[16]

Centre Market's opening was an extravaganza for the city's social elite. For a $5 ticket, a gentleman and two ladies could attend the opening ball, and people reportedly scalped tickets for $25. The ladies' tickets were engraved in gold with a representation of the new market building, Cupid, wreaths, and the names of the market managers. The long corridors over the market were brilliantly illuminated, and tables were covered with fine foods. As the newspapers claimed, "The whole world—that is, the eating world—will be there, and a great affair it will be. No sirloins or rump steaks only, but all the delicacies of the season will be displayed in the most tasteful and fashionable style." More than a thousand people attended the opening, including the mayor and members of the corporation. De Voe described the crowd as "a class of rich, substantial citizens, and all have received good educations, with the usual accomplishments."[17]

While the city's epicures celebrated the new Centre Market, butchers at Clinton Market, still embroiled in the meat shop controversy, refused to pay rent until the city either suppressed meat shops or refunded their premiums. In 1842, when Comptroller D. D. Williamson announced that the city could not afford to refund premiums, Edward Phillips, butcher at stall no. 28, Clinton Market, reported to the common council that he was "at a loss as to know the school of morals [Williamson] was educated in." Phillips also alluded to the identity of meat shop butchers—basically established butchers who were fed up with the city's practice of auctioning stalls to the highest bidder. They had been "driven out" of the public markets "by the very power that placed them there," intending to hold out in their shops only temporarily, with the hope that the city would enforce the current market laws. Phillips accused the city of managing markets that were "private instead of public" and concluded, "I think you will perceive from this simple statement that the butchers have been, in all this premium business, mere creatures of the power of the Corporation." Much to the surprise of the corporation, Phillips also presented a petition from over three hundred journeymen and apprentice butchers declaring that they preferred existing market laws because they preserved "peace, health, and morality."

Partisan Politics

Despite the butchers' petition, growing public sentiment for repeal of the market laws mounted in the early 1840s, particularly among the Whigs, who believed that the public markets, among other city services, provided a lucrative vehicle for the infamous patronage system of the Democrats.[18] Advocates for repeal argued that Thomas Jefferson had mandated "a wise and frugal government, which shall restrain men from injuring one another, and shall leave them otherwise free to regulate their own pursuits of industry and improvement." They argued that there was "no good public reason why the trade in fresh meats should not be left perfectly free. The demand would occasion supply, and competition would ensure the greatest degree of cheapness." Addressing public health concerns, meat shop supporters welcomed government inspection of shops, but that was all. Any further intervention, they contended, did "not come within the legitimate scope of government. Prevent men from injuring one another, but leave them otherwise free to regulate their own pursuits of industry and improvement."[19]

Throughout the meat shop controversy, however, market laws remained in effect. Perhaps in a show of strength against a Whig-dominated council, on December 14, 1841, Democratic Mayor Robert H. Morris detailed twelve marshals "to aid in the suppression of the violation of the Market Laws."[20] Mayor Morris, however, ultimately failed to impress the public with his supposed commitment to law enforcement, and the city's public markets remained constant reminders of municipal neglect. The large ones, such as Washington Market, were stressed for space and lacked adequate facilities, while the smaller ones, such as Weehawken, Franklin, Monroe, and Union, had high vacancy rates or were abandoned altogether by disgruntled butchers. Moreover, with the increasing uptown movement of residential neighborhoods, the city failed to build small markets within walking distance for housewives—a proposal the Market Committee of the Board of Alderman had urged, unsuccessfully, the previous year.[21] Rapid social changes also disrupted the municipal market system. Native-born market men complained of being pushed around by Irish clerks, municipal weighers, and policemen, and they disliked the growing competition from German and Irish food vendors. Caught between Democrats who sought the political support of the city's growing foreign-born population and Whigs who favored dismantling the market system, the native-born market men joined the American Republican Party.[22]

Repeal of the Market Laws

Although the legalization of meat shops and the repeal of the market laws appeared to be a goal of the Whigs in the late 1830s and early 1840s, these "reforms" finally transcended partisan politics as both parties gradually came to favor less government involvement in business.[23] On New Year's Eve 1842, meat shop promoters celebrated their impending victory in a series of articles in the Democratic *Weekly Herald.* Reporting that the ordinance to license meat shops had just passed the Board of Assistant Aldermen, the paper asserted, "Whatever may be the final action of the Corporation . . . , the question is certainly forever settled with the people. They have determined to tolerate [meat shops], and to use them. They have become a part and parcel of this city, and cannot be eradicated."[24]

The *Weekly Herald* also celebrated impending changes to the city's overall system of urban food distribution, including a proposal for suburban slaughterhouses. Meat shop supporters favored them because they would make it easier to distribute meat to their shops and alleviate congestion downtown. As it stood, butchers continued to receive animals arriving by boat in lower Manhattan and to drive them through the streets, "lowing, bellowing, bleating, and squealing—running under the wheels of carriages, and between the legs of horses—upsetting children, and frightening the women—and in short creating a general panic and disturbance." The proposed suburban slaughterhouses, accessible to wharves farther north on each side of the island, would eliminate animal drives through the city's streets and keep the business of slaughtering out of the back rooms of the shops and away from residential areas.

Finally, after years of debate, on January 20, 1843, the city passed a revised market ordinance repealing the market laws that restricted the sale of fresh meats to the public markets. This ordinance allowed the mayor to issue licenses for "the sale of fresh meats in places other than the Public Markets" to butchers who were not required to have served an apprenticeship. In an effort to dissociate these places from meat shops—though of course they were the same thing—the ordinance specified that places for the sale of meat other than the present "public markets" would simply be called "markets."[25]

Reflecting the current nativist ideology, the revised ordinance specified that a shop license would be issued only to a butcher who was "an actual resident of the city, a citizen of the United States of the age of twenty-one years." The ordinance required butchers to place signs with their names painted on them over their shops. In an effort to assure the public that municipal regulations applied to shops, butchers also had to keep scale beams and weights suspended conspicuously in the shop. Furthermore, the street inspector or deputy health warden of each ward was required to visit the shops daily, and the aldermen and assistant aldermen had the right to inspect them in their wards. The meat shop promoters, much as they believed in "free trade," therefore knew that widespread public acceptance of private shops would be possible only if they were subject to the same rules, regulations, and routine inspections as the public markets.

The shop butchers also took measures to duplicate the experience of shopping in the public markets and create a familiar atmosphere for their customers. Typically operating from a converted lower floor of a house, shop butchers stood behind a long wooden table that served as both counter and cutting board and hung meats so as to allow close inspection.[26]

The legalization of meat shops coincided with the city's proposal to build two municipal abattoirs along the Hudson and East Rivers, "based on the Parisian model," where the meat would be inspected and stamped with a seal of approval before going to markets and shops. The rivers would make convenient dumping grounds for the slaughterhouse refuse.[27] City officials claimed that the presence of private shops and municipal slaughterhouses was "a measure of such immense public importance" and had already brought down the price of beef. They also declared their intention to refund the butchers' premiums based on "an equitable indemnification of real damages."[28]

Last Chance for the Market Butchers

During the term of nativist mayor James Harper in 1844–1845, the market butchers once again tried to return to their old arrangements by petitioning for a repeal of the ordinance that licensed meat shops.[29] A committee of butchers, including Thomas Winship, Charles DeVoe (Thomas De Voe's cousin), J. C. Bayles, and Leonard L. Johnson, reported to the common council that "butchers occupying Stalls in public Markets have felt themselves aggrieved, and we think justly so, in relation to the course the Common Council has pursued in regard to their rights, as well as the interests of our citizens at large." The market butchers had paid approximately $80,000 for stall premiums, in addition to annual rent, which they stopped paying when "they conceived their rights were put in jeopardy, and that, too, in violation of the pledge given on the purchase of the good will of the stands." The butchers believed that when they paid for stall premiums they

> would be protected in all their rights, as guaranteed by the Ordinances, which provided that the sale of meats should be exclusively confined to the public Markets. But how sadly they have been disappointed! The entire system has been invaded. The shop Butchers are authorized by Ordinance to locate themselves in any part of our City, whether in the great thoroughfares, or in the by-streets. What a commentary upon our Municipal consistency! What a commentary upon our Police regulations! That a well regulated Market system should be thus broken up and destroyed, by our predecessors, and by what motive prompted, whether for political purposes, or to gain popularity, we are unable to say; but whatever the motive, the ruinous consequences are before us.

They also stressed that meat shops, numbering over four hundred by 1845, threatened the public health because they were "scattered" all over the city, making health inspections difficult. However, citizens were "perfectly secure from this imposition" of unsound meat in the public markets because "it is the direct interest of each Butcher to guard against the exhibition and sale of unsound meats; and when any one is detected, the individual guilty of the act is immediately expelled from the Market by the Clerk."

The Market Committee also reported that shop butchers favored returning to the public markets if the common council would abolish the system of licensing meat shops. The inducement to return was the hundred or so vacant stands. The Market Committee asked the Common Council "to act definitely on this subject, and to make no compromise to accommodate any particular clique, or any class of politicians, or to take into view the question of monopoly or anti-monopoly, but to have an eye solely to the true interests of the City." The committee recommended "placing our Market system upon its original basis, sanctioned many years before our time, and which have proved to be a good one; one that was beneficial to our city treasury; one that secured to our citizens the procurement of good and wholesome meats, and just and equitable weight for all they purchased; and in short, your Committee challenge a scrutiny of the minutest character into that system which has stood the test of a century or two." This proposal, they claimed, was "based upon correct and just principles, and . . . proves most beneficial to our citizens at large."

Market reform was highly unlikely during Harper's administration; his basic strategy for municipal reform of any kind was law enforcement. Harper

FIGURE 4.3 *Progress of Reform!* No. 1, 1844. Lithograph by James Baillee, New York. Library of Congress.

resurrected many long ignored and unpopular ordinances, including restrictions against the commercial use of sidewalks by peddlers and shopkeepers. Such police practices discriminated against widowed apple sellers and other poor street vendors, many of whom were foreign-born (fig. 4.3). With no visible improvement of city services, and growing fear that ethnic violence similar to the Philadelphia riots of 1844 would erupt in New York, the market butchers saw no signs of reform.[30]

Laissez-Faire

By the mid-1840s, the city was in no position to return to the laws that required butchers to sell only in the public markets. Such government involvement in business was highly unlikely in an atmosphere of laissez-faire at both the state and the local level. In 1846 the revised New York state constitution reorganized the legislature, abolished a "host of useless offices," decentralized the patronage of the executive government, and revised the judicial system. The revised constitution also rid the state, once and for all, of privileges inherited from the colonial legislature, such as the offices of weights and measures, licensing, and royal land grants, and the "repugnant" remnants of English common law. Such changes had the intention of guiding the state, "rapidly increasing in arts, culture, commerce and population," into the modern era.[31] After the closing of the state office of weights and measures in 1846, as well as the legalizing of meat shops three years earlier, the public market system in New York entered the second half of the century without the primacy it had always enjoyed. Not only did the revised state constitution aim to annul the powers and privileges that reeked of New York's colonial past, but so did revisions to the city charter.

Weakening the priority of public markets at the local level was a provision in the revised city charter of 1847 that gave the common council, in very general terms, the power to establish, regulate, and maintain markets—but without specifically mentioning their number and location as previous charters had done.[32] The charter amendment was undoubtedly influenced by an opinion of Chancellor James Kent, who argued that the public market system was antiquated and too restrictive for the needs of a growing city. Kent, a well-known American jurist and the author of *Commentaries on American Law* (1826–1830), believed that the city charter provision authorizing the authorities to establish and maintain markets in specified places was "irrelevant." Furthermore, "under the great change in localities, which the growth and commerce of the city has produced, the adherence to the specification would have been idle and absurd."[33]

The revised city charter amendments bounced the position of superintendent of markets between various entities such as the Department of Streets and Lamps and the City Inspector's Department, to the point where even the common council was never sure who was responsible for nominating market clerks, collecting fees and rents, and authorizing extensions to market houses.[34] Weakened market laws, vague wording in the 1847 city charter, and the revised state constitution muddled the city's responsibilities over public markets, making any major improvements to the market houses doubtful and paving the way for private speculation in urban food marketing and distribution.

Proposal to Sell or Lease the Public Markets

The New York market butchers faced an uncertain future when Comptroller Azariah C. Flagg proposed leasing the city's markets to wholesalers in

1854. Flagg had been influenced by the practice in New Orleans, which farmed out its market houses to private individuals. Since New Orleans produced $200,000 a year from its leases, Flagg was convinced that a city the size of New York could produce at least $500,000.[35] In addition to increased revenues, leasing markets would leave "all the market arrangements to be made on enlightened, liberal and simple business principles, and having the power of the municipal government interposed only to protect the weak and virtuous against the strong and vicious, and to enforce such wholesome regulations as are required for the preservation of the public health, and the enforcement of good order."[36] Precisely because supplying food to the city was such important business, Flagg believed that "our security, after all, rests on the *business man,* rather than on the government official. Why, then, not withdraw the bungling hand of government from the meats which are wanted for the daily consumption of the city, and in this, as in other matters, let trade regulate itself?" Flagg believed that enlightened business enterprise not only would supply customers with food more conveniently and cheaply than before but also would upgrade market facilities to a level equal to the city's "splendid hotels."[37]

In 1855 the subject of "letting, leasing, or doing away with the Public Markets" caused Thomas De Voe to take up his pen in the *New-York Daily Times.*[38] He was particularly angered by official reports that the markets failed to generate sufficient revenue for the city, especially since he himself was a victim of various clerks at Jefferson Market who issued illegal permits to favored individuals for bribes. Such "foul play," De Voe argued, was costly to the public, for market revenues went into individual pockets rather than into city coffers.[39]

De Voe's article on the "true value" of the public markets was intended to expose the absurdity of the city's calculations and its misconceptions about the system. He began by dismissing Commissioner Heman W. Childs's calculations that the markets operated at a loss in the mid-1850s.[40] De Voe contended that public markets increased the value of nearby property and that the city would lose tax revenues if it destroyed them. To illustrate his point he calculated that the Jefferson Market property, without the public market, would be worth only $30,000, as opposed to its current value of $73,000, taking into consideration the value of space used for the police station, city prison, harness and paint stores, hose companies, and bell tower (fig. 4.4). More important than the markets' financial advantages, however, was De

FIGURE 4.4 Jefferson Market, New York. From *Ballou's Pictorial Drawing Room Companion*, October 17, 1857.

Voe's claim that market property could not be sold. He took his argument back to the "Olden Time," when the city's inhabitants placed their property in the care and protection of the municipal corporation for the exclusive use of public markets.

Deaf Ears

De Voe not only was swimming against the laissez-faire tide but also was opposing the demagogic Fernando Wood, mayor from 1855 to 1858, whose antimonopolist policies and calls for modernization aimed at the heart of the city's oldest public service (fig. 4.5). Wood appealed to the council to abolish the entire system, which New York had "inherited from its two old-fashioned paternal ancestors, the Hollander and Britisher." Having lost its purpose, according to Wood,

> the ancient mode of supplying the people with places in which to obtain meats, vegetables, &c., by erecting buildings for that purpose, is, in my opinion, wrong in theory, and unsuitable to the cities of this country. It is derived from the practice of the old cities of Europe, where it was originally established for the pur-

FIGURE 4.5 Fernando Wood, mayor of New York. Portrait from Xavier Donald MacLeod, *Biography of Hon. Fernando Wood, Mayor of the City of New-York* (New York: O. F. Parsons, 1856), frontispiece.

poses of revenue, or part of a system of taxation. . . . Whilst we have improved upon many European customs, we have not only adhered to the errors of this, but so improvidently conducted it as to make it a source of expenditure, and objectionable in almost every other respect.[41]

Wood pointed to the more than five hundred meat shops as justification for asserting that the market system had strayed from its original purpose. He stated that meat shops were created by "the energies and necessities of individuals" and resulted from "personal enterprise." By the 1850s they were not only prolific but also fashionable, as were grocery stores and fish and oyster stands.[42]

Claiming numerous objections to public markets, the mayor continued:

Our market system is obnoxious to a great republican principle, which is, that government shall not interfere with private enterprise; that that is the best government which governs least; that government should avoid becoming a proprietor, or restrict the free exercise of individual rights, so long as no encroachment is made upon the rights of others, or of the community. We should no more build market houses for the transaction of the business of a butcher or of a vegetable monger, than for the conducting of any other trade of life.

Wood also objected to the expense of a public market system, especially when city debt exceeded $14 million. He referred not only to operating expenses, but also to lost revenue from the markets' tax-exempt property. He therefore recommended "the abolition of the present system, and the sale of the market property, and the adoption of the free trade principle; permitting any individual to open a shop for the sale of meats and vegetables, the same as he is allowed to sell dry goods or boots and shoes."

Wood was responding to popular complaints about a monopoly on stalls, inflated prices, and little sanitary oversight in the public markets—the same complaints that had been used against centralized markets in Paris and London. He was also motivated by his disdain for driving cattle through the streets, "another evil calling for prompt action." In reality, however, behind a smokescreen of free trade and accusations of mismanagement and unsanitary conditions, he was offering the markets for sale or lease in order to bail the city out of its enormous financial crisis.[43]

The mayor portrayed an honest and efficient city government whose role in food marketing was to inspect markets, slaughterhouses, and shops—not to build, lease, license, or own them. Knowing that such measures were drastic, Wood gave his potential opponents the benefit of the doubt:

> [If] the continuation of public markets is persisted in, there should be what may be termed a market avenue, not less than two hundred feet wide, commencing at about Fourteenth street, running parallel with the Hudson and East rivers toward the Harlem, with corresponding ones at convenient distances to be placed on the cross streets, at right angles with the avenues. In these avenues should be placed the markets, and the one running northward be extended as the population extended on either side, and demanded its accommodation. This location would be equally accessible to all.[44]

Such a scheme, he added, could be financed by the sale of the present market property, which he estimated would yield $1.5 million. At the time of his proposal, the city was operating thirteen markets, all concentrated at the lower end of the island.

Wood may have been calling the bluff of certain members of the council whom he expected to insist on maintaining public markets. He could not seriously have proposed a market avenue that in all probability would have interfered with his stronger desire to develop a major park.[45] In fact, he concluded his discussion of public markets in his 1856 inaugural address by insisting that the city adopt the "New Orleans plan . . . of leasing the market stalls at public auction." But he clearly preferred that the city get out of the

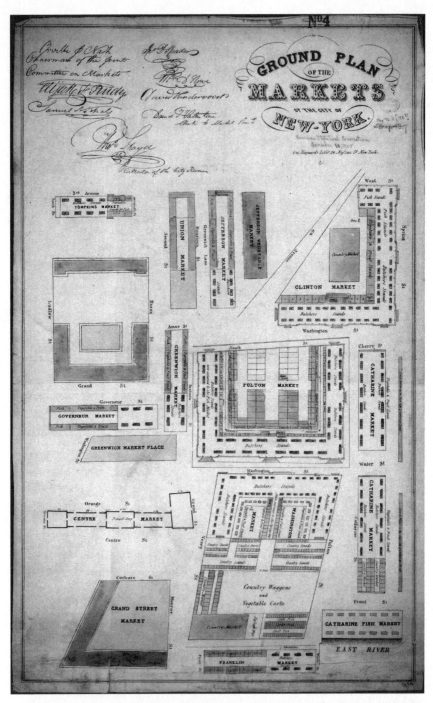

FIGURE 4.6 *Ground Plan of the Markets of the City of New-York*, 1850s. Lithograph by George Hayward. Courtesy of the Trustees of the Boston Public Library.

market business altogether, for in concluding his proposal for a market avenue he said, "I am to be understood as meaning this suggestion to be adopted only in the case the present system of public markets is persisted in. My earnest desire is, that there be no such houses furnished by the Corporation, but that the whole matter be left to private enterprise alone."[46]

Fernando Wood's position on public markets—that there be none—failed to receive enough support to implement such a drastic change. The issue was ultimately submerged by plans for Central Park, which opened in 1859. The development of the 843-acre park attracted real estate speculation far more promising than downtown market property, and his vision of a marketless metropolis drifted into oblivion.[47]

New York's market system survived the meat shop controversy and remained a public institution, though weakened by inadequate facilities. At the outset of the controversy in the 1830s, thirteen markets served a population of 202,589; by the 1850s the same thirteen markets served a population that had more than doubled, to 515,547 (fig. 4.6).[48] De Voe and his followers felt a strong moral and legal obligation to save the system, winning the battle against the elimination of public markets but losing to the legalization of meat shops. According to De Voe, however, the shops did not totally destroy the public markets, because patrons began to return to them soon after the meat shop controversy was settled.[49]

Still, the public market system in New York was never the same. Municipal market ordinances were weakened so much that the city's absolute control over urban food retailing ended.[50] Butchers, moreover, were forced to adapt to changes in their trade. Although they still preferred to slaughter their own animals, large-scale privately owned slaughterhouses replaced the neighborhood slaughterhouse, forcing many butchers to specialize in dressed meat. The only thing in favor of the New York butchers in the 1850s was that some cattle yards and slaughterhouses remained in the city, making New York the most extensive cattle market in America and keeping alive a demand for meat that was fresh, not packed.[51] Looking back on the way New York City government had handled the public markets during the antebellum period, De Voe remarked with regret, "I cannot avoid the conclusion, that if our public markets were properly conducted, they would be highly advantageous, not only to the city and citizens, but to all who have occasion to obtain supplies, as they facilitate the voluntary inspection, as well as the comparison of every article offered for sale in them, and they also concentrate the trade by which people are protected from imposition."[52] De Voe believed that public markets were not obsolete but that they had lost their effectiveness because the city failed to run them properly.

Furthermore, the public market suggested the old village days, when animals roamed the streets and carts and wagons blocked major thoroughfares. Particularly offensive were street markets, which conflicted with the vision of a modern city. At midcentury, Philadelphia businessmen were discontented with the old-fashioned public markets. They believed they had found the ultimate answer for guaranteeing public order, health, cleanliness, and comparison shopping: not private meat shops scattered about the city, but mammoth privately owned market houses.

Market House Company Mania in Philadelphia

Since the city has determined to provide no more public markets, the business is falling into the hands of companies and private individuals, in which probably the public will be better accommodated than by having all the markets in one street.

Philadelphia Public Ledger, March 24, 1859

In 1859 two events occurred in Philadelphia that would have been unimaginable only a decade earlier. The famous High Street Market sheds were demolished, and the Pennsylvania legislature authorized the incorporation of thirteen market house companies. Several factors led to these events: the railroads' demand for access to the streets, widespread acceptance of the private corporation, and lack of faith in municipal government. These factors were not new or unique to Philadelphia, but they were particularly influential at midcentury, when the consolidation of twenty-four boroughs and districts of Philadelphia County with Old City Philadelphia created investment opportunities and a climate for change.

Urban Philadelphia in the 1840s, when the movement for consolidation began, was a growing port and mill city whose population was rapidly increasing and becoming socially and economically diverse. It had grown from 232,000 in 1840 to 389,000 in 1850—an increase of 68 percent in just a

FIGURE 5.1 Washington Market, about 1844. Philadelphia. From *A Full and Complete Account of the Late Awful Riots in Philadelphia* (Philadelphia: John B. Perry, 1844), 19.

decade. Moreover, the city encountered the usual problems caused by rapid growth and industrialization, as exemplified by the riots of 1844.

Market houses, because of their central location and high visibility in the city's streets and squares, were vulnerable to the volatile social forces that characterized big cities of the time. These forces included nativist activities, gangs, and strikes by labor. In some cases the market house itself was a victim of civil unrest, such as Philadelphia's Washington (Nanny Goat) Market, an important rallying point for hundreds of striking Irish weavers that retaliating nativists burned in 1844 (fig. 5.1). Nearby a famous gang known as the Killers would strike clubs against the hollow cast-iron pillars of the Hubbell Market shed to alert their members.[1] Markets were such common sites of civil unrest that several riots were named after them, not only the Nanny Goat Market Riot in Philadelphia, but also the Northern Liberty Market Riot in Washington, D.C., in 1857, and later the Haymarket Riot in Chicago in 1886.[2]

In addition to the sensational events surrounding market houses were the everyday affronts to middle-class sensibilities. Public markets, such as the Delaware Avenue Fish Market near the docks attracted loiterers, vagrants, alcoholics, and prostitutes (fig. 5.2). Equally offensive were foul odors from decaying fish and produce, numerous rats, and loose animals (fig. 5.3).

FIGURE 5.2 Representation of the Philadelphia Fish Market, about 1860.
The Library Company of Philadelphia.

FIGURE 5.3 Runaway pig on Front and Market Streets, Philadelphia, about 1848.
The Library Company of Philadelphia.

The 1854 consolidation was intended not only to restore order in the streets but to unify and modernize public services. Its proponents hoped that eliminating the old committee system of councils, extreme localism of politics, and large numbers of elected offices would move the city in a new, forward-looking direction. They aimed to improve a number of public services—not only waterworks, schools, and police security but also public markets.[3]

A New Vision for Market Street

On the eve of consolidation the principal market still stood where it had since the eighteenth century—in the middle of High Street—though now it was a continuous row of sheds extending from Water Street to Eighth Street, with two more sheds from Fifteenth Street to Seventeenth Street (fig. 5.4). High Street was so deeply associated with the market that an ordinance was passed on September 1, 1858, changing its name to Market Street. This belated recognition was ironic; the city demolished the market houses the following year.[4]

Merchants and city boosters envisioned Market Street as a broad business thoroughfare, unencumbered by traffic and lined with professionally designed commercial buildings of uniform character, proportion, and design. Improvements in this regard began as early as 1853, when merchants invested in elaborate three- to five-story buildings with imposing cast-iron facades, designed by established architectural firms such as Philadelphia's Sloan and Stewart and Collins and Autenrieth.[5] The city's mercantile elite, however, hesitated to invest further in Market Street until the city removed the market sheds. Its members argued that the street's extraordinary width of one hundred feet was ruined by the presence of the sheds. Removing them was considered a move toward modernity, one that would encourage new development and change the neighborhood's village appearance. Market Street promoters believed that the two-mile-long street, if "given up entirely to our increasing commerce, would be a business thoroughfare such as few cities could boast of." In this vision of a metropolis there was no place for open-air markets.[6]

Planning Demolition

Most of the market houses scheduled for demolition were those rebuilt from 1835 to 1837 under the direction of architect William Strick-

FIGURE 5.4 Bird's-eye view of Philadelphia, about 1850. The line of market sheds can be seen in the middle of Market Street, *at the right.* Toned lithograph (hand colored) by G. Matter. Amon Carter Museum, Fort Worth, Texas, 1971.40.

land, who also served at that time as the city's "engineer of the rail road." Sharing Market Street with the sheds was a new branch of the Philadelphia and Columbia Rail Road, which passed the sheds to the north, from Eighth Street to Third Street, before turning down Dock Street to its Delaware River terminus. City ordinances of the late 1830s restricted railroad cars to three miles an hour and forbade trains altogether on market days. Strickland had chosen a slender design for the market houses— basically sheds supported by columns and capped with slightly convex metal roofs without projecting eaves (fig. 5.5). His design incorporated the latest architectural features such as cast-iron columns, popular for market houses in England and on the Continent and highly regarded for their beauty and utility. Strickland's market houses replaced the earlier ones that had brick piers supporting gable roofs with plastered ceilings. At the eastern market terminus stood the 1822 Jersey Market, still admired in the 1830s for its classicism and its ornate cupola decorated with cornucopias (fig. 5.6).[7]

FIGURE 5.5 Market sheds in Market Street, between Fifth and Sixth Streets, Philadelphia, about 1859, just before their demolition. Free Library of Philadelphia.

On December 8, 1853, less than two months before the consolidation act passed, the common council authorized the Committee on City Property to secure sites for new market houses in four quarters of the city with a view toward removing the Market Street sheds. Moving quickly to secure funding, the city council passed an ordinance on January 30, 1854, authorizing $1 million in debt for the project.[8]

Any practical, or even visionary, reason for removing the sheds from Market Street was quickly swept away by accusations from the market vendors that the city was committing itself to an unnecessary capital project in order to take advantage of the impending consolidation. Two sections in the proposed consolidation act gave rise to these claims. Section 6 prohibited new debt after the passage of the act, and section 36 provided that the current debt of the various municipalities would be consolidated into a shared debt pool. These provisions tempted local authorities to initiate

FIGURE 5.6 Jersey Market, Market Street at Front Street, Philadelphia, 1854.
Free Library of Philadelphia.

last-minute capital projects. On February 2, 1854, a special committee of
the city councils announced contracts with four property owners for new
lots and with John Rice for new market construction, for a total project
cost of $650,000. Governor William Bigler was awakened just before mid-

night on February 2, 1854, to sign the consolidation act into law before the city councils authorized any more debt.[9]

Litigation Ensues

The following week Edward Wartman, who had leased a stall in the market for twenty-five years, and John F. Gross, a "taxpayer," filed a bill in equity in the Pennsylvania Supreme Court for a special injunction to restrain the city authorities from proceeding with the contracts. Joining the city as defendants were property owners of the future market sites, George W. Brown, John Mc-Crea, Anna Hertzog, and the First Reformed Dutch Church, as well as contractor John Rice. At the same time, Thomas Pratt and his fellow residents of the counties of Delaware, Chester, and Montgomery—all of whom rented stalls to sell produce from their farms—filed a second motion in equity to prevent the city from demolishing the market houses. The plaintiffs argued in both cases that the city's plan to remove the sheds and to contract for new market houses would interfere with the legal rights of farmers, increase taxes in the newly consolidated city, and harm the public interest.[10]

In addition, the plaintiffs argued for the superiority of open market sheds over "close walled and roofed houses, which the experience of other cities has not recommended." According to Thomas Pratt, "the plan of open well ventilated market houses" allowed for "free and unobstructed circulation of air, such as cannot be had in buildings of the latter kind." An open plan, he added, was "indispensable to the preservation of meats and other provisions when brought together in large quantities in warm weather." Beyond addressing the popular concern for public health and sanitation, Pratt also hoped to win the court's sympathy by pointing out that the "open" and "public" market shed was the very feature that had given the Philadelphia markets their high reputation. Architectural issues aside, Pratt also argued that the city had no authority from the legislature to remove the sheds and that their removal would injure the market's business. The Pratt motion, moreover, claimed that the few people who supported the move were chiefly wholesale merchants who lived in "remote parts of the City and adjoining districts" and who had "but little occasion to use said Markets, and . . . no regard for the many families who are now dependant upon them." In conclusion, Pratt reported to the court that the city had received 4,831 petitions to keep the street markets versus 2,835 petitions to remove them.

Mayor Charles Gilpin, defendant, felt otherwise. The present market houses, he believed, interfered with the street's use by "a railroad, connecting with the improvements of the Commonwealth, as well as private corporations, and the consequent daily increasing demand upon that street for the convenient transportation of merchandise and produce." Gilpin's remark implied that railroads took priority over markets. Whereas the city had earlier protected markets from traffic by blocking off streets or restricting wagons, and later trains, during market hours, by midcentury it hoped to eliminate street markets so that trains could travel on Market Street on what had been market days.

John Rice, contractor for the proposed off-street market houses, naturally sided with the city on the grounds that "it is believed that in every large city, it has been found wise and not pernicious to remove the market houses from the public highways." Rice's high regard for off-street market houses was predictable, coming from a recent founder of the Broad Street Market House Company, newly incorporated by the state legislature on May 2, 1853.[11] The company's market house, built by Rice on the southwest corner of Race and Juniper Streets, was purchased by the city for the new market project. In rejoinder, Pratt pointed out to the court that the city had purchased the Rice property in order to bail out Rice's "deserted" market.

On April 3, 1854, Chief Justice Jeremiah Sullivan Black decided in favor of the city of Philadelphia (fig. 5.7). As he himself stated, it was the responsibility of the court to judge not the moral nature of the city's actions but their legality. The court argued that

> a municipal corporation, comprising a town of any considerable magnitude, without a public market subject to the regulation of its own local authorities, would be an anomaly which at present has no existence among us. The state might undoubtedly withhold from a town or a city the right to regulate its markets, but to do so would be an act of mere tyranny, and a gross violation of the principle universally conceded to be just, that every community, whether large or small, should be permitted to control, in their own way . . . the daily supply of food.

Black emphasized that the authority to establish public markets was "seldom, if ever, vested in individuals," referring to Pratt and his fellow plaintiffs, who were trying to stop "the progress of a contemplated improvement which concerns so many other persons." The city acted within the law by its decision to remove the market sheds and to replace them with four off-street

FIGURE 5.7 Jeremiah Sullivan Black (1810–1883), chief justice of the Commonwealth of Pennsylvania. Pennsylvania Historical and Museum Commission, Publications Division, Photograph File.

market houses. Its actions may not have been just, Black concluded, but they were legal.[12]

These two cases, *Wartman v. The City of Philadelphia and Pratt v. The Same,* demonstrate that the public market imperative was still alive in the commonwealth in 1854. Neither the court nor the plaintiffs questioned the right of a municipality to establish, maintain, or regulate public markets. The consensus was that public markets were necessary, but that they did not need to stand in the middle of a main thoroughfare. At question in these two cases was whether the city was behaving justly in replacing the Market Street sheds with four new off-street market houses at such great expense to the taxpayers and alleged inconvenience to retailers and customers.

The City Stalls

Despite the court's sanction in 1854, the city did not remove the sheds until 1859, nor did it ever construct the four public market houses. During the intervening years, inaction best describes the city's handling of the market issue, beginning with the administration of Robert T. Conrad, first mayor of the newly consolidated city.

Although the city unified the markets under one department, W. D. Newell, the market commissioner, repeatedly complained that the old municipal ordinances, still in effect, rendered consistent enforcement all but impossible.[13] The councils therefore spent more time discussing the need for uniform market ordinances than considering plans for the new market houses; moreover, inaction was cheap. Although the city had purchased the market house properties before consolidation, the new administration was reluctant to spend money on the necessary construction. Builder John Rice had to remind the councils of his contract with the former city government to build the four new market houses.[14] Besides being unwilling to spend the money, officials of the newly consolidated city continued to receive numerous petitions against removal of the Market Street sheds. Until that issue was resolved, there was no rush to complete the new market houses.[15]

Hostility and impatience nonetheless ran high among the city's leading merchants, who demanded that the "blemish" of the market sheds be removed so that the Pennsylvania Railroad could build tracks down the street to the Delaware River. "We ask for room," they demanded of the councils. "We ask for a removal of this unsightly obstruction! Only give us what we require, and we pledge ourselves, as the merchants of Philadelphia, to perform our part, to place our cherished City *second to none in the land.*"[16]

Despite the merchants' demand for removal of sheds and construction of off-street market houses, the matter also lay dormant under the administration of Richard Vaux, mayor from 1856 to 1858. During Vaux's tenure, such a large building campaign would have been unpopular, particularly during the panic of 1857. Moreover, Vaux hesitated to build new market houses at a time when private stores or market establishments, called "provision stores," were becoming "daily more numerous."[17]

Despite the alleged popularity of provision stores, in 1857 the city still owned and managed thirteen markets with a total of 3,442 rented stalls—885 in Market Street alone—for which there was increasing demand. In addition to stalls were the city's curb markets, with their estimated five thousand farmers' wagons. Farmers who had no desire to run a year-round shop or market stall sold their goods in curb markets. The public market remained the primary source of urban food supply and distribution, and market houses continued to be unquestionably more profitable than any other city investment.[18] According to the journals of the common council from 1854 to 1858, annual market revenues averaged about $65,000.

Market rents contributed so much money to city coffers that the councils, in response to applications for additional stalls and a desire for more revenue, passed an ordinance to permit the sale of fish at the west end of the market houses at Fourth, Seventh, and Seventeenth Streets. Mayor Vaux vetoed the ordinance, chiding the councils for trying to rent portions of the public streets at high fees. Such action, Vaux argued, "cannot be sanctioned by any principle of public justice or municipal policy." Vaux concluded, "Until the present system of renting the use of the highways to private citizens for private uses, outside the Market Houses, receives serious consideration of the Councils, and some legislation based on sound principles [is] enacted, I cannot approve this spasmodic legislation." Vaux alluded to the unresolved issue of whether railroads, let alone fish vendors, could use the public highways for their own gain.[19]

Railroading the Market

Supporters of a railway on Market Street included not only the merchants but also the suburbanites who lived across the Schuylkill River in West Philadelphia. This pioneer suburb, boosted by real estate developers and land speculators between 1850 and 1880, attracted residents seeking a retreat from their urban workplaces.[20] The West Philadelphia Passenger Railway promised to meet the increasing demand of commuters and began its "march" downtown in 1858, when the company received legislative authority to lay rails over the Market Street Bridge. In response to the encroachment, a defeated Mayor Vaux sighed, "We are fast becoming a corporation growing country. Our State Legislature devotes itself each winter to creating those irresponsible, power-accumulating monopolies." It was "dangerous," Vaux had decided, to try to stop them.[21]

Any question whether the railroads could use Market Street was settled during the administration of Mayor Alexander Henry, the Whig who defeated Vaux in the 1858 election and under whose tenure the market issue finally came to a close. In a fiery session on November 26, 1858, the select councils considered an ordinance to remove the market houses on Market Street. Some councilmen offered amendments to stagger demolition over a year, beginning with the two sheds between Fifteenth and Seventeenth Streets, since the public was not expecting destruction of the entire market. Others, however, opposed the ordinance altogether, like a Mr. Handy, who knew that in doing so he would be considered an "old fogy." Councilman William C. Kelly opposed the ordinance because it benefited only a railway corporation. Kelly reasoned that for all the railroad's promise of making Philadelphia into a great depot, "Who could tell but that at some future day, a bridge would be constructed over the Delaware river and trade, by this means, be diverted to New York." Kelly offered a compromise amendment that provided for the erection of eleven replacement market houses in various wards. This idea did not sit well with Councilman W. P. Hacker, who "thought the erection of buildings for the sale of meats and vegetables should be matters of private enterprise." In agreement with Hacker was Councilman William L. Dennis, who believed that removing the sheds would not cause "one cabbage less raised and sold," implying that the ordinance would have no significant impact on the city's food supply or distribution.[22]

The bickering came to an abrupt and dramatic end when Councilman John Krider, who opposed tearing down the sheds, publicly announced that someone (whom he would not name) had offered him a $200 bribe to vote in favor of the removal. This statement caused considerable excitement, loud cries, and a final vote on the ordinance, which passed forty-nine to twenty-eight.

Repercussions from the council's decision to remove the sheds appeared two days later in the *Sunday Dispatch*. Losers of the vote blamed the "greedy, stingy, mean, and snobbish commercial classes of Philadelphia." "The grand philosophers of the Board of Trade," they argued, had ideas that were "not more elevated than the opinions of hucksters ought to be. It was these men who have long since imagined that they discovered that the whole prosperity of the city depended altogether upon the removal of markets from High Street." They blamed the loss of a great convenience to the city, not to mention the anticipated loss of $30,000 in annual market revenues, on the "aristocrats" and "their parasite organs of the press." The "commercial classes" had gotten their way at last—not by honest means, but with "corporation assistance." That assistance came when the Market Street Railway Company received its charter from "a venal Legislature" for a "whole monopoly of what might indeed be a splendid street if it were clear of railroad tracks, all to themselves."[23]

How could the appearance of Market Street, the article continued, possibly benefit from "four railroad tracks in the center, and with turn-outs breaking up the pavements in every square? What inducement will there be for anybody to walk in it, and to stumble over tracks crossing the pavements? What pleasure can it be for drivers of vehicles to ride in it, and damage their wheels on the rails . . . ? Take away the crowds that must go into it to attend the markets, and it will become the most silent, deserted, profitless street in the city." The years-old controversy over the market sheds had just been settled in "the most disgraceful hurry" to accommodate the railroads, with the result that "corporations, purse-proud dealers in merchandise, and would-be market house builders" would now have control of Market Street. The latter referred specifically to builder John Rice, who "stands ready, no doubt, to build all the market houses in the city."

Having covered the controversy closely for many years, the *Public Ledger* reported from experience that the question of removing the market houses was almost as difficult to settle as the issue in Congress over statehood for the territory of Kansas. Despite a majority vote to remove the sheds, bickering still ensued in spring 1859 over the timing of the demolition, and over paying for it, as well as the salvaging of materials, particularly the valuable metal roofs and iron posts and lintels.[24]

The Incorporation of Market Houses

With demolition pending, Mayor Alexander Henry assuaged any anxiety in the councils over the expected loss of market revenues. That loss, he stated, would be offset by increased trade along the city's chief business thoroughfare. Henry also laid to rest any notion that the city would build new market houses to replace the sheds. In his mind, providing public accommodations for individual businesses—no matter how profitable—was "questionable." Celebrating Henry's position was the *Public Ledger,* which announced that "since the city has determined to provide no more public markets, the business is falling into the hands of companies and private individuals, in which probably the public will be better accommodated than by having all the markets in one street."[25]

The notion of market companies also sat well with the state judiciary and legislature in Harrisburg. In 1859, when the Pennsylvania Supreme Court decided yet another case, hopefully the last, involving Philadelphia's market controversy, the court's opinion was completely the opposite of Chief Justice Black's opinion of five years earlier. In *Twitchell v. The City of Philadelphia,* Justice John Meredith Read reported on the property dispute case that "none of the market-houses contracted for [by the city] have been or ever will be built, and the Broad street-market house has as yet produced no revenue."

Accordingly, "the whole [market] scheme has utterly failed, with a most serious pecuniary loss to the city and their constituents." Philadelphia's "costly outlay for nothing" (referring to the $650,000 spent on new market property in 1854) "is now entirely superseded by private corporate enterprise, which promises to supply the old city proper with well-arranged and convenient market-houses." After Read's decision, the state legislature hastily considered bills for the incorporation of market house companies in Philadelphia, and before the year's end thirteen companies received legislative charters.[26]

By 1859 it was clear that corporations, which could raise capital with limited personal financial risk, offered unprecedented opportunity for speculation in food retailing and market house construction. With their legal authority to issue stock, officers of market companies raised the capital needed for property and new buildings, including the latest innovations in refrigeration, lighting, ventilation, and construction. The corporate ownership once reserved for a small group of directors acting for the public good had become a popular means by which the state promoted economic individualism.[27]

Market house company charters followed the trend in the antebellum period of transferring economic power to private entities by modifying the legal system. State legislatures, for example, revised not only the laws of "eminent domain" and "nuisance" but also corporation law to favor entrepreneurial groups and individuals with capital. In the colonial period, corporations enlisted private capital to construct such public works as canals, bridges, turnpikes, and urban water systems, with investors entitled to revenues from tolls and user fees.[28] According to the public market tradition in America, some cities and towns financed market houses in much the same way, but the investors' claim to market revenues expired after construction costs had been met. Moreover, it was always clear that such financing schemes did not entitle investors to participate in the affairs of the market, because local authorities maintained the right to regulate it and oversee its daily operation. For example, the William Penn Market Company, chartered by the Commonwealth in 1838, was subject to "the control and supervision of the proper municipal authorities of the city of Philadelphia" with respect to weights and measures and the soundness of provisions. After the company's twenty-five-year charter expired, the city had the right to take its stock, "whether the said company shall agree or not."[29]

The market house company charters of 1859, however, typically yielded all responsibility for the market house to the company. The charter of the Western

Market Company, for example, vested authority for the ownership, maintenance, use, and management of the market house to a board of seven managers elected by the stockholders. Overriding traditional municipal market laws, the legislative charter also gave the company full power over the location of the market house, the selection of tenants, and the rules governing farmers.[30]

The Rise of the Businessman

The concept of a market house as a private business venture was new and could not have existed without widespread faith in the hero of the mid-nineteenth century—the "business man."[31] According to the principles of the moral economy, consumers had always expected government to protect the public markets, to enforce the ethics of trade, and to regulate the merchants and middlemen who stood between them and the producer. Now individuals who used to warrant close regulation were heroes. Merchants and middlemen, with legal protection from the state and the ability to raise capital through stock corporations, took the lead in urban food retailing and distribution. They were the same people Azariah Flagg and Fernando Wood declared would save New Yorkers from a failed public market system.[32]

Despite economic and political advantages, food merchants (as opposed to small retailers) still needed a public relations campaign to win the public trust. A new genre of "success" books promoted, among other things, laissez-faire, faith in the merchant and businessman, and the profitability of market gardening. Among them, Mrs. L. C. Tuthill's *Success in Life: The Merchant* (1850) touted the qualities of a good merchant—one who was engaged in "self-government," "economy," "courtesy," and "integrity."[33] More prolific was Edwin T. Freedley, whose works read like handbooks for would-be capitalists.[34]

Freedley praised the merchant and businessman by drawing analogies between their activities and those of the popular huckster and public market vendor. In *A Practical Treatise on Business, or How to Get, Save, Spend, Give, Lend, and Bequeath Money* . . . (1852), Freedley offered a broad definition of "merchant" as one "who buys and sells; who buys to sell, and sells to buy the more." Merchants, Freedley explained, were important members of the community because they distributed goods between the classes. Within his definition of "merchant" fell "the whole class who live by buying and selling, and not merely those conventionally called merchants to distinguish them from small dealers. This term comprises traders behind counters, and traders behind desks; traders behind neither counters nor desks. There are various grades of merchants. They might be classed and symbolized according as they use a basket, a wheelbarrow, a cart, a stall, a booth, a shop, a warehouse, a countingroom, or bank. Still, all are the same thing—men who live by buying and selling."[35] Capitalizing on the public perception that the "small" dealer was more trustworthy than a "large" one, Freedley relied on the imagery of the public market to defend the international merchant, noting that "a ship is only a large basket; a warehouse, a costly stall. Your peddler is a small merchant going round from house to house with his basket to mediate between persons; your merchant is only a great peddler sending round from land to land with his ships to mediate between nations." By the terms of traditional market laws, the scope and method of trade Freedley described would have fallen into the category of the illicit practices of hoarding, engrossing, and forestalling. Now the formerly despised middleman was portrayed as an accepted, legitimate, and valued member of society.

Perhaps to assuage any fear that cities would be deprived of an adequate food supply while merchants sent goods wherever they commanded the best price, even abroad, Freedley made a direct pitch for market gardening. In *Opportunities for Industry and the Safe Investment of Capital, or A Thousand Chances to Make Money* (1859), published in the same year that Philadelphia was tearing down the market sheds, Freedley argued that "the cultivation of fruits and vegetables, especially in the vicinity of large cities, is, if skillfully managed, almost uniformly a profitable business." Market gardening was an attractive occupation because "the attention of producers is so exclusively devoted to the raising of staples, that the markets of the cities are often illy supplied with garden fruit and vegetables." Best of all, according to Freedley, market gardening required little experience, for "it is a singular fact, that many of the most important improvements made in Agriculture are traced to men who are not professional farmers." Freedley advised the successful market gardener to base agricultural decisions on a careful reading of commercial journals and comparison of price currents. Market gardening was particularly profitable in the South, Freedley added, because "strawberries, peas, potatoes, etc, will ripen at least six weeks earlier in the Southern than in the Northern States; and a very profitable and extensive business may be done in shipping them to Philadelphia, New York, and Boston."[36]

Perhaps heeding Freedley's advice was Thomas H. Elliot of Georgia, a former purser who in 1859 established a business on Market Street above Eleventh selling country produce from southern agents.[37] The Philadelphia firm of Arthur, Burnham and Company also boasted a year-round business in fresh produce, importing from regions with long growing seasons.[38]

The "success" literature of the period suggests that some critics worried that privatizing markets would disturb the city's food supply by creating more distant markets and sources for food. Despite some skepticism, however, investors in market house companies eagerly awaited the business of Market Street's displaced food vendors while the city planned to remove the sheds. Both parties closely coordinated their efforts, and the entire process took roughly one year, from April 1859 to April 1860.[39]

The March Down Market Street
Western Market

The first to organize was the Western Market Company, financed by butchers from the city's two market sheds on Market Street west of Broad. The company hired architect John M. Gries and builder John Rice to construct a market house on the northeast corner of Sixteenth and Market Streets.[40] On November 16, 1858, at the laying of the cornerstone, Philip Lowry, chairman of the committee of the Butchers' Association, remarked that those gathered were helping to inaugurate "a system of conducting the markets that must, sooner or later, be adopted by all the principal cities in our Great Union." Claiming that Philadelphia led the movement toward market privatization that was characteristic of large cities, Lowry remarked that a growing trade demanded use of Market Street and that the butchers had finally yielded their "time-honored rights" and consented to demolition of the old markets, as long as the new market house would be subject to the same municipal regulations.[41]

At the inauguration, Mayor Henry commented on the importance of markets in general, conveniently (and deliberately) leaving out the word "public." He claimed that the market was "closely associated with the progress of civilization, and, by the character, abundance and variety of its commodities, may justly be estimated the prosperity, wealth and refinement of the community in which it is established." He described the market as a place that provides food to satisfy "the cravings of hunger, to give sinew to the arm of the work-

FIGURE 5.8 The municipal market sheds on the eve of their demolition, with the new Western Market just visible in the background. Market Street, West of Fifteenth, Philadelphia, 1859. Free Library of Philadelphia.

man, or to delight the palate of the luxurious." He called the act of the Butchers' Association in building a market an "unostentatious deed of charity." Councilman Dennis also offered a toast, saying that unsightly street markets would be "remedied by the erection of closed markets."[42]

Opening day, April 20, 1859, was tense as the public watched the Western Market Company coordinate removal of the city's market sheds (fig. 5.8) with the opening of its new market house. At 10:00 A.M. occupants of the sheds moved into the new Western Market, at 11:00 A.M. gangs of laborers tore down the sheds, and at 4:00 P.M. the new market house opened for business. The press noted cynically, "The city would have to talk about it for several years before that much work could be accomplished, and its performance would then be the work of weeks instead of hours."[43]

FIGURE 5.9 The streets are cleared for the new Western Market, Philadelphia, 1859. Free Library of Philadelphia.

Press accounts described the Western Market as a "market palace," rivaling Quincy Market and by far the best market in the Union (fig. 5.9). Constructed of load-bearing brick walls supporting a clerestory and arched roof, the Western Market was praised for reflecting the "skill of our Philadelphia mechanics." Inside, the market house boasted 280 stalls with Italian marble countertops, divided by wide paved aisles. Four underground vaults running the length of the building housed the wholesale trade of Jersey produce. John H. Jones operated a restaurant on the Market Street front. Two galleries 150 by 20 feet at each end of the building accommodated the sale of flowers, seeds, and ice cream. Sheds for selling fish stood on the east side of the building. Iron-framed doors with wicker inserts for air circulation lined the entire perimeter of the market house. One newspaper account reported that "the means of ventilating this market are so perfect that all objections to close[d] markets will no doubt, be removed."[44]

Eastern Market

The concept that markets need not be built and managed by the municipal authorities had indeed arrived in Philadelphia, but not everyone immediately accepted the idea. The market butchers east of Broad insisted on remaining in the city-owned sheds. The city, by now determined to get out of the market-building business, hoped that the first phase of the demolition, from Fifteenth Street to Seventeenth Street, would encourage the butchers east of Broad to organize their own market as their fellow butchers to the west had done. Only then could the city proceed with a "general sweep of all the sheds from Eighth street to Front."[45]

As soon as the sheds between Fifteenth and Seventeenth Streets were gone, the West Philadelphia Passenger Railway Company laid tracks where the sheds had stood and awaited passage of a bill in Harrisburg to extend their tracks to Front Street.[46] With the railway on their heels and the city just standing by, the butchers east of Broad had no choice but to organize to build their own quarters. On February 18, 1859, they incorporated as the Eastern Market Company, whose principal shareholders included former mayor Richard Vaux as well as Edward Wartman, plaintiff in the 1854 case against the city.

According to the incorporation act, the Eastern Market Company was authorized to construct a market house on the block bound by Market, Chestnut, Fourth, and Fifth Streets. Officers had to be citizens of Pennsylvania, and farmers of the state would be entitled to occupy half of the stalls. The act also limited farmers to a maximum of three stalls each but declared no restrictions on the quantity or terms of their sales. The company received a thirty-year charter "unless extended or renewed by the legislature."[47]

The new market was equipped with 431 stalls that the company auctioned to the highest bidders on November 8, 1859. The next day the *U.S. Gazette* reported that the auction drew a large crowd: "Of course they were all males, females having no direct interest in the trade in chops and sirloins." Bidders were "composed almost wholly of butchers," one of whom paid a premium of $5,150 for a pair of stalls, in addition to annual rent.

Farmers' Market

Farmers from the neighboring counties of Chester, Delaware, Montgomery, and Bucks, displaced by the removal of the city's market sheds and not in a position to pay such high premiums for a stall in one of the new private market houses, met to discuss the matter. Feeling that the private market houses were governed by directors whose interests were inimical to their own, the farmers chose to incorporate as the Farmers' Market Company. Located at Twelfth and Market Streets, the new Farmers' Market, designed by Samuel Sloan and built by H. Phillippi, combined modern structural tech-

FIGURE 5.10 Farmers' Market, Philadelphia, designed by Samuel Sloan, about 1880. Free Library of Philadelphia.

niques, including a sheet-metal roof and a ventilator that ran the length of the building, with a "false" facade inspired by the Venetian Renaissance (fig. 5.10). The pediment featured a lunette that held a marble relief carving of the farmers' coat of arms. (Similar architectural and iconographic embellishments, such as reliefs of bulls' heads and cornucopias, were popular features of market houses at this time.)[48] The interior was laid out like the grid of a city, with six broad aisles running lengthwise and eighteen narrow cross aisles. The company numbered the 428 stalls in much the same way as the houses of the city. The market's avenues were numbered from east to west, and the stalls ran northward, with even-numbered stalls on the west side and odd-numbered stalls on the east.[49]

The companies of the Western Market, Eastern Market, and Farmers' Market were among the twenty incorporated in Philadelphia from 1859 to 1861.[50] De Voe's unpublished essay, probably written after he returned to New York from a visit to Philadelphia in 1862, offered a skeptical view of the market house company mania. He was impressed by the beautiful market houses built by private enterprise, but he also feared they were too "numerous and costly." He pointed out that they had "nearly all proved themselves unsuccessful for market purposes" and had only short life spans.[51] Eastern Market, for example, was practically empty of vendors within two years of operation, and the property was sold. Likewise Western Market, hailed at its opening as one of the greatest market houses in the country, survived for only twelve years before the Pennsylvania Railroad converted it into a depot in 1871.

De Voe predicted that market companies would fail to survive in the long term because they were overcapitalized and highly speculative. Investors, he warned, "were led into the erection of these elegant and commodious buildings, from the fact that some of the first sold their stalls at public auction for high premiums, besides ground rents; which gave them the appearance of such a profitable nature, that it created a mania for them, and they grew up like mushrooms in every part of the city." Eventually, however, few remained successful because of "their great expense, their excessive numbers, and [lack of] the proper knowledge to conduct them."[52] One exception was the Farmers' Market, whose "perfect success" De Voe attributed to the farmers who were the exclusive owners and managers. His verdict on market companies was premature, however, for little did he imagine that they would proliferate throughout Pennsylvania and ultimately reach his home city of New York.

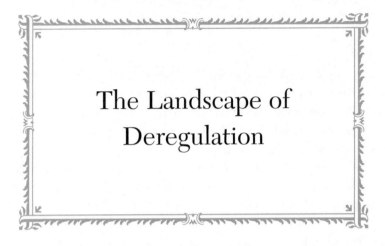

SIX

The Landscape of
Deregulation

I claim that public markets under Municipal rule are a failure, and
must give way to private enterprise such as the Manhattan Market
Company has demonstrated in the erection of their magnificent
building.   PAUL J. ARMOUR, New York, 1873

A distinct characteristic of the private market house, distinguishing it
from a public market, was its splendid (and costly) facilities. Market
companies hoped to attract families and middle-class shoppers by advertising
the latest in construction, lighting, ventilation, and refrigeration as well as orderly aisles and luxurious stalls. Such features were affordable to a corporation, whose power to issue stock provided the initial capital. In contrast, city-
owned markets suffered from the bad reputation of city government in
general, which by the 1850s was understood as an inferior public entity, lacking in rights, privileges, and immunities.[1] Caught in a vicious circle, cities
could not afford to repair or improve markets because revenues were declining owing to unexpected competition from private markets.

Different management styles in the public and private markets also contributed to the landscape of deregulation and reinforced a public/private divide. Owners of market companies considered themselves modern and for-

ward-looking, while those who defended municipal ownership were labeled old fogies. Citizens watched as their old market sheds were torn down, never to be replaced. Some watched with delight, others with regret.

The public/private divide was nowhere more apparent than in Pennsylvania, where more market house companies were incorporated than in any other state of the Union. City council minutes reveal the fears and anxieties expressed by mayors and councilmen who struggled with the movement to privatize. Most were left with little choice but to remove their market sheds from the middle of streets or town squares and leave the construction of markets to private enterprise. The Commonwealth of Pennsylvania is a particularly rich site for the study of the public/private struggle over market houses. The market house company mania that began in Philadelphia in 1859 continued unabated throughout the rest of the state, particularly during the 1870s and 1880s. Cities and towns tore down their market sheds, and in their place there sprang up new off-street market houses owned and run by private companies. The story was repeated over and over, and by the end of the nineteenth century more than one hundred market house companies had received legislative charters from the Commonwealth.[2]

Deregulation played out differently in New York City, where public markets suffered not so much from competition from meat shops and private companies as from corruption, mismanagement, and neglect. It is here that De Voe enters the story again, not as an antiquarian and amateur historian, but as a bureaucrat charged with resurrecting New York's public market system. In short, De Voe understood that private shops, market house companies, and public markets were not mutually exclusive and that there was a need in New York for several forms of food distribution. Unfortunately, as De Voe pointed out, the potential of public markets had been compromised by corruption, inefficient public officers, and the lack of a coordinated system for marketing and distributing food. His opinions, naturally, were not popular with city officials, who ran the markets only to siphon off revenues for themselves or for other public projects—a fact that would come to light with the downfall of the Tweed ring and De Voe's appointment as superintendent of markets in 1871.

The Public/Private Divide in Philadelphia

In 1875 Earl Shinn praised the private market houses in his history of the architecture, life, and manners of Philadelphia, written for the forthcoming

FIGURE 6.1 Farmers' Market, Philadelphia, about 1875. From Edward Strahan [pseud. Earl Shinn], *A Century After: Picturesque Glimpses of Philadelphia and Pennsylvania* (Philadelphia: Allen, Lane, and Scott and J. W. Lauderbach, 1875), 156.

national centennial. His chapter on market houses touted the privately owned Farmers' Market at Twelfth and Market Streets as a dazzling sight of continuous color, movement, and life—with an inexhaustible supply of food, high ceiling, large stalls, good ventilation, and crowds coming and going in the main aisle (fig. 6.1).[3] In contrast to the splendor of the privately owned markets were Shinn's descriptions of the municipal markets still owned and operated by the city of Philadelphia: New Market, on South Second Street between Pine and South, was described as small and dingy, with low ceilings, and as lacking modern conveniences.

The press, too, assured readers that the private markets "combine all the advantages of being light, clean, comfortable, well ventilated, and last, though not least, of not being built in the middle of the street and in everybody's way."[4] In contrast, the city's street markets not only stood "in everyone's way" but also offended the middle class, who shunned them for their chaos and their appeal to the lower sort (fig. 6.2). The press heaped insults on the city market vendors who had "monopolized" the stalls with the sale of goods that were incompati-

FIGURE 6.2 "Mrs. Livewell and the Farmer," from a short story by T. S. Arthur. Courtesy of the Roughwood Collection.

ble with family needs, such as chops, soup, stewed oysters, fried sausages, cake, gingerbread, cheese, coffee, and spruce beer.[5] These vendors, the press argued, chased away the families and housekeepers and catered primarily to "errand boys and heavy clerks [who] resort to the sheds to procure a cheap meal."[6] The middle-class consensus in Philadelphia, popular by the 1870s, was that the preferred market houses, in terms of service, modern facilities, and atmosphere of civility, were those owned and managed by private companies.

Privatization Moves Inland
Harrisburg

One of the earliest market companies established outside Philadelphia was in Harrisburg, where William Verbeke, a Dutch émigré and pharmacist, and Jacob Haehnlen, a former resident of Philadelphia, founded the West Harrisburg Market House Company in 1860. Haehnlen may have gotten the idea from his native Philadelphia or from the local Harrisburg paper. The *Patriot Union,* for example, regularly printed bills that were before the legislature, including those for the incorporation of the Philadelphia market house companies.

Verbeke had begun building a stone market in the part of Harrisburg known as "Verbeke town" in 1856, but he ran out of money. The Haehnlen family contributed property and funds to the enterprise, and together they formed a stock company, chartered by the legislature on April 2, 1860.[7] The stone market house in the middle of Broad (today Verbeke) Street, between Third and Elder Streets, three blocks from the Susquehanna River, opened for business in 1864. When the market opened, the number of stockholders had grown from the original ten at incorporation in 1860 to over fifty, including five women.[8]

Extant company records show that the Broad Street Market operated in much the same way as a municipal market, with a salaried superintendent, fixed public hours, and strict rules for tenants and farmers. The market was successful for several reasons. Stockholders were local, construction costs were modest, and the market was closely regulated by dedicated long-term superintendents. In addition, it was in a growing neighborhood, where it was closer to consumers than markets in the commercial district.[9]

Borough and city council minutes reveal, however, that the local government in Harrisburg, not to mention vendors from Market Square, had deep

FIGURE 6.3 Broad Street Market, Harrisburg, about 1880.
Pennsylvania State Archives.

anxieties about the incorporation of the West Harrisburg Market House Company. Several months before the company received its corporate charter, the town council unanimously passed a resolution opposing the incorporation bill. The council argued that "there seems to be a general hostility to said measure because the same is not necessary and will seriously prejudice the revenues of the Borough."[10] Harrisburg's own charter from the Commonwealth required the city to maintain public markets, which it had been doing on the square since 1807.[11]

The legislature did not consider the council's opposition, and competition from the West Harrisburg Market House Company was felt almost immediately. The company was so successful that it expanded its facilities with a new brick market house just east of its original structure (fig. 6.3). In addition, several other companies formed to build and manage market houses in Harrisburg.[12]

FIGURE 6.4 City-owned sheds in Market Square, Harrisburg, 1880.
Pennsylvania State Archives.

Having suffered from declining revenues, the city-owned sheds at Market Square (fig. 6.4) had deteriorated so much that in 1884 retired Pennsylvania senator Simon Cameron called them "a disgrace to the city; they are things of the past, and could not be permitted to exist in this age of progress."[13] Nonetheless, some residents still demanded the right to an adequate and convenient *public* market on the town square. After receiving a lengthy citizens' petition in favor of a new market house on the square, the city contracted for a building 65 feet wide by 173 feet long, with a ventilated roof supported by iron trusses. But the project prompted opponents to take the matter to the Pennsylvania Supreme Court. In October 1887 the court declared the existing structures a nuisance, not because they were unsightly but because they obstructed a public thoroughfare. State intervention therefore forced marketing on the square to cease, and the city tore down the sheds in early February 1889.[14]

In the midst of the demolition, the *Daily Patriot* declared that corruption in the office of Thomas G. Hargest, city solicitor, had delayed the removal of the sheds. The Hargest ring had been blocking the removal of "these old eyesores" for years, but now the taxpayers would finally "see the debris of the sheds and the Hargest ring both 'cleaned up' together."

The market sheds not only stood "in the way of progress" but also were visual reminders of corruption in the city government. The purge of market sheds from the town square symbolized the purge of cronyism and old alliances in the city government. It also paved the way for the streetcar, which completed the transformation of the street from a meeting place to a conduit for transportation and a traffic artery (fig. 6.5).

York

A similar movement to demolish the market sheds on the main square in York, just thirty miles south of Harrisburg, came as no surprise. On May 20, 1887, the York common council resolved that the market sheds "greatly interfere with the convenience of public travel, and have become a public nuisance" (fig. 6.6). Pushing the councils to remove the sheds was Edward D. Ziegler, a prominent York attorney and officer of the stock company that had built the privately owned City Market House in 1879. City Market House, aptly named to attract York residents, was an imposing structure designed in the High Vic-

FIGURE 6.5 Market Square, Harrisburg, 1906. Pennsylvania State Archives.

torian Gothic style by John Augustus Dempwolf. Located on the southeast corner of Duke and Princess Streets, not far from the center square, City Market House was a death blow to business in the municipal market sheds (fig. 6.7).[15]

Fearing demolition of the market sheds on the square was the antiquarian Henry L. Fischer, who explained in his celebratory publication of 1879 the reason for "Market sheds, butchers' stalls and sheep shambles, instead of statues and fountains in our Centre Squares." Steeped in the German tradition, some of the Pennsylvania towns, Fischer argued, tolerated "no suggestion of removal" of markets from their squares. As in England, "the very thought of removing these ancient marts . . . would be denounced as a violation of the Constitution, the Declaration of Independence and the sublime sentiments of Washington's Farewell Address."[16]

York, Fischer declared, "adheres to its central idea—its Centre Square market houses with a stubborn yet commendable tenacity, semipatriotic." He defended the market against the "shortsighted people" who knew little "of its history, its high and royal origin, its Revolutionary associations, the revenues and the countless substantial blessings, and luxuries which it has brought and must 'forever' bring to the citizens of York."

FIGURE 6.6 Market Square, York, about 1875.
The York County Heritage Trust, Pennsylvania.

FIGURE 6.7 City Market House, York, about 1880.
The York County Heritage Trust, Pennsylvania.

Fischer's strongest claim in favor of York's public market was its benefit to the common man. Without the market sheds, he asked,

> where would the average, hungry, York County Pennsylvania-Dutchman pro-
> cure a cheap dinner? Where would the Sallie Puddings, the Schmack-worschts,
> the vendors of Fresh roasted Pea-nuts, Ginger-cakes, Pretzels, Hard boiled
> eggs, Cold Puddings, Pop, Raspberry-ade, Oysters and Coffee and their suc-
> cessors forever find a "commodious" place for their business? Where would the
> Dixie Pluffs the "City Kraffts" and the other loafers "and their successors for-
> ever," find a "commodious" place to loaf? Where would the unemployed street
> laborer, woodsawyer, coal heaver "and their successors forever," find a "com-
> modious" place and shelter to spend a rainy day and sit and talk and tell their
> simple stories o'er? Where would the Pennsylvania-Dutch boys and girls "and
> their successors forever," find an equally "commodious" place to meet and
> spend their Whit Mondays and their small change for the exquisite luxuries
> above in part recited? And where, oh! where, would that last refinement of

modern civilization, the respectable Tramp, in search of employment "and his successors f-o-r-e-v-e-r," find a "commodious" and comfortable place to lay their weary heads . . .[17]

Fischer published his commemorative in the wake of the by now familiar movement in the Commonwealth to remove market sheds from town squares.

While the councils bickered indecisively over the "market shed matter," the local butchers claimed the right to some protection. Anxious about the uncertainty of having their leases renewed, the butchers claimed that until a final decision was made on the removal of the market houses they demanded their basic right to a clean, regulated, and policed market.

The matter came to an end on June 27, when a vote of fourteen to ten in the councils resolved that the market sheds in the Centre Square "encroach upon a public highway of the City, thereby greatly impeding and rendering dangerous travel through the said square." The York councils declared the market sheds a public nuisance, and Mayor D. K. Noell ordered their immediate removal.[18]

The councils also passed a resolution of thanks to Mayor Noell "for the noble and fearless manner in which he made effective the concurrent resolution for the removal of the market sheds, thereby subserving the will of the people, and ridding the City of that which has so long disgraced its public square and the spot made sacred by many revolutionary memories."

Despite the councils' confidence that the mayor had acted in the public interest, the mayor signed the resolution for removal of the sheds on June 30 at 12:05 A.M., and by 2:00 A.M. the demolition team began its work "under cover of darkness." Firemen and people in the vicinity arrived on the scene after someone sent in a fire alarm from the Centre Square call box. The event created a public uproar, as "some threatened arrest for destroying public property, others frantically searched for the county judges to secure last-minute injunctions." Efforts to stop demolition failed; laborers flattened the sheds by 3:00 A.M., and by dawn the market's skeletal ceiling beams were all that remained (fig. 6.8).[19]

Reflecting on the year's activities, Mayor Noell reported on December 31, 1887, that "some of these changes and improvements were at the time they were made, especially the removal of the market sheds, quite severely criticized by a few, whose hearts cling fondly to the relics of the past, but the young people, to whom so strongly belongs the spirit of progress, said, 'the

FIGURE 6.8 Market Square, demolition of the sheds, York, 1887.
The York County Heritage Trust, Pennsylvania.

sheds must go,' and the Mayor obedient to the direction of the Councils, in-
stantly removed them." The mayor also bragged that those who had most vi-
olently opposed the removal had since congratulated him. Among his advocates certainly must have been investors in the City Street Railway Company,
which received the mayor's support to move its tracks to the center of the
square just six weeks after demolition of the market sheds.

Harrisburg and York were not alone in the Commonwealth in joining the
movement to rid their streets and town squares of "unsightly" sheds. In southeastern Pennsylvania alone, street markets were demolished in West Chester
(1869), Reading (1871), Hanover (1872), and Lebanon (1884), as were the
open-sided but off-street market sheds in Columbia (1869) and Carlisle
(1878). Much of the pressure for their removal came from prominent local
businessmen who either had a personal stake in a private market house com-

pany or had investments that would profit from improved railway service through the town.[20]

The Pennsylvania German preference for convenience and economy over beauty and ornament, however, interfered with the movement to remove market sheds from the main squares in some of the smaller, more conservative towns such as Lancaster. In 1873, when a group of investors approached the Lancaster city council to build a new market house on the city's market square, Mayor William D. Stauffer refused to succumb to private interests. Stauffer vetoed an ordinance that would have charged the Lancaster Central Market Company $2,000 per year for a ninety-nine-year lease on market square—property that yielded the city over $5,000 a year in net income. Stauffer, having done the math, could not believe the city council was willing to forfeit $3,000 "of the people's money every year for ninety-nine years to a company of private individuals." "This money," he added, "belongs to the public; it is for its use and cannot be given away without perverting the trust for which it is held."[21] Stauffer concluded, "If at any time within this period or after it, the citizens of Lancaster want new market buildings, they can erect them as cheap and as good as any company, without the payment of a large bonus."[22] The veto was sustained, and the city did not lease its market property to the company, although it was fifteen years before municipal funds built Central Market.[23]

Return of the Mixed-Use Market House

As one would expect, the removal of city-owned market sheds typically coincided with the construction of private market houses. Company managers, as they attempted to win the public trust, searched for a distinctive look that would distinguish their buildings from the old market sheds. At the same time, they looked for ways to combine rent-producing functions under one roof. Their solution was to revive the mixed-use market house, the two- or three-story building with marketing on the ground floor and public meeting space above. Companies chartered for this purpose were established in Altoona (1863), Mechanicsburg (1865), New Castle (1866), Williamsport (1866), Lock Haven (1866), Germantown (1868), West Philadelphia (1868), Milton (1870), Mantua (1870), Wheatland (1871), Sharon (1871), Bridgeport (1874), and Hanover (1887). These companies supplemented market revenues by renting the upper hall to numerous social and ethnic clubs, professional entertainers, church groups, and political parties.

FIGURE 6.9 Kelker Street Market, Harrisburg, 1889. Pennsylvania State Archives.

Likewise, fire companies and "opera house" companies financed new buildings by renting market space on the ground floor. Fire companies that received legislative charters to erect market houses in Philadelphia included the Mantua Hook and Ladder Company (1863), the Lincoln Steam Fire Hose Company (1867), and the Union Fire Company (1867). The Grand Opera and Market House Company of Reading incorporated in 1879 to maintain an opera house and a market, as the Fourth and Kelker Street Market Company of Harrisburg did in 1889 (fig. 6.9). The term "opera house" was highly flexible, an affectation that companies used to describe the market's upper floor— basically a meeting hall with a gently sloping floor, balconies, and elaborate decorative schemes.[24]

Investors flooded the Pennsylvania Assembly with so many bills for the incorporation of market houses and other profit-making ventures that it passed a general corporation law in 1874. This law permitted the general establishment of corporations for a "hotel and drove yard or boarding house, theatre, opera and market house, livery or board stable," so that companies no longer had to apply for individual charters from the legislature. Companies incorporated under the act had the power to buy property, erect buildings, and borrow money equal to their capital stock.[25] The West Harrisburg Market House Company, for example, erected its second market house under the new incorporation law.[26]

New York City

While the market house mania confronted small-town officials throughout the Commonwealth of Pennsylvania, the situation was quite different in New York City, which envisioned itself as one of the great food depots of the world. Unfortunately, the city had a long way to go before living up to its claim. Even Junius Browne, in praising the "great metropolis" in 1869, was doubtful that New York's market houses could impress anyone. He found more hope in the markets of Philadelphia, where "the City of Brotherly Love may be an overgrown village; but its market-houses are what they should be, and its municipal government won't steal more than fifty cents on the dollar. Would we could say the same for Gotham!"[27]

On December 15, 1871, Thomas De Voe was appointed superintendent of markets of the city of New York.[28] This was no routine appointment. De Voe was charged with restoring the public markets from near physical and ideological collapse after years of corruption and neglect. His appointment coincided with the establishment of the Committee of Seventy, whose larger task was to topple the Tweed ring.[29] Armed with a strong commitment to well-regulated public markets, and in the spirit of the Committee of Seventy, De Voe aimed to seek out the abuses, collect outstanding revenues, and appoint new clerks, with the hope of making the public market system work again.

De Voe was prepared for the task. He came to the job at age sixty, after decades of experience as a butcher. He had also made a name for himself as an expert on the history of public markets with his two books, *The Market Book* (1862) and *The Market Assistant* (1867). Beyond his research in the confines of the New-York Historical Society, De Voe had accumulated knowledge about markets in other parts of the country. He conducted fieldwork, sketching floor plans and collecting stories and anecdotes from the established vendors and their customers in Philadelphia. He also solicited copies of market laws and ordinances from city clerks in Baltimore, Boston, Chicago, Cincinnati, Louisville, Montreal, New Haven, New Orleans, Philadelphia, Raleigh, and Providence and issued circulars asking for information on the types of food sold in their markets. In 1867 he and his wife journeyed west to Illinois, Iowa, Minnesota, Missouri, and Ohio, documenting markets along the way, most notably the large markets of Chicago and the new Union Market in St. Louis. The trip also enabled him to gather information for his voluminous manuscript "The History of Cattle in America."

When he was appointed superintendent of markets in 1871, De Voe was a well-known "market man," noted for the books he enthusiastically promoted, his lectures on public markets and abattoirs, and his opinions in the newspapers. He had a reputation for honesty and good citizenship, to which his fellow butchers and his customers attested. Anyone who visited the Jefferson Market could find "in the recess of one of the avenues . . . , the excellent and abundantly supplied stand of Colonel De Voe—a noble specimen of an American citizen, military as well as civil."[30]

Congratulating De Voe just a few days after his appointment, John C. Wandell, a retired officer of the New York State National Guard, wrote:

> I think the Political Melenium [sic] is close at hand, having laboured for the last 25 years for not Whig nor Democrat nor Republican but Political Reform in regard to our City affairs. I begin to realize that my labours have not been in vain. You my dear Colonel [De Voe] have the experience and the ability to rescue our Markets from the deep slough of corruption which, for many years past has steadily and surely made them highly unpopular with our citizens and has compelled many worthy men to sacrifice their business in order that they might cease to be black-mailed by the hand of Clerks, Collectors, Inspectors, etc. I for one have the confidence that you will speedily put an end to such practices.[31]

Wandell alluded to the frequent frauds committed at Washington Market, as well as the "system of terrorism" exercised by the Tammany Ward at Clinton Market. Market clerks and superintendents randomly revoked stall permits, issued fines, and demanded unjustified stall premiums from any vendor whose political leanings they considered incorrect. These unexpected "costs" of doing business in the public markets had given many vendors little choice but to move elsewhere.[32]

Hope for Market Reform

A demand for market reform had been in the air since Peter Cooper proposed selling the public markets in 1867. Cooper, then president of the Citizens' Association of New York, calculated that the city was losing an important source of revenue by wasting valuable commercial real estate on public markets. According to his calculations, the market property was worth $5 million but generated a paltry average net annual revenue of $110,000. Cooper complained to the notorious comptroller Richard "Slippery Dick" Connolly (ultimately to no avail): "It is unnecessary to detail the method by which the city has received so small a portion of the revenues actually collected from the markets—it forms part of the system which has been the growth of dishonest and incompetent government for thirty years. If the custodians themselves are dishonest, who shall watch them?"[33]

The remedy Cooper proposed was selling the market property, for he believed that the original intent of public markets—for government to provide "a common ground for the meeting of producer and consumer"—was irrelevant in a city as large as New York. Farmers were crowded out of the markets and forced to occupy the public streets in the neighborhood, while the market houses themselves were occupied by self-seeking wholesalers. Cooper reported that the markets were misplaced downtown in the heart of the commercial district and that the 5,473 uptown meat shops and stores were forced to charge consumers a premium for the high cost of trucking goods from downtown. Cooper praised the markets in Paris, which were located so as to keep down the price of food in the shops. In Paris, Cooper reported, fresh food was retailed at a markup of 24 percent, while shops in New York and Brooklyn commanded 100 percent.

It was to be expected that Connolly would disregard Cooper's proposal to sell the markets—especially since they offered a wide range of jobs for Connolly's political cronies who looked for a place on the public payroll. Connolly's "gang of rogues" included street sweepers, market clerks, and finally, in 1870, the superintendent of market rents and fees—a job he had given to his loyal supporter (and renowned street fighter) former alderman Richard Croker.[34]

De Voe's appointment as superintendent of markets on December 15, 1871, immediately followed Connolly's arrest and the downfall of the Tweed ring in November. With a newly cleansed Tammany Hall, Andrew H. Green, deputy comptroller during the crisis, charged De Voe with reforming the market system under his leadership. De Voe's appointment was publicly endorsed by the market vendors and by the commission merchants in West Washington Market, who were convinced that De Voe was "the right man in the right place."[35] De Voe did not share Peter Cooper's idea of selling the market property as a remedy for corruption and lost market revenues. On the contrary, he aimed to purge the markets of "thieves" so that honest men could return to their stalls knowing their rights would be protected. Within days of his appointment, he began to receive pleas for retribution from victims of the corruption.

Cleaning House

De Voe's first task was to dismiss the "worse than useless officials" who managed the individual markets. Washington Market, one of the oldest and the largest in the city, employed a clerk, an assistant clerk, and a deputy clerk. During his investigation, De Voe reported that the head clerk ignored basic standards for order and cleanliness and the assistant and deputy clerks seldom reported to work. De Voe reduced the staff from three to two and increased the number of private watchmen, all selected for their "respectability and integrity." He also identified several sweepers and cartmen who collected their pay without working for it.[36] He concluded this after making random unannounced visits to the markets. The words of an angry sweeper confirm that De Voe made surprise visits and insisted on high standards of cleanliness. In his letter to De Voe, "Take the Hint" wrote:

> Will you ever come into the market like a man you Steal in like a Snake to see if you would catch your Sweeppers idle no Shuperintend ever acted so you dont want to give us a minuts rest our business is to sweep the market and not the work of the common Street Scavengers by sweeping haf the streets it dont do you to sweep the market but we must sweep the ro[o]f also and do the work of every Tom Dick and Harry of the Tinkers Now you out to get a long ladder made and send us to sweep the dust of[f] the clouds when you come to the market come like a man and dont be Stealin in lik a Snak or a Spy.
>
> [Signed]
> Take the Hint[37]

De Voe was not bothered by such threats and remained determined to improve conditions and increase worker efficiency at any cost. After two years in office, he proudly reported a reduction from eighty-four to forty-two market employees on the city payroll.[38]

Improving the Facilities

In his 1873 report on the condition of the public markets, De Voe detailed every market's sad story of years of physical neglect. According to the public market tradition, market revenues were supposed to support the cost of routine maintenance and repairs. The "tradition" in New York, however, was to direct market revenues into the pockets of "official political sinecure vampyres" and "leeches." Washington Market was the most notoriously corrupt. De Voe claimed that most of its 528 stands generated bonuses of $500 to $5,000 for market officials, who blackmailed vendors in exchange for permit renewals for their stalls. Market officials also pocketed money from vendors who occupied unofficial spaces in the public passages and gangways.

Whereas Washington Market was declared the "greatest in the world" in 1853 (fig. 6.10), by the time De Voe took office twenty years later it had earned the title as one of the "mean-looking markets of New York."[39] *Harper's Weekly* reported on November 30, 1872, that order was impossible because of the market's irregular lanes and makeshift sheds, descriptions that corresponded to official reports from the city's Office of Public Markets. As De Voe described it, Washington Market's neglected, insufficient, and exceedingly narrow passageways were congested with produce wagons and teams loaded with market refuse—those "obnoxious vehicles rapidly driven through the various passage-ways, spilling portions of their offensive load along their route, and thus creating a continual and intolerable nuisance."[40]

Much of the chaos occurred because the city had not upgraded the market for several decades. Although it had considered rebuilding Washington Market in 1851, the plans were caught up in rivalries and disagreements over design. Wholesale merchants wanted a cast-iron market "after the manner and plan of the Hudson river railroad depot." Some members of the Committee on Repairs and Supplies preferred the plans of Frederick A. Petersen, who proposed two stories of shops plus a third story that could be rented for offices to help offset construction costs. Butchers disliked the idea of shops on the second floor because they believed their customers would not bother to climb the stairs. They argued that although Petersen's plan "may have been

FIGURE 6.10 Washington Market, New York City. From *Gleason's Pictorial Drawing-Room Companion,* March 5, 1853.

drawn by a skillful architect," he was "unacquainted with the wants of the occupants and customers." Plans were finally set aside altogether in 1854, when Mayor Fernando Wood vetoed the ordinance to rebuild the market, and the facilities had been ignored ever since.[41]

Shaming New Yorkers even further was the superior appearance of market houses in Europe, which the press described as "high-storied, arch-roofed, iron, stone, and glass built triumphs of architecture and convenience."[42] The writer was perhaps alluding to Les Halles, the central market of Paris, designed by Victor Baltard with cast-iron and glass pavilions, which served as a model for market houses throughout France and the rest of Europe (fig. 6.11). In New York, however, widespread demand for improved market facilities was not just a superficial desire to keep up with the Europeans. The city was indeed the nation's largest market for fresh food, particularly meat. The estimated weekly per capita consumption of fresh meat in the 1850s and 1860s ranged from 2.9 to 3.6 pounds for beef and 4.2 to 4.9 pounds for all meat.[43] Promoting New Yorkers' reputation as the foremost meat-eating population in the world were the popular journals, which claimed that they spent $180,000 a day on meat, that over eight million pounds of livestock entered the city each week, and that a single hog slaughtering establishment—at Fortieth Street along the North River—generated annual sales

FIGURE 6.11 Les Halles, Paris, about 1853–1858. Courtesy Bibliothèque Nationale de France.

of $15 million. Any city whose demand for fresh, affordable food was that high would have a big stake in ensuring that its markets could handle volume with the greatest efficiency.[44]

Solon Robinson, social reformer and agriculturist, called for more space, at least for the country wagons. As it stood, limited parking and crowded conditions hindered farmers from coming to the market or staying for any length of time. As a result, low-income shoppers accustomed to buying directly from the farmers had to bull their way into the market, where prices were higher. The high cost of food worried Robinson, who warned that food deprivation among the poor "breeds discontent, dissipation, crime, and ruin to any civilized society."[45]

With De Voe's campaign to collect outstanding revenues, he was happy to report that after he had been in office two years the Washington Market had received repairs to the roofs, flooring, doors, steps, and walks, and the sewerage system was improved with additional branches, drainpipes, and water hydrants.[46] But that was about all he could do. He understood that public expenditure on new market buildings was unthinkable until faith in (and revenues from) the system was restored. Until then, he looked for alternatives to new construction, at least for his first few years in office.

Alternative Reforms

De Voe saw immediate hope for improving certain market buildings by accommodating the growing demand for armories. Jefferson, Essex, Centre, and Tompkins Markets were already home to National Guard regiments that rented their upper floors for drills, storage of equipment and uniforms, and meeting space. Tompkins Market, for example, was home to the Seventh Regiment, which in 1861 had persuaded the city to rebuild the market and give the regiment exclusive use of the upper floors (fig. 6.12). Constructed by Theodore Hunt according to the plans of Bogardus and Lafferty, the market was near the Cooper Union on the square bounded by Third Avenue and Sixth, Seventh, and Hall Streets. At the time of construction it contained the largest drill room in the country.[47]

FIGURE 6.12 Tompkins Market Armory, New York. From New York Infantry, Seventh Regiment, *The Manual of the Seventh Regiment, National Guard, S.N.Y.* (New York, 1868).

After the Civil War, as more and more members lived uptown, regiments found downtown market houses inconvenient and inadequate, so they pressured the city to finance new uptown quarters for their exclusive use. Comptroller Andrew H. Green, however, firmly opposed using taxes to build new armories while the city debt was so large. De Voe thus received the city's support for any proposal that encouraged the use of extant market houses for armories. In 1873 he proposed repairs to the second floor of Jefferson Market so it could "serve for any public use, or otherwise offer superb drill-rooms and armories for one or more of the state military organizations, by which many thousands of dollars would be saved to the city." Other cities employed a similar strategy of combining market houses and armories. Baltimore's Fifth Regiment, for example, persuaded local officials to build a new market house that would provide it with space on the upper floors, and the Richmond Market Armory opened in Baltimore in 1873.[48]

De Voe's boldest move as superintendent of markets was his strong support for long-term leases of public market property to stallholders' associations, an experiment that began in 1868 with the establishment of the Fulton Fishmongers Association. This organization built its own market house on city property with a ten-year lease at $5,000 a year. According to De Voe, these arrangements removed politics from the markets because vendors themselves were responsible for allocating stalls and setting rents. The leasing of market property would also ensure "that American citizens owning property in our public markets, and applying it to legitimate purposes for the benefit of the public at large, can retire to their beds and rise in the morning to find that what they owned yesterday is secured to them to-day."[49] A guaranteed long-term lease would encourage vendors to make improvements to their stalls without fear of random eviction.

The Manhattan Market Company

Much as he preferred public ownership of markets, De Voe was powerless against wholly private speculation in new market house construction. On April 28, 1871, shortly before he took office, the New York Assembly, like its counterpart in Pennsylvania, passed a general incorporation act for organizations "to carry on the business of marketing in the city of New York." This act gave five or more persons the right to erect buildings for public markets and to rent stands, stores, and stalls in them for no more than fifty years. The markets of any company organized under the act would be subject to the sanitary rules and supervision of city health officials.[50]

De Voe delivered a short speech on January 22, 1872, at the opening of the Manhattan Market, one of the earliest private market houses in New York. The mammoth structure, funded entirely by private investors, covered a five-acre lot bounded by Thirty-fourth and Thirty-fifth Streets and Eleventh and Twelfth Avenues, including a bulkhead along the North (Hudson) River (fig. 6.13). The imposing brick, iron, and stone structure was capped with a series of graceful turrets, which made a visual contrast to the city's unsightly market houses. At 160,000 square feet, it could accommodate up to a thousand wholesale and retail dealers in stalls of varying sizes. Twenty entrances gave access to the grand interior, illuminated by one hundred windows and a central dome fitted with two thousand electric lights. An ornate vestibule with an iron staircase led to company offices on the second floor, there were restaurants at each end of the building, and an ice cellar was constructed underneath the eastern end.[51]

For all its grandeur, the Manhattan Market was not the kind of "large speculation" De Voe welcomed, perhaps accounting for his short speech at the opening. He had encouraged capitalists to invest in market houses, but specifically those that already existed.[52] Given that all the public markets (still south of Fourteenth Street) needed major repairs or rebuilding, capital expenditure for mammoth market houses as far north as Thirty-fourth Street seemed frivolous to him. Moreover, the Manhattan Market Company, as well as the newly incorporated East River Market Association, did not involve the vendors as De Voe would have hoped.[53] New markets, he believed, should be established by a select number of "practical men from our several public markets, to assist in locating such buildings where most required, or at points most accessible to the greatest number of citizens."[54]

Sour Grapes

One year after the opening, Paul J. Armour, president of the Manhattan Market Company, wrote a scathing letter to the editor in the *New York Times* opposing the city's plans to improve West Washington Market. Perhaps fearing that the municipal venture might hurt his own investment, Armour heaped insult after insult on Comptroller Green and Superintendent De Voe:

FIGURE 6.13 Manhattan Market, New York City, about 1872. From Frederick
Lightfoot, *Nineteenth-Century New York in Rare Photographic Views*
(Mineola, N.Y.: Dover, 1981).

Both [are] equally ancient in their ideas when they write upon the subject of
markets. Mr. Green proposes that all the great commercial interests of this Metropolis shall be subservient to the article of food. Mr. Devoe believes in the
same doctrine, but would distribute the markets all along the river front, from
Fulton to Fourteenth-street, in the face of the earnest demand of commerce,
which is rapidly being driven to New-Jersey, owing to the blockade of the water
front by just such nuisances as West Washington Market.[55]

Referring to the city's plan to expand West Washington Market, Armour
opined, "What a farce! Does Mr. Green know that two-thirds of the stand-

holders of Washington Market to-day are residents of New Jersey, and pay no taxes in New York! Does he know that the greatest portion of all the beef and mutton is slaughtered above Fortieth-street, and has to be carted down town, there sold, and then carted back to the great points of consumption!" Armour criticized the city for taking its lessons from the markets in Paris and London, "cities that are entirely different from New-York as to topography, being nearly as broad as they are long, while here we have but a narrow strip." Furthermore, Armour argued that the markets in Paris and London were located where the densest part of the "consuming population dwells," whereas in New York "it is exactly the reverse." Armed with statistics, he showed that the downtown population was steadily declining, while the up-town population was on the rise. The population in the First, Second, and Third Wards was 36,754 in 1850 and had declined by almost half to 19,487 by 1870. In contrast, the population in the Eleventh, Seventeenth, and Eigh-teenth Wards was 119,070 in 1850 and 219,239 in 1870—an increase of 90 percent. The population of the Twentieth and Twenty-first Wards more than doubled, to its current 96,000 inhabitants. Armour's conclusion: "Nine-tenths of all the food eaten in New-York is consumed above Fourteenth-street. Where, then, is the parallel between the Paris and London markets? The comparison is absurd."

Armour accused Green of visiting Washington Market for the sole purpose of giving speeches to the butchers to gain their votes for the mayoral nomi-nation. His boldest claim, however, was that "public markets under Munici-pal rule are a failure, and must give way to private enterprise such as the Manhattan Market Company has demonstrated in the erection of their mag-nificent building, to which Mr. Green never refers, and entirely ignores, never having seen it himself, and going to England and France for patterns to our people." Armour may not have approved of Green's tour of model market houses in Europe, because Green would have learned that the most success-ful ones were owned, built, and managed by government, not by private in-dividuals.[56]

Despite the Manhattan Market Company's promise to allow stallholders to share in its profits, the venture never attracted enough vendors to survive. In 1877, only five years after it opened, the market was tomblike inside, lacking both dealers and customers. It was soon converted into a slaughterhouse, which survived until the acclaimed fireproof building burned in 1879 and the property was sold to the New York Central and Hudson Railroad.[57]

Hope for New Public Market Construction

De Voe was highly critical of the New York market companies because they failed to manage their operations in the long run, and their vast capital expenditures had not resolved the city's market problem. As he complained in 1873,

> The first and great fault has been with the city authorities, by their not providing buildings that would be a credit to our city, or otherwise the present buildings should have been kept in proper order and repair. The city should have not only replaced these with suitable erections, but also placed one or more such in every ward in our long neglected city, and in places that would be most convenient to our citizens, so that provisions or every kind used for human food could or should be forced by law to be taken into these several marts, where they would be properly inspected or supervised daily; which can only be done successfully in large quantities thus collected and exposed.[58]

Still a believer in the public market system and in the principles of the moral economy, De Voe thought New York residents "should be protected, as well as have equal accommodation secured to them in all public markets." He argued that the system would benefit not only the consumers but also the vendors, many of whom were wasting $10 to $20 a week in rent at shops or private market houses, while weekly rent at the public markets was only $1 or $2.

The famous Washington Market was finally rebuilt soon after the city recovered from the depression of 1873. Designed by architect Douglas Smyth, the attractive Victorian structure opened for business in 1884. According to *Carpentry and Building*, iron and glass were the principal materials used. On the inside Smyth employed the latest in "modern construction" to meet the city's demand for "a maximum of room, light and ventilation with a minimum space consumed by construction as well as the smallest amount of material."[59] Butchers from the old Washington Market celebrated their new quarters with great fanfare, confirming their allegiance to the city (fig. 6.14).

De Voe Leaves Market Politics

In 1881, ten years into his job as superintendent of markets, De Voe was promoted to the collateral post of head of the Bureau for the Collection of City Revenue and head of markets, two jobs that he soon found overwhelming, not to mention "annoying and unsatisfactory." Unable to collect the estimated

FIGURE 6.14 Butchers celebrating the opening of Washington Market, New York City, 1884. From *Frank Leslie's*, December 27, 1884.

$600,000 in outstanding market revenues, De Voe asked Comptroller S. Hastings Grant to divide the two positions. On October 20, 1883, Grant appointed De Voe deputy superintendent of markets at the same annual salary he had been paid before—$2,750. Francis Tomes, former importer of cutlery and fancy goods, was appointed to the higher position of collector of city revenue and superintendent of markets. De Voe, however, resigned out of frustration within a few months. In a letter to Mayor Franklin Edson, dated February 8, 1884 (and marked by De Voe as "not sent, too much politics"), De Voe intended to inform the mayor that he was resigning because Tomes meddled too much in market matters by hearing complaints and issuing unwarranted permits.[60]

De Voe's departure guaranteed a return to business as usual. No sooner had he left office than Comptroller Grant authorized Tomes to erect a corrugated metal awning along two sides of the recently built Fulton Market in order to rent outside stalls. The market vendors were outraged, for several reasons. First, they objected to such an unsightly addition to their attractive new quarters, another Victorian brick and terra-cotta market designed by Douglas Smyth in 1882. Second, they believed that outside vendors would obstruct the entrances and sidewalks with their oyster shucking and fish cleaning, thus deterring the customers who were *"just beginning* to come from uptown in their carriages to leave orders."[61]

City officials also received criticism for their handling of the new West Washington Market, built by a private association on public property near Washington Market (fig. 6.15). Accommodations were insufficient compared with the old market, and in 1888 twenty-three market men joined in a complaint against the comptroller and the superintendent of markets for denying them permits in the new market. Moreover, the Dock Commission was angry because the comptroller had sold city property to the West Washington Market Company—property that the commission had been using for a depot and equipment storage.[62]

According to the Report of the Department of Public Works for 1879, the city's ten markets—Washington, West Washington, Fulton, Catharine, Union, Essex, Tompkins, Jefferson, Clinton, and Center—collectively averaged $354,000 per year in revenue from 1874 to 1878, while expenditures for the same period amounted to $57,554. Although business was tremendous, the facilities decayed to such an extent that the 1886 *Report on the Social Statistics of Cities* declared that "there is no capital city where the market accommodations, both for seller and for buyer, are so badly managed as here [in New York]." Bad as they were, New York's public markets still survived privatization, giving the city a chance to launch a progressive campaign for improved public markets at the end of the century.[63]

Thomas F. De Voe was ahead of his time. Although he managed to implement a few short-term improvements and to expedite new market house construction, his broader vision for public markets did not come to fruition until

FIGURE 6.15 West Washington Market, New York City, 1885. From Mary Black book, neg. no. 50756. Collection of the New-York Historical Society.

after his tenure. He predicted in the early 1860s that large public market houses could provide more affordable downtown retail space than could shops. He also predicted the potential of public markets to service the whole-sale trade, supplying not only the uptown shops but also the large steamers, hotels, and boardinghouses that demanded food in bulk. Washington Market, for example, became the city's largest wholesale market by the 1930s, doing a greater volume of business than all the other markets in the city combined.[64] Likewise, the downtown public markets provided a service to thousands of residents and daily commuters seeking quick meals and snacks from stands and sidewalk vendors.[65]

In Pennsylvania, the privatization frenzy had a different outcome than in New York. The numerous private market houses of Philadelphia, for exam-ple, continued to earn the city high praise, especially from the 1886 report, which declared that "the provision supply of Philadelphia is superior to that of most cities, and her markets have always had a wide celebrity." Likewise, other cities throughout Pennsylvania reported successful market houses, both public and private.[66] By generating large-scale, highly capitalized buildings, the market companies of Pennsylvania reinforced the concept of marketing under one roof, with the result that the market house, regardless of its form of ownership, remains an important feature of the urban landscape in the Commonwealth.

"Cracks in the market walls" were most visible in New York and Pennsylvania, but they were also found elsewhere as cities throughout the country faced similar pressures to privatize market houses and to legalize shops. However, a few years of experience with the negative repercussions of deregulation had given other cities pause. Faced with potential losses in revenue, lack of control over food costs, and threats to public health, they looked for ways to strengthen, not abandon, their public market systems in order to maintain control over urban food supply and distribution.

PART III

Regaining a Share
of the Marketplace

SEVEN

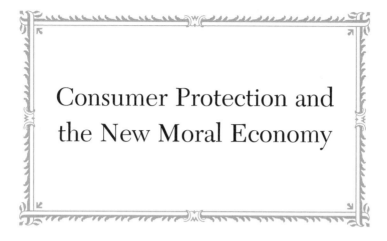

Consumer Protection and the New Moral Economy

Having gone so far in the control of the market business, the government must go farther.

Committee on Free Markets, Boston, 1870

<p>

D espite the dramatic events in Philadelphia and New York, local officials elsewhere resisted the fad of privatizing, particularly during the
last quarter of the nineteenth century, when public market deregulation
proved disastrous. The first and most obvious reason for their resistance was
that public markets were still a major source of municipal revenue, if not the
primary one. Unless alternative sources of income could be found, city leaders hesitated to disturb the system. Second, there were public health concerns. Several years of experience with suburban slaughterhouses, dispersed
retailers, and food transported by railroad proved that the loose market laws
of a deregulated era could provoke a public health crisis. And third, the city
still had an interest in securing affordable food for the workingman, something private enterprise had yet to deliver. Shops had been legalized under
the promise that they would bring down the price of meat, but they failed to
do so. In short, city officials realized that privatizing had failed to guarantee
the urban populace a healthful, affordable food supply. Although the public
market was no longer the principal source of provisions, municipalities still

looked for ways to maintain their share of the market in food supply and distribution, and they based their strategies on the individual city's needs within a regional, national, and international food marketing system.

The Need for Nationwide Market Reform

Raising awareness of the need for market reform from coast to coast was Horace Capron, commissioner of the United States Department of Agriculture (USDA) from 1867 to 1871. After the Civil War, high food costs and neglected marketing facilities prompted Capron to review the country's current "market systems"—the entire process by which food moved from the source to the dinner table. These systems included not only public markets but also stockyards, slaughterhouses, commission houses, and grocery stores, as well as the rails, roads, and waterways that connected them. His study marked the beginning of scientific management applied to food marketing and distribution, in which eliminating waste and inefficiency depended on understanding the entire system and its parts.

To understand current practices, the USDA sent food marketing questionnaires to local authorities throughout the nation, including municipal officials, food dealers, agricultural society members, and journalists. Capron reported only the results from sample cities such as San Francisco, Boston, Newark, New York, Philadelphia, and Chicago, since the mass of material was too difficult to present in its entirety.

The responses convinced Capron that in general food marketing and distribution were much more difficult in cities with populations over 100,000. As he explained it,

> When a place returns a population of about 100,000, from the nature of things, the length of streets, the enhanced value of lands near the city, the influx of crowds indifferent to the quality of their food or ignorant of the characteristics of sound meats and fresh vegetables, the market usages undergo a change, and the problem of furnishing great metropolitan centers with food in abundance, on moderate terms, becomes one of the first practical importance.[1]

In general, survey respondents from cities under 100,000 reported no problem with securing a varied, affordable food supply. The nature of small cities—with their homogeneous class of shoppers, proximity to farms, and uncongested streets—promoted direct trade between farmer and consumer. In

Capron's words, "The very hands that dropped and dug the potatoes may measure them out by the bushel or the barrel at the door of the merchant, the lawyer, and the capitalist." Such was the market system in Albany, New York, which reported fine farmland within a mile in several directions from the farmers' stands on Capitol Hill. Furthermore, the principal thoroughfare was so broad and steep that a street market did not lower its "tone" or health-fulness as a place for upper-class residences. The New York State capital had little cause for complaint in its answer to the USDA circular, reporting that nine-tenths of its food came directly from farmers. Norfolk, Virginia, reported favorable marketing conditions for similar reasons.

According to the responses from large cities, however, food marketing and distribution were more difficult where the population exceeded 100,000—places like New York, Newark, Boston, Chicago, and San Francisco. Nearby farms could not meet the demand, and farmers found it impractical to spend the day in the city, preferring to sell their wagonloads to middlemen and hucksters. As a result, prices were high because middlemen took a dispro-portionate share of profits and certain customers were wealthy enough to pay the price. This was the case in New York, where three distinct classes of shoppers affected food prices and quality in the public markets. First were "the upper 20,000, who live in five-story brown-stones, and spend from $5 to $10 daily in the purchase of perishable food and as much more for pantry ar-ticles. For such, nearness to a market-house is a prime necessity; hence the steady increase in the number and neatness of outfit of grocers' and butch-ers' establishments on or near fashionable streets." Although shoppers in this class did not directly patronize the public markets, the proprietors of their neighborhood grocery stores and meat shops did, especially the wholesale stands in Washington, West Washington, and Fulton Markets. Storekeepers took "the cream of all that comes, the tenderloins, the fat chops, the finest chickens, the fattest turkeys, paying well and expecting their customers to pay better."

Next was the middle class, which valued high quality in food but always practiced thrift. According to the New York respondent, this class suffered most from inadequate market accommodations. Not only did shoppers waste an hour in round-trip travel to the public market, either they paid a premium for high-quality meat at a fashionable stall or they bought "at a third-rate stand, where the million go, where the vegetables are wilted, the chickens are blue, and the beef Texan." The "million" referred to the third class of shoppers—the poor masses who shopped only for low prices, since they could rarely afford quality.

Newark suffered from its proximity to New York because the nearby metropolis "draws everything, and gives its citizens the first cuts of beeves, the fattest of the chops, and the largest peaches." On an average daily wage of four dollars Newark's artisans and laborers could afford local cabbage, beets, lettuce and tomatoes, but not bread or wholesome meat. Flour dealers, for example, sold only by the barrel, so storekeepers divided the flour into family-size bags and charged an exorbitant price for their work. Butchers who operated "cheap meat-shops" in the poor parts of the city slaughtered "low-priced cattle, poor, miserable, lean, stringy, diseased, over-driven beasts." Newark's informant reported that the city's meat trouble began during the Civil War, when some operators bought large numbers of cattle from New Jersey's principal stockyard at Communipaw, shipped them to Albany, and "dribbled them out at their own prices." Newark butchers could not afford the artificial prices and opted for inferior cattle, while expensive cattle went to New York, where wealthy patrons could pay the price.

The San Francisco respondent reported a similar dependency on middlemen for fresh meat and produce. The closest farmland was in Alameda, where farmers preferred to sell their produce to commission merchants rather than make the long ferry ride across San Francisco Bay. The convenience of middlemen came with a price to both producer and consumer. As reported, "Of one dollar paid by the consumer, the producer generally gets 70 cents on butter, cheese and eggs, 65 cents on apples and hard pears, 35 to 45 cents on soft fruit and berries, and on green vegetables 50 cents. Out of this [the producer] must pay the freight to the place where the fruit sale is made in the city, provide the packages, pay return freight on them, incur all the expenses of picking and packing, and all the risks of loss previous to the first sale." The same products then passed through the hands of wholesalers and retailers, who in turn took their profits before the goods finally reached the customer at the store or market house.

Business was slow in San Francisco's five market houses, where ideally "one large stall could do all the business at less expense." According to the respondent, however, rather than give a sole proprietor "the monopoly of privilege" in the market house, the price of food could be better protected by controlling the number of middlemen and regulating their business. "Middlemen are and always will be indispensable, and they must be paid," he remarked, because producers and consumers generally could not meet face-to-face in large cities. However, the respondent believed that the number and profits of middlemen were disproportionately large and needed to be controlled, since middlemen "contribute nothing to production." As it stood, the only municipal market laws of San Francisco were those that established license fees for peddlers in wagons and for stallholders in the market houses.

Respondents to the USDA survey generally agreed that a reasonable profit for middlemen should range from 25 to 50 percent, as it did in Cincinnati, St. Louis, Buffalo, and Louisville. Regulations were necessary only when profits reached 100 to 200 percent. At that point, Capron recommended that cities adopt the "better features of the best-regulated markets." In the 1870s Philadelphia's market system was still the country's model, as it had been since the eighteenth century. According to Capron, despite its large size, "the second city of the Union has better marketing than some towns of one-fifth her population." Philadelphia's market laws encouraged farmers from Delaware County, Chester County, and other nearby counties to bring produce into the city. Space in the market houses was set aside for their use, parking for wagons was ample, and there were no longer restrictions on the type and quantity of food they could sell. As a result, Philadelphians enjoyed fresh local meat and produce raised within thirty miles of the city.

Equally praiseworthy were Philadelphia's "elegant, cleanly, sweet-smelling, though expensive, buildings in which the Pennsylvania farmer meets the consumer face to face," as opposed to the "musty old rookeries" and market sheds of New York and Baltimore. Capron also admired the Philadelphia market houses in contrast to the meat and fish shops "scattered promiscuously over that most vigorous and thrifty metropolis"—Chicago. One could see the absence of a well-ordered market system in Chicago, where "next to a great hardware-house you buy a roast, and the latest novel is side by side with white fish caught in Lake Superior."

In some cases topography hindered development of an efficient market system, as authorities in Charleston and Mobile reported. Both cities lacked access to the countryside in all directions. Charleston was situated on a low, narrow peninsula formed by the confluence of the Ashley and Cooper Rivers, and a wide interval of marshes and barrens separated Mobile from its productive farmlands. Although seafood was readily available, these cities lacked affordable fresh fruit, meats, vegetables, eggs, and milk because farmers preferred to sell these products to middlemen, who in turn charged consumers

100 to 200 percent of cost. Capron recommended that cities reconsider the "oppressive regulations" that often discouraged farmers from selling direct because of burdensome licenses, fees, and restrictive market days and hours.

The Inefficiencies of Transportation

After describing the country's diverse market systems, Capron reported one practice that was consistent from coast to coast: the abuse of animals on cattle trains and in stockyards. This situation aroused his concern more than any other market problem and prompted him to propose specific recommendations for reform. Another participant in the crusade against cruelty to animals was William F. Channing, secretary of the Rhode Island Society for the Encouragement of Domestic Industry, who described his astonishment at "the system of wholesale torture" on cattle trains. Channing claimed that "the horrors of no slave ship ever exceeded the suffocation, starvation, maiming, and trampling on the cattle trains, save that the victim in one case is human in the other a brute beast."[2] Urging Capron to investigate and resolve the matter were members of the United States Senate Committee on Agriculture, including Charles Sumner and Simon Cameron, who received alarming reports that "the rising generation in our eastern cities have been so accustomed to diseased meat" from animals sickened by transit to market.[3] Consumers, knowingly or not, bought yellow and bruised meat from animals that were crippled and exhausted by the time they reached the butcher's mallet. Enormous quantities of such meat were sold daily in New York's Washington Market.[4]

Texas beef had a particularly bad reputation. The Civil War cut off Texas cattle ranchers from their ordinary markets in the South, causing a cattle surplus in the state. After the war, ranchers flooded the eastern markets with their surplus of millions of Texas longhorns. Unfortunately for the longhorns, drovers literally shoved them into the markets, where they were barely alive after a series of long and abusive train rides.[5] Texas ranchers were also eager to take advantage of the epidemic that banned the sale of eastern cattle from January 18 through May 1, 1871. By the fall of 1873, Texas and other western cattle arrived at Brighton Market, just outside Boston, at the rate of three thousand a week.[6]

The USDA's interest in more humane treatment of cattle in transit to markets was connected, of course, to its desire for "healthful meats at fair prices to the dwellers in American cities." Capron estimated that four million people in eastern cities depended on meat from cattle that had traveled 1,000 to

1,200 miles by rail. Cattle transportation therefore required strong regulations because it was "guided solely by immediate self interest; it is incapable of far-sighted wisdom; it is blind to the essential and permanent good of the greatest number." He insisted that improving cattle transportation was "a subject of national importance" and urged Congress to appoint a commission to examine current practices, determine the abuses, and suggest improvements.

One way to prevent sick and abused cattle from arriving at eastern markets was to slaughter the animals closer to their source and then transport the dressed meat. In describing the challenge, Capron remarked that "the natural course of pastoral agriculture in such a country is, that the grass belt should produce the cattle, and the corn belt should finish them and fit them for the knife. . . . The real difficulty to be solved is, how to bring corn-fed beeves from the Mississippi, the Ohio, the Illinois, and the Wabash to the tide-water cities."[7] His answer: a "well-regulated beef express" that would connect eastern cities with slaughterhouses in Chicago, St. Louis, Springfield, Burlington, Kansas City, Omaha, and Abilene. "In this way, within forty to fifty hours from the time the beef is killed, his quarters, in perfect condition, could be hanging in an eastern market-house." Such a system required improvements in refrigerated railcars, so Capron recommended that the USDA offer a prize to the inventor of the best method for year-round transportation of dressed meat over long distances.

National Market Reform Loses Momentum

Concluding his annual report, Capron announced that "marketing thus grows into a special trade, requiring special confidences with railroad men and a knowledge of cities that the working farmer has neither the time nor the tact to acquire." Unfortunately, the momentum for national reform in market systems and cattle transportation was lost when Capron resigned as commissioner of agriculture in June 1871 to accept a position as agricultural adviser to the Japanese government.[8] His successor, Frederick Watts, commented briefly on marketing concerns in his annual reports, but he just reiterated the problems and lacked the fervor of his predecessor. Capron's recommendations to limit the profits of middlemen and to reward the best designs for refrigerated railcars thus fell into oblivion.[9]

Furthermore, the possibility of national market reform—ranging from the need for price controls and restrictions on the profits of middlemen to a nationalized transportation system for urban food distribution—was unlikely under the administration of Ulysses S. Grant, president from 1869 to 1877. Grant's administration was shamelessly corrupt and had an unprecedented commitment to private enterprise. When federal inaction on market reform followed Capron's resignation as commissioner of agriculture, each city was left to deal with the "market problem" in its own way. While Philadelphia basked in the glory of its magnificent new market houses and New York City struggled to resuscitate its public market system, events in Boston exemplify a city on the offensive—a city that declared its commitment to regulated food marketing and distribution for the common good.

Boston: The Failed Promise of the Railroad

Echoing Capron's sentiment on the need for a nationalized food transportation system was Josiah Quincy (1802–1882), son of the mayor who oversaw construction of the great Faneuil Hall Market in the 1820s. Quincy followed in his father's footsteps by also serving as mayor from 1845 to 1849, and he later maintained a public profile as president of the Boston Social Science Association. Throughout his public career, Quincy held that only state ownership and regulation of the railroads, not private enterprise, could control the high cost of food transportation. His concern for the public welfare extended not only to his various railroad proposals but also to his later crusade for co-operative banks.[10]

In his 1869 address before the Boston Social Science Association, Quincy spoke out in support of cheap food for city workers who had little or no chance of maintaining their own kitchen gardens. High food costs, he believed, were due to the railroad companies' taking advantage of their quasi-monopoly by charging an unfair price for transportation. The daily welfare of Boston's citizens was at the mercy of railroad presidents and managers, who stood "between us and the food required by our daily necessities." Quincy continued, "If plain nourishing food is made inaccessible to the poor, and diminished in quantity for a large portion of the community, as is the case at present, it is an evil that strikes vitally at the best interests of society."[11]

Boston, he believed, did not suffer from high food prices for lack of sufficient and varied food outlets. On the contrary, the city was well stocked with a series of public markets (fig. 7.1), more than eight hundred shops, and hun-

FIGURE 7.1 Public markets in Boston, with Faneuil Hall Market as the centerpiece. From *Ballou's Pictorial Drawing-Room Companion*, August 15, 1855. Collection of David K. O'Neil.

dreds of farmers' wagons selling door to door. Since "the arrangements of our Market are as perfect as can be devised," the problem was not with the system but with the high cost of food transportation, of which "the railroads do not give honest accounts."

The government, he concluded, should take control of the food supply from "the hands of those whose interest is only in increasing the gains of a small class, and place [it] in the hands of the representatives of the people." In Ireland, the railways "will soon be purchased by the government, and they will be in America, as soon as the people can understand the amount of taxes imposed on their daily bread by monopolies."

Quincy also argued for government ownership of the railroads before the Boston Board of Trade, where he hoped to find that a conscience still existed in Massachusetts. After all, he remarked, "we live in Massachusetts, where, it is to be hoped, the notorious immorality attributed to New York legislators is unknown." He had hoped that Massachusetts was morally superior not only to New York but also to Pennsylvania, which "sold out her public works to joint stock companies." "Let us beware," Quincy warned, not to "permit such an overgrown power to exist in Massachusetts." Going to the heart of the matter, Quincy proposed that the state purchase the Boston and Albany Railroad Company in order to control the cost of food transportation.[12] Attempting to argue the advantages of government ownership of the railroads, Quincy turned to the success of the United States postal system, which conveyed mail in the same way that the railroads conveyed people and goods. Someone could send a book across the country at post office rates for about four cents, but it would cost more than fifty cents at railroad rates.

Although the state legislature gave Quincy decent hearings on his proposals for state ownership and regulation of the railroads, ultimately, of course, it rejected them. The final responsibility for a fair and equitable system of urban food marketing and distribution once again fell on local government, as did the blame for the problems.[13]

Boston's Committee on Free Markets

Despite continued private ownership of the railroads, the public/private struggle over markets continued in Boston for most of the 1870s. Sparking the issue was an 1870 petition from citizens who demanded a "free market" and an investigation of alleged price fixing at Faneuil Hall Market. A committee was established to conduct the investigation, although it was uncertain from the beginning what constituted a "free market." Contemporary uses of the phrase varied widely, including markets free of government regulation, markets free of price fixing and monopoly, and markets open free of charge to any seller. The committee set out to address all three possibilities, knowing, at least, that the citizens were generally dissatisfied with food facilities and prices.[14]

The committee's first task was to investigate the factors that led to the current state of food provisioning in Boston. In 1825, when the cornerstone of Faneuil Hall Market was laid, the city's population was 58,277, with most residing within one mile of the market. The surrounding countryside was thinly populated and devoted mostly to farms that provided the city's fruits and vegetables. Meat, too, was supplied from within the state, as well as from neighboring Vermont and New York. By 1870 Boston's population had grown to 648,525, and the increase was accompanied by a change in the character of the market business. As the committee explained, over the previous twenty-

FIGURE 7.2 Faneuil Hall Market, Boston, 1914. National Archives, RG 83-G, neg. 4028.

five years Faneuil Hall Market had been transformed from an almost exclusively retail market to a wholesale and jobbing center, having become "the great provision exchange for New England."

It was common knowledge that Faneuil Hall Market was now in the hands of middlemen devoted primarily to the wholesale trade, but the committee found no evidence of price fixing. On the contrary, the concentration of hundreds of farmers' wagons at a single space in the city had guaranteed healthy competition (fig. 7.2). Most stall owners purchased all or part of their stock directly from the farmers' wagons, as did three-fourths of the city's grocery stores. This concentration virtually guaranteed that producers would sell out their stock. The committee reported that the source of high food prices was the small stores, which kept prices up until they were forced down by quotations at Faneuil Hall.

These findings confirmed the local and regional benefits of a city-owned central wholesale market. Summarizing the economic role of Faneuil Hall Market, the committee found that in "this small space—eight hundred and fifty feet by two hundred feet—having come to be the centre of the market business, not only for Boston and the cities and towns immediately adjoining, containing a population of about 650,000, but for the chief cities in New England during portions of the year, the producer knows that he can always sell promptly what he sends to that centre."[15] The concentration of business promoted competition, not hindered it.

To verify the committee's conclusions, several members visited markets in the major cities of New York, Philadelphia, Baltimore, Washington, Cincinnati, Albany, Chicago, and St. Louis, where they gathered printed market laws and ordinances. After reviewing the regulations of other cities, the committee asserted that those in Boston were not unusual, as the petitioners had argued. It admitted, however, that some regulations could be modified or removed to encourage competition. It suggested extending the market hours for street stands, permitting farmers and stallholders to sell at wholesale or at retail, and allowing the sale of goods not necessarily the product of one's own farm.

Faneuil Hall Market continued to generate enough revenue for the city so that its transfer to private enterprise was out of the question. The market had produced $1,948,955 since its opening in 1826. After deducting the interest on the cost of the building and the land for forty-four years at 5 percent ($983,400) as well as operating expenses ($264,957), the committee concluded that the city had made a profit of about $700,000, or 8 percent per annum, on its investment without taking into account the increased value of the property. Although petitioners favored privatizing the market, the committee believed that "laissez-faire was inappropriate for the supply and distribution of meat and vegetables, where government has no greater duty than to regulate." It was particularly concerned with "the great mass of the people in cities" who were directly affected by the price of necessities.

Still, the concentration of trade in one location had rendered Faneuil Hall Market inefficient by the 1870s. To encourage additional market nuclei in other parts of the city, the committee proposed that "having gone so far in the control of the market business, the government must go farther." It recommended purchasing suitable lots in various sections of the city—in the Highlands and at Dorchester, South Boston, and East Boston—where new market houses could be operated by the city or by private corporations under municipal regulations.

The Sale of Bad Meat

Shortly after the report of the Committee on Free Markets, Bostonians rallied again in 1871 when they received news of the sudden death of a butcher at a slaughterhouse in Brighton, Boston's principal source of meat.

The coroner determined that a diseased animal had given the butcher blood poisoning during slaughtering. Whether or not this was true, the common council ordered yet another committee to investigate the city's markets. Where the previous investigation had focused solely on Faneuil Hall Market and its influence over food prices, this one focused on public health—extending the committee's scope to include all food markets, not just those owned by the city.[16]

The investigation found no evidence of bad meat for sale in Faneuil Hall Market. Testimony from vendors asserted that "it don't pay to sell inferior meat," because "it would be known and a man would lose his business." Vendors at Faneuil Hall were under the constant eye of other vendors, patrons, and city market officials. Informants argued time and again that the sources of bad meat were the private markets, over which the city's Board of Health had no direct authority. In fact certain ones, such as Blackstone Market, actually specialized in meat that was unfit for sale anywhere else.[17]

The bad meat sold at Brighton Market was attributed to the lack of standards in slaughtering. Charles Bohn, a German butcher who had practiced the trade in Saxony and Weimar, was astonished at the lack of regulation in the United States compared with his experience in Europe. In Germany, for example, laws forbade a butcher to dress dead animals, and elsewhere in Europe commissioners were required to inspect animals before they were slaughtered. He also recalled that cattle were not overcrowded in railroad cars in Germany as they were in the United States.

Dr. R. M. Hodges, another informant, declared that in France "the arts of cooking, slaughtering and inspecting meats are carried to great perfection." The only solution in the United States was "for municipalities to exercise a control over the kind and quality of meats consumed. A great central slaughter-house, under strict superintendence, with intelligent inspectors, having full powers, could accomplish more in this respect than anything else."[18]

Following the way of other cities, the committee proposed a new abattoir inspected by government officers. Quoting George T. Angell, president of the Society for the Prevention of Cruelty to Animals, the committee's report stated that "for the immediate protection of our citizens, I think a sanitary police should be established, as in Europe and at Chicago. The Jews of our city eat meat of no animal that has not been examined, before killing, by their Rabbi, and the meat, after killing, stamped as good with his seal. What the Rabbi does for the Jews, let the sanitary police do for the Gentiles."[19]

George Derby, secretary of the State Board of Health, considered the idea of a government-inspected abattoir a "life saving reform."

The committee's report prompted immediate results, for in 1872 a new abattoir was built in Brighton along the Charles River. Considered state of the art, the multistory buildings had the capacity for three hundred beef cattle each day. After slaughter the meat was hung for two or three days in cold storage, cooled by a ventilated dropped ceiling that held fifteen to twenty tons of ice. In the slaughtering area, workers disposed of hides and offal through trapdoors that led to cars on tracks, which took them to an adjacent rendering house.[20]

The notion of well-regulated markets under the inspection of local government had come full circle in Boston. During the 1850s and 1860s, city officials had tolerated a certain number of private markets, stores, and slaughterhouses, since Faneuil Hall Market had exceeded capacity and could not meet the city's provisioning needs. However, years of experience with loose market laws gave local officials reason to believe that the "laissez-faire" principle was inappropriate for urban food marketing and distribution. By the 1870s Boston reaffirmed its commitment to public markets, not only to secure a source of revenue, but also to protect consumers.

Faneuil Hall Market's Semicentennial

Although Faneuil Hall Market was exonerated by the investigations, vendors still looked for ways to promote the market's reputation. That opportunity came in 1876, when they joined with the city to sponsor a parade in honor of its fifty years of public service to the citizens of Boston. On August 26, four hundred ticket holders formed a procession that began in South Market Street, passed through Merchants' Row and Commercial Street, and ended at Faneuil Hall Square (between the market and Faneuil Hall) for a public ceremony. Flags of various nations adorned the market's exterior, and the interior was decorated with additional flags, bunting, arms of several states of the Union, shields, Masonic devices, and emblems.

The program began with the presentation of ceremonial canes to four veterans of the market house—J. Herman Curtis, Harrison Bird, Ebenezer Holden, and Nathan Robbins—all of whom had occupied stands when the market opened in 1826. After the presentation the honorees were photographed (fig. 7.3), and an elaborate banquet followed in Faneuil Hall. The

FIGURE 7.3 Mayor Samuel Cobb honoring the veterans of Faneuil Hall Market at the semicentennial celebration, Boston, 1876. From Abram English Brown, *Faneuil Hall and Faneuil Hall Market* (Boston: Lee and Shepard, 1900).

bill of fare was a sampling of the market's bounty, including mock turtle soup, a fish course, a boiled course, a roasted course, entrees, assorted game, pastries, ice cream, fruits, and coffee.

The after-dinner speeches revealed the true meaning of the celebration and the recent debates that had mounted over the market's future. Josiah Quincy Jr. returned to the scene with his passionate declaration of the market's success. "The lesson of this anniversary is *confidence*. Judicious expenditures for facilitating exchanges are never wasted. The cost of land for public purposes is never to be measured by its cost for purposes of individual monopoly. Whatever adds to the attraction of a city and to the convenience of its citizens must be remunerative in the end."[21] Quincy alluded to the numerous complaints about the extravagant cost of the buildings and property since the market opened in 1826 but claimed that Faneuil Hall Market had paid for itself "over and over again."

Governor Alexander Rice acknowledged the market's contribution to the region, noting that "it has encouraged the neighboring farmers to a systematic and scientific cultivation of their lands, and helped to develop the market gardens, so numerous in our suburbs." Rice also praised the market as a major tourist attraction and noted that visitors to Boston always included it on their tours. Likewise, Curtis Guild stated that "the building itself is to tourists one of the lions of Boston."[22]

Merchants emphasized the market's impact beyond Boston and the Commonwealth, where "its supplies are drawn from cities, towns and villages, in nearly all the States in the Union, from Texas to Maine, from Oregon to Florida, and from islands and countries beyond the borders of the States." They were proud, too, that the Committee on Free Markets found no evidence of a monopoly at Faneuil Hall Market. Claiming to act in "the best interests of their fellow citizens," the Faneuil Hall merchants boasted that "it is the pride of the market that it is free, open and untrammelled by rings or cliques or 'corners.'"

Self-congratulation was not enough to sustain the market's reputation as a major wholesale center for the city and region. The building's 132 stalls and twenty-two basement cellars were home to eighty-six firms. In addition, thirty-four firms occupied the ground floor of the adjacent Faneuil Hall itself, which contained twenty-three stalls and eleven basement cellars. All in all, the city was landlord for 120 firms in this single location, which in 1876 generated approximately $71,000 from rent plus $19,000 from other market revenues.[23] Given the scope of this major enterprise, the city looked for ways to strengthen its management.

George E. McKay was appointed superintendent of Faneuil Hall Market in April 1877. McKay had no experience with the market business, but other qualifications soon made him successful in the job. His ten-year partnership in the tailoring establishment of McDonald and McKay had required him to combine face-to-face interaction with careful behind-the-scenes bookkeeping—skills that prepared him for the duties of market superintendent (fig. 7.4). McKay immediately began to enforce the market laws he was sworn to uphold, and after one year of service the stallholders and porters presented him with a decorative cane in recognition of their appreciation. At the presentation address, J. Herman Curtis remarked that "within sixty days after your appointment I became convinced that in appointing you the mayor had filled the bill to a T." Curtis also knew of no previous market superintendents who were as "faithful, able, and gentlemanly" as McKay, "particularly one who could say no without giving offence." In carrying out the public market tradition, McKay was called on to pass judgment on disputes between buyers and

FIGURE 7.4 George E. McKay (*left*) superintendent of Faneuil Hall Market, Boston, in 1876. From Brown, *Faneuil Hall Market.*

sellers, and his decisions were considered just and final. During his twenty-year tenure, his performance enhanced the reputation of Faneuil Hall Market not only in the United States but also abroad, where his methods and manners as a market superintendent were considered exemplary.[24]

Market Regulation in the Midwest and South

Outside Boston, other cities defended the public market system and renewed the moral and practical arguments for keeping urban food retailing under the wing of government. This was true particularly in the Midwest, where, according to the Tenth Census of the United States, the distribution of public markets in 1880 was regionally strong, as it was in the South and the Northeast.[25] Although laissez-faire policies had weakened government regulation of markets in the antebellum period, after the Civil War the moral economy and the notion of regulated trade still were part of American legal discourse. Strict market laws were established, for example, in Detroit, St. Paul, Cincinnati, Dubuque, Pittsburgh, and St. Louis. Showing even more strongly that laissez-faire was generally not tolerated in the Midwest, market laws against private shops were still upheld in the courts. In 1869 Missouri justice Philemon Bliss upheld a fine against a private butcher shop in St. Louis, arguing that regulated public markets in "larger towns" were necessary to "public order, cleanliness, and health."[26] Although the city of St. Louis ultimately permitted meat shops in 1870, they were not allowed within five blocks of any city market, and operators were required to pay the city collector $100 a year for a license. Moreover, the ordinance declared that "all meat-shops shall be under the control also of the Board of Health." This body had the power, by a majority vote, to revoke someone's license to operate a meat shop for sufficient cause.[27]

Midwestern cities were also motivated to protect their investment in market houses, which were new relative to those in the East. St. Louis, for example, had an incentive to fight for its right to limit sales to the regulated public markets in 1869, since it had just built an addition to Soulard Market in 1865 and built Union Market in 1868 (fig. 7.5).[28] Likewise, the enforcement of market laws was pressing for other cities that had recently established public markets, such as Dubuque (Central Market, 1856), Pittsburgh (North Side Market, 1864, South Side Market, 1868), and Cincinnati (Findlay Market, 1860).[29] Where establishing a market house enhanced the success of surrounding shops and businesses, members of the socioeconomic elite were motivated to maintain the market's monopoly of place by rigorously defending the enforcement of regulations. Overall, anti–public market sentiment was not strong in the Midwest, where the public market was still the centerpiece of the city's boosterism.[30]

The attitude concerning public markets in the South was affected by the peculiar municipal leadership of cities by nonlocals during Reconstruction. For example, from 1870 to 1874 Houston, although on the fringes of the Confederacy, was under the mayoral administration of Timothy H. Scanlan, an ambitious entrepreneur who used the Republican cause to reap the fruits of the government's distribution programs.[31] During his tenure, Scanlan hoped to replace the low, moss-covered market house (see fig. 2.10) with a mammoth city hall and market. After a tour of several American cities to survey city hall designs, Scanlan proposed a combined market and town hall that would reflect Houston's close ties between government and the mercantile economy. Considered one of the most elaborate buildings in Texas and an unnecessary extravagance, Scanlan's city hall and market was short-lived: it

FIGURE 7.5 Union Market, St. Louis, about 1870. Missouri Historical Society.

burned down on July 8, 1876 (fig. 7.6). Nonetheless, it was replaced a few months later by a new city hall and market, designed by Galveston architect Edward J. Duhamel (fig. 7.7). Larger than its 1872 predecessor, the 1876 structure featured Italianate detailing and a three-story central block, 100 by 125 feet, flanked by asymmetrical towers and two-story market wings. The increasing power of government is represented in the building's formal features, such as the tall clock and bell tower, which also may have served as a lookout tower for fires, a lower tower with balconies for public ceremonies, a weather vane, a flagpole, a landscaped square with walkways and fountains, and wide projecting eaves around the market wings. The building provided a powerful civic icon for a city eager to give shape to its postwar prosperity.[32]

FIGURE 7.6 City hall and market, Houston, 1872. Courtesy Houston Metropolitan
Research Center, Houston Public Library.

Local officials in Mobile, Alabama, also used the public markets to express
their political and economic strength. After the Civil War and throughout Reconstruction, the city experimented with repealing laws that restricted the
sale of fresh food anywhere within the city limits except public markets. Mobile's opposition to public markets during this period has been attributed to
the city's leadership by nonlocals. Instrumental in the experiment with deregulation, for example, was Gustavus Horton, the first of three successive mayors appointed by either the United States government or the Alabama legislature after the war.[33] The city council under Horton believed that eliminating
the "market monopoly," a plan that was "adopted and working in other cities,"
would stimulate the food supply and normalize prices. In 1867 Mayor Horton, a committed Unionist and Republican (not to mention a commission
merchant from Boston), supported a "greengrocery" ordinance that would
allow fresh food retailing anywhere in the city.

The effect of the ordinance was immediate, as market vendors chose not to
renew their stall leases. By 1870 annual revenues at Southern Market—the

city's largest public market—dropped from an average $75,000 to $8,000 owing to empty stalls. A concerned city council responded by proposing an ordinance that would combine the market and greengrocery system, but Horton's successor, Martin Horst, vetoed it. Horst's business interest in the wholesale trade of liquor, cigars, tobacco, and groceries gave him a stake in preventing the revival of the public market system. He argued successfully that a return of public markets would revive the market monopoly as well as high prices.

In 1885, when Mobile reached a financial crisis, the city's new *local* management returned to a "municipal" market system, bringing an end to the twenty-one-year experiment with the greengrocer system. Under the new city charter, the market system enacted by an ordinance of 1888 was the "municipal market system," as opposed to the "public market system" that had ended in 1867. The ordinance strengthened the monopoly on fresh food sales at municipally owned and controlled markets throughout the city by establishing zones around each city market. These zones excluded independent retailers from setting up their businesses close to the markets and were meant to shield the markets from competition. The 1888 ordinance was intended to make the municipal market system bigger, better regulated and enforced, more effi-

FIGURE 7.7 City hall and market, Houston, about 1880. Courtesy Houston Metropolitan Research Center, Houston Public Library.

cient, and more lucrative to the city than the old public market system. Opponents of the ordinance, including greengrocers and commission merchants, challenged its constitutionality, but the Alabama Supreme Court ruled in the city's favor, arguing that it fell within the powers of the new city charter. Mobile's municipal market system was a planned institution that local officials considered vital to the city's mission of handling its own affairs, modernizing, and making civic improvements.

During the last quarter of the nineteenth century, in an era that predated routine health inspections of private food markets and manufacturers as well as national pure food and drug laws, the municipality was still the primary polity responsible for ensuring a healthy, adequate, and affordable food supply. The concentration of marketing not only facilitated food inspection, street cleaning, and waste removal, it also justified the city's right to police weights and measures, food packing, slaughtering, and the use of docks, wharves, and streets for the food trades. Contrary to popular predictions, meat shops and private market houses did not replace public markets. Public markets survived the impulse to modernize and continued to challenge local governments to consider their moral and practical benefits. They remained a valuable source of provisions for the large immigrant and working-class populations that preferred them for their accessibility, affordability, and familiarity. As a result, the late nineteenth-century city in the United States, as well as in Europe, attempted to standardize market houses, extend them into the suburbs, coordinate them with rail service, and develop distinct building types for the wholesale and retail trade. New market houses, usually major public works projects, remained part of the city-building process as architects and engineers experimented with ways to incorporate them into a growing and changing urban infrastructure.

EIGHT

Rebirth of the Municipal Market

The science of city market establishment and management is only
in its infancy.   J. W. SULLIVAN,
                                   American Federation of Labor, 1913

The municipality in the late nineteenth century rediscovered that public markets could improve—not hinder—public order, hygiene, and urbanity while providing cheap, affordable food for wage earners and their families. Unlike private food shops and grocery stores, market houses encouraged
interaction and bargaining between buyers and sellers. Their multiple entrances invited public access, and they fostered solidarity among vendors, who
shared the same landlord. These features had been part of the system for centuries, but they gained particular relevance at a time when high food costs,
sanitation problems, and traffic congestion were paramount.

Realizing the potential of public markets was only half the battle, for ultimately municipalities had to secure public control and build confidence in
food provisioning. To do so, they built sophisticated market houses that were
bigger and more numerous than ever before, in order to satisfy diverse
vendors and customers. Center Market in Washington, D.C., for example,
constructed between 1871 and 1877 and reportedly the country's largest,
comprised 57,500 square feet of floor space, compared with New York's

Washington Market (52,000 square feet), Philadelphia's Farmers' Market (32,400), and Boston's Faneuil Hall Market (27,500).[1] At the same time, the nation's capital established two smaller market houses, each approximately 10,000 square feet, in the growing eastern and western sections of the city.

Dozens of other cities built enclosed municipal markets in the last decades of the nineteenth century, including Buffalo, New York (Broadway Market, 1883); Cleveland, Ohio (Broadway Market, 1878); Columbus, Ohio (North Market, 1878; East Market, 1888; West Market 1890); Dayton, Ohio (Central and Wayne Avenue Markets, 1878); Denver, Colorado (City Market, 1889); Indianapolis, Indiana (Central Market, 1880); Lexington, Kentucky (City Market, 1879); Roanoke, Virginia (City Market, 1887); Savannah, Georgia (City Market, 1872); and Winston-Salem, North Carolina (City Market, 1876).[2] Likewise, New Orleans added fifteen market houses to its already extensive public market system between 1880 and 1911, primarily in the most densely populated outer zone of the city.[3] Even the model industrial town of Pullman, Illinois, chose a centrally located, fully enclosed market house (1881), with stalls rented by independent retailers, as an alternative to the company store.[4]

These efforts were piecemeal, but ultimately they laid the foundation for a nationwide campaign for improved municipal markets promoted by the National Municipal League and the federal government during the Progressive Era. The rebirth of the municipal market system in the late nineteenth century was more than just a defensive move by local government to keep financial and physical control over the food supply. It represented an important victory over laissez-faire in food provisioning and secured a future for the public market system in the twentieth-century American city.

The All-in-One Market House

The late nineteenth-century market house was ambitious in design and scope. Architects and engineers hoped to accommodate a wide range of individuals and functions under one roof, including farmers, retailers, hucksters, wholesalers, upscale shoppers, bargain hunters, cold storage, and public meeting space. The large, light open spaces of exposition halls, train stations, and other nineteenth-century building types worked well for market houses too by fostering a streetlike atmosphere that encouraged shoppers to stroll and inspect the goods. Mammoth market houses—with stalls numbering in

FIGURE 8.1 The new Center Market, Washington, D.C. (built 1871–1877). Washingtoniana Division, D.C. Public Library.

the hundreds—also aided the market clerk, whose office, usually in a second-story gallery, provided an unobstructed bird's-eye view of the market floor. Improvements in cold storage extended the life of perishables, enabling vendors to expand their hours of operation and the season for their goods, and better heating and lighting enhanced comfort and convenience. In short, the market house had evolved into a recognizable building type characterized by the classification of space by goods, separate facilities for the wholesale and retail food trades, parking for farmers' wagons, and cold storage.[5]

Washington's new Center Market epitomized the all-in-one market house of the 1870s and 1880s (fig. 8.1). Stretching from Seventh Street to Ninth Street along Pennsylvania Avenue, the city's most prominent thoroughfare, Center Market embodied the revived notion that a grand market house, if well designed, could be both functional and aesthetic.[6] Officials in Washington had reached this conclusion after a complicated sequence of political decisions and demanded a market house that would rival the great markets of New York, Boston, and Philadelphia. They also hoped an impressive market house would help Washington rank with the great European capitals.

Several steps paved the way for the capital's dream of market houses. In 1866 the city revised its market ordinances to allow wholesale purchases in the old Center Market—a long, low frame structure with whitewashed walls and moss-covered roof dating from the 1820s. Until then, it was illegal to buy goods in the market for resale. Although the 1866 ordinance encouraged gro-

cers, hoteliers, restaurateurs, and boardinghouse owners to make their wholesale purchases at the old Center Market, it also had the negative effect of increasing business beyond capacity.[7] To relieve congestion and better distribute
market activity, in 1872 the city established Eastern Market and Western Market. These neighborhood markets served the growing residential sections of a
city whose population had increased from 75,000 in 1860 to 132,000 in 1870.[8]

According to Congress, however, a new building for Center Market, located as it was on the ceremonial avenue that linked the Capitol and the
White House, was beyond the means, vision, and capability of the local government. After the Civil War, Washington was in debt and in deplorable physical condition. New wartime congressmen suspected that the city was a
hotbed of secessionists. Congress, for fear of leaving the city to manage its
own affairs, abolished the office of mayor and established a territorial government, which ran the District from 1871 to 1874. During these tumultuous
years Alexander "Boss" Shepherd, head of the Board of Public Works from
1871 to 1874 and governor of the Territory from 1873 to 1874, launched a
massive urban development program. Likened to the reconstruction of Paris
under the infamous Baron Georges-Eugène Haussmann, Shepherd's program
for Washington involved extending water mains, grading and repaving streets,
installing new sidewalks, landscaping prominent avenues, and dredging the
canal that ran along the north side of the Mall. Backed by Congress, the Board
of Public Works accomplished its mission by ruthlessly demolishing old land-
marks as it paved the way for public and private building construction, including a new central market.[9]

Center Market's reconstruction soon became a reality once Congress authorized an act to incorporate the Washington Market Company in 1870. This
private company, chartered by an unprecedented act of Congress, was empowered to construct and manage a new market house to replace the old city-
run Center Market within two years. It was also authorized to issue $1 million
in capital stock and received title to the market squares for ninety-nine years,
after which the property and buildings would revert to the United States unless Congress chose to extend the agreement. Although the new Center Market was an anomaly because of its federal legislative charter, it was still typical
of the reformed public markets of the 1870s and 1880s, in which government
officials (in this case members of Congress and the Territory of the District)
worked with the architect, engineers, and local merchants to create a modern
all-purpose market that would accommodate the needs of a varied public.[10]

The promise of a building with architectural refinements dominated congressional debate over the incorporation of the Washington Market Company, which proposed to erect "instead of the loathsome pile of rubbish . . . , a stately and elegant structure [with] magnificent entrances and porches to the edifices. . . . Nothing will be seen of the Market and its operations, by passers along Pennsylvania Avenue, and no evidence of the existence of such a place will be observed, except the flood of people, entering and retiring from the capacious space within."[11]

The company hired German-trained architect Adolf Cluss to design the new market. Cluss was known for designing numerous city schools, churches, and residences, including that of his neighbor and client Alexander Shepherd. Before working for the Washington Market Company, Cluss also designed the first Agriculture Department building, slightly west of Center Market and just across the Mall. He worked in the eclectic Victorian style, often imposing a French mansard roof on a building in the German Renaissance Revival *Rundbogenstil,* or round arch, style—a combination he employed at Center Market.[12]

According to the final plan, Center Market consisted of three retail wings connected in a U shape, with twelve wholesale storefronts enclosing a central courtyard (fig. 8.2). It had more than 57,500 square feet of floor space, contained over six hundred stalls, and covered more than two acres of ground including the metal awnings.[13] Unlike earlier market houses, Center Market had few alleys and driveways—a feature that vendors ultimately criticized. According to Cluss, driveways "would have been a ruin to the market, an anomaly, and a great danger to life and limb of the market-going public, and would, before this, have exposed the architect and officers of the company to the charge of manslaughter." Cluss also justified his omitting a second floor over the Seventh and Ninth Street retail wings, for it enabled the company "to introduce those large ventilating skylights, opening through the whole length of the roof, which are most appreciated by the market men, by the public, and by the sanitarian, and have elicited flattering comments from the most competent authorities of this country and elsewhere" (fig. 8.3). He was also proud of the large icehouses along the courtyard side of the retail wings, which he considered "indispensable appendages of a modern market in a southern climate." Placing the icehouses outside relieved "the interior of the building of incumbrances preventing the free circulation of air, an unobstructed view, and affording hiding places for rats and vermin."[14] In 1886 the

Washington Market Company responded to growing demand for cold storage by increasing the height of the B Street wing to three stories, insulating the wing, and installing modern refrigeration equipment. The market also had a steam-heating system and its own electric plant, which powered the lights, meat grinders, fans, and ice-making equipment.[15]

Another new feature of Center Market was separate facilities for the wholesale and retail trades. Describing the ornate fixtures in the front row of wholesale stores, Cluss remarked that they were designed "without regard to expense" for a certain "class of market men" from the old market. The style of the three retail wings also "varied to suit the wants of the different trades." They were equipped with "tasty modern market stalls," such as stall no. 226, John Ockershausen's condiment stand (fig. 8.4). Outside, the "country people," as they were often called, preferred to furnish their own benches under the eaves and awnings and to occupy their space for a nominal fee (fig. 8.5). According to Cluss, providing modest space for this type of vendor was "a feature which is held in supreme importance by all owners of markets and by the public, and is participated in by intelligent market men, since it draws the great mass of purchasers to their business places." Center Market, in short, provided an enclosed, hygienic, controlled environment for the wholesaler, retailer, and bourgeois shopper while offering modest facilities for vendors and consumers of low-cost goods.[16]

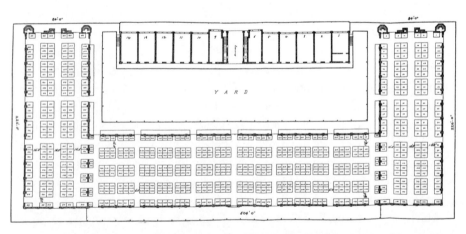

FIGURE 8.2 Plan of Center Market, Washington, D.C. From U.S. Senate Committee on the District of Columbia, *Papers relating to the Washington Market Company . . .* , 60th Cong., 1st sess., 1908, S. Doc. 495.

FIGURE 8.3 Interior view of Center Market, Washington, D.C., 1923. National Archives, RG 83-G, neg. 6721.

The Washington Market Company also reached out to middle-class women by installing an elegant ladies' lounge, equipped with stylish wicker furniture and a telephone (fig. 8.6). This feature set a new standard—or at least expectation—for other markets in the city. In 1891, for example, J. Eldridge Burns, market master for the municipally owned Western Market, requested $5,000 from the city commissioners "to put the market in condition to meet the wants of the dealers as well as the patrons, as it is situated in the center of the West End and patronized by a class of people who require a first-class market." Evidently Burns's request went unheard, for in 1902 he insisted that "there is still needed, to put it in first-class order and provide for public comfort, a ladies' retiring room, for we must depend upon ladies marketing for our future success."[17]

Even the most modern facilities, however, could not totally satisfy Washington's middle-class women. According to the African American newspaper the *Bee*, most of the public markets in Washington, especially the Saturday

FIGURE 8.4 Stall no. 226, John Ockershausen's condiment stand, Center Market, Washington, D.C., 1917. National Archives, RG 83-G, neg. 3653.

night markets, "have largely grown to be resorts of loose characters, young men and women, young boys and girls who promenade through them using improper language, flirting, and by a system of handkerchief signs communicating their evil thoughts and purposes." Informants for the *Bee* reported that "naturally, these young girls, embryo fast women, carry their market-house flirtations into the public avenues and streets, and there, by making signs of recognition and invitation, degenerate into the most foul vice." Hundreds, perhaps thousands, of young female streetwalkers, "white and colored alike," frequented the city streets, and parents were called on to guard their daughters closely from "night market-house promenading," especially since the police were "not mindful of their duty in these important matters."[18]

Domesticating the Public Markets

Indeed, one of the principal features of new market houses in the late nineteenth century, not just those built in Washington, was their middle-class character. Architects strove to create a safe, attractive environment for the bourgeois consumer, whose expectations about shopping had risen, perhaps from the experience of the department store. New market houses, public and private, were promoted as a bourgeois sanctuary—a space where respectable middle-class women could feel safe in public.[19] Architects Daniel Burnham and John Wellborn Root took this into account when they designed Chicago's Central Market for developer Wilson K. Nixon in 1890–1891 (fig. 8.7). On the east side of State Street, just south of the bridge over the river, Central Market contained wholesale cold storage vaults on the ground floor and a retail market on the second floor. The retail entrance on State Street was decorated with a roundel representing a bull's head and elegant gold and green glass mosaics executed in Paris from Root's designs. Inside, the retail market offered a bright, unobstructed view of the stalls, which were tastefully decorated with plants and sparsely furnished with simple counters and shelves.[20]

FIGURE 8.5 Hucksters selling outdoors from makeshift stands, around 1900. Center Market, Washington, D.C. Washingtoniana Division, D.C. Public Library.

FIGURE 8.6 Ladies' lounge, Center Market, Washington, D.C., 1917. National Archives, RG 83-G, neg. 3633.

Creating an atmosphere of civility was difficult in the old, established public markets. Women were particularly aware of this and criticized vendors for failing to maintain standards of orderliness, cleanliness, and general appearance. Four members of the Chautauqua Society held a symposium on the topic in 1896. Although they praised the artistic arrangement of fruits and flowers at Baltimore's Lexington Market (fig. 8.8), they scoffed at San Francisco's market buildings, with their ceilings "artistically festooned with cobwebs . . . , floors a mosaic of soggy sawdust . . . , and enough vegetables wasted every day to make free soup for the city's entire poor." They also noted the lack of tasteful displays and artistic decoration of booths at Faneuil Hall Market, which needed a "woman's touch."[21]

Women were also concerned that the public markets had ignored the needs of the average housekeeper. In 1885 a short-lived New York magazine, the *Cook,* posed the question, Are the markets doomed? It recognized that New York's public markets, particularly Fulton and Washington, had suffered from

FIGURE 8.7 Central Market, Chicago (1890–1891). 1. Fish and oyster department; 2. fresh meats; 3. main entrance; 4. a glimpse of the interior; 5. view from the river. From *Graphic,* November 14, 1891, 314.

FIGURE 8.8 Lexington Market, Baltimore, about 1895. State Historical Society of Wisconsin, neg. (A62)7225.

the numerous private markets established uptown, and for good reason: "The keepers of those [uptown] establishments know the individual tastes and requirements of numerous patrons in their vicinity, and, as a rule, treat their customers—even the smallest buyers—with a degree of attention and courtesy that is to be feared are not customarily shown in the public markets, except to large purchasers." Even though prices were higher in the shops than in the markets, household buyers preferred the one-stop convenience of shops "instead of being compelled to travel from stall to stall, and department to department, through the narrow lanes of a big public market." The housewife also saved time and carfare by not having to travel downtown to the public market. And finally, she could keep a monthly account with a shop, "practically a necessity where the buying is entrusted to servants." The public market men, on the other hand, kept few accounts, except for larger purchasers.[22]

Despite the benefits of uptown shops, the *Cook* still expressed hopes for the public markets if market men would make an effort to attract the average consumer. The journal recommended better treatment of the "humble buyers of small quantities of cheap goods." It warned that unless the market men took action in this area, "it is to be feared that the public retail markets are doomed to pass away before a great while."[23]

The *Cook's* skepticism about the future of New York's public markets was justified in the 1880s and 1890s, for the system limped along under poor municipal management, shifting neighborhoods, and changing practices in the retail and wholesale food trade. New York's old public markets competed not only with new private ones but also with the small suburban grocery stores that gave consumers an alternative to traveling downtown to a public market. Likewise, commission merchants used the improved railways to bring produce directly from farmers and sold on commission to retailers, taking away some of the wholesale business typically carried on at the public markets. In addition to competition from private food retailers, public markets suffered from shifting downtown populations and physical deterioration. As Deputy Comptroller Edgar J. Levey of New York said in 1899, the public market was a feature of local government since the city's founding, but it was time to "go out of the public market business."[24]

Public Market Reform in Europe

In the aftermath of the market house boom of the 1870s and 1880s, skepticism about a future for public markets in the United States prevailed both at home and abroad. In 1891 England's Royal Commission on Market Rights and Tolls reported that the United States was the only major power that lacked state authority over public markets. Since the right to establish markets was the prerogative of the individual municipality, they often fell into the hands of private individuals or trading companies, as they had done primarily in the western states. England's Royal Commission on Market Rights and Tolls also reported that American wholesale markets were particularly susceptible to private ownership and speculation and were rarely coordinated with public services. Chicago's South Water Street, for example, was in constant gridlock from the market wagons that lined Wholesale Row (fig. 8.9). Even New York's wholesale West Washington Market (see fig. 6.15), despite its waterfront location, lacked adequate facilities for receiving goods by water and had direct connection to only one railroad—the New York Central. Thus most dealers bought their goods at nearby railroad yards and piers and trucked them by wagon to their markets or shops.[25]

FIGURE 8.9 Traffic congestion at Wholesale Row, South Water Street, Chicago, 1915. National Archives, RG 83-G, neg. 3716.

England and the European nations shared an interest in the comparative systems of food marketing and distribution at a time when conflicts over the food supply threatened the public order. The high cost of living was a source of widespread discontent and was often a central theme of strikes and worker protests. Moreover, the growth of armies, civilian employees, and national and provincial capitals fueled a demand for food services and supplies.[26] Each European nation therefore developed its own strategy for maintaining physical and financial control of the food supply—an important element in the state-making process. In England, construction of public markets reached a peak in the 1870s, when sixty-six new market halls were constructed—11 percent of all new markets built during the century. This building boom has been attributed to a combination of factors, including cheap and plentiful food, railway expansion, rising real wages, continued urban growth, and improved methods of public funding. England also favored a more decentralized market system than other countries when it passed the Local Government Act of

1858. This legislation let many towns purchase markets from their manorial owners.[27]

France preferred a highly centralized public market system, with Les Halles at its core. By 1870 the Paris central markets comprised twenty acres, with nearly half covered by ten iron and glass pavilions. Each pavilion accommodated the special needs of the wholesale trade; some were equipped with movable benches and tables to handle large auctions of fruit, butter, or vegetables. Although the city permitted retailing in designated areas at Les Halles, the market's principal function was to supply the neighborhood public markets and stores.[28] By the late 1880s over sixty retail markets were scattered around Paris—and many copied or improved on Les Halles. Architects repeated the iron and glass construction for markets throughout France as well as in Brussels, Florence, Milan, Madrid, Vienna, Berlin, Frankfurt, and Leipzig. A variety of English, French, and German architectural journals contributed much to the dissemination of construction techniques, plans, and elevations for market projects.[29]

The iron industry also contributed to the proliferation of covered markets throughout Europe and in the French and British colonies. Schneider et Cie, the great iron foundry at Le Creusot, France, exported prefabricated cast-iron markets to cities throughout the world, including Madrid, where two markets patterned after Les Halles were constructed in 1872. Andrew Handyside and Company of Derby, England, exported similar prefabricated cast-iron markets to the English colonies, advertising them in its trade catalog along with other prefabricated iron structures.[30] By the end of the century the young nations of Latin America, including Mexico, Brazil, and Argentina, also embraced the prefabricated iron market house as a means of imposing order to the streets and as a statement of modernity.[31]

While European architects promoted market house designs in a variety of journals and handbooks, it was the civil engineers and municipal authorities who tried to grasp the public market's administrative demands, complex social and economic networks, and reciprocal relationship with the urban infrastructure. These amateur economic geographers believed in a system of government-controlled retail markets supplied by a central wholesale market. The union of wholesalers under careful municipal administration and regulation, they argued, would stabilize food prices and supply throughout the city. According to the advice literature, cities needed to understand the economics of the public market—both retail and wholesale.

Otherwise their costly mistakes would bring abandoned market houses and high food prices.[32]

Promoting a market typology were bureaucrats like Theodor Risch, a member of the Berlin city council, whose extensive 1867 handbook (more than five hundred pages long) provided architects, civil engineers, and municipal authorities with descriptions of the present market systems in twenty-five European cities. Lengthy charts listed each city and its population with the number, location (in the center of the city, along a river, or by a railroad), type of ownership (public or private), stall dimensions, and type of trade (wholesale or retail) of the market houses. Additional charts compared food prices among cities.[33] The choice of style was also a matter of interest; the chapter titled "In What Style Should Markets Be Built?" was Risch's effort to bring public markets into the decades-old architecture debate in Germany.[34]

Risch's attempt to create a classification system for public markets was a logical response to the demand for market reform in the major European cities, where inadequate markets and distribution systems inherited from their ancient past strained efforts to modernize. Risch's handbook and others like it offered planners a comparative guide and encouraged them to consider ways of integrating the market house into the new urban infrastructure.

The greatest challenge was integrating railroads into the market system. Vienna, for example, built a central wholesale market in 1865 to create a hub for the city's food distribution network, but it failed to coordinate the new market with rail service, so the city lost out on its share of the food commerce.[35] Likewise in Paris, Les Halles was equipped with two underground levels—one for cellars and cold storage, and below that, another level for direct connection to the principal railway stations, but the latter feature was never used.[36]

Berlin, shortly after becoming the capital of the German empire in 1871, rationalized the distribution of food by taking railroad technology into account. Between 1886 and 1891 it closed seventeen open square markets and replaced them with thirteen retail market houses. All wholesaling, formerly conducted in the open squares, was subsequently removed to a new central market house that, unlike the one in Vienna, was equipped with its own railroad depot.[37]

England was exemplary in its integration of rail service with wholesale market halls. Smithfield Market, London's principal market for meat, had an underground freight terminal with loading docks from which meat was hoisted to the shops above. City architect Horace Jones reported that the hoisting mechanisms were hidden in the corner towers, which were ventilated to prevent railroad fumes from contaminating the market. According to the plan, Smithfield Market was serviced by the London, Chatham and Dover, Great Northern, and Metropolitan railways.[38] The British rail system also promoted the regional supply and distribution of food. If there was a food shortage in a London market, the London Committee on Markets and Tolls would telegraph its counterparts in other cities to ascertain their supplies. If the market in Penzance had a glut of fruit, for example, the Great Western Railway would send freight cars of fruit directly from the market house to a needy London market.[39]

American efforts to coordinate a public system of food marketing and distribution with rail service were lame by European standards. In 1892, when the Philadelphia and Reading Railroad built a market under the sheds of its new terminal in downtown Philadelphia, the unlikely combination of railroad and market prompted ridicule from investors and shareholders, who saw a future in railroads moving people, not food.[40] In reality, however, railroads moved food all across the country—which still alarmed public officials, who had been complaining for decades that uncontrolled freight rates were passed on to the consumer as high food prices. The Pennsylvania Railroad's produce terminal in New York, for example, handled an average of 35,000 tons of fruit and vegetables a month, not to mention tons of butter, poultry, and dry goods.[41]

Municipal Market Reform in the Progressive Era

Market reform finally reached national proportions in the United States as part of the larger municipal reform movement, generally dating from the 1890s to the First World War. Municipal reformers aimed to improve not only city government but also the quality of city life by eliminating the urban "evils" of rising food costs, lack of fresh food, traffic congestion, and poor public hygiene. These problems were paramount in and around the public markets, compelling various groups and individuals to put markets on their agendas. Advocates for public markets included members of the National Municipal League, leaders of the City Beautiful movement, consumer protection groups, chambers of commerce, sanitary engineers, and civil servants. They valued the public market system for its efficiency, economy, and equity, and rather than abandoning it, they looked for ways to improve it.[42]

FIGURE 8.10 George Waring's proposal for a combined market and playground. Drawn by W. A. Rogers. From *Harper's Weekly* 39
(December 28, 1895): 1237.

Local initiatives varied in scope and effectiveness. In 1895 George E. Waring Jr., the great sanitary engineer, proposed to the mayor of New York a combination of market and playground (fig. 8.10). To address several municipal problems at once, Waring proposed market stalls that were suspended by chains from the ceiling of the sheds. At the beginning of the day business would open for marketing. At noon, city street sweepers would raise the stalls to the ceiling and sweep the floor clear of debris. Then children could use the cleared floor as a playground.[43]

Local government also considered reform for aesthetic reasons, believing that modern, attractive markets would enhance a city's national and international image. It was commonly believed that the deplorable condition of city markets was an *American* problem, and that no market in the nation matched the magnificent ones such as London's Smithfield Market or Les Halles in Paris. In 1909 a writer for the *Atlantic Monthly* declared that "the Fulton or Washington [markets] in New York, or the Faneuil Hall Market in Boston, are not in the same class with the great modern markets of the European capitals." This belief was a product of the City Beautiful movement, whose promoters hoped that physical improvements would enhance the country's image abroad and inculcate moral values and civic pride in its citizens.[44]

The City Beautiful movement gave impetus to new municipal market construction across the country.[45] In 1909, for example, the city of Madison, Wisconsin, built a new market to remove a disruptive and unaesthetic open-air farmers' market from the downtown streets. A contemporary newspaper praised the "catchy" color scheme of the new market, designed by local architect Robert L. Wright, and considered it "the most artistic piece of property owned by the city" (fig. 8.11).[46] In Cleveland, Ohio, the architectural firm of Hubbell and Benes designed one of the finest municipal retail markets produced by the City Beautiful movement. Completed in 1912, the city-owned West Side Market was 123 feet wide by 245 feet long and boasted an impressive vaulted ceiling 44 feet high and decorated with Guastavino tile. The market was equipped with 110 stalls and was graced by a monumental 137-foot water tower and a matching market shed for farmers (fig. 8.12). Having completed his survey of hundreds of municipal markets in 1918, Samuel L. Rogers, director of the Bureau of the Census, remarked that the West Side Market was "one of the most pretentious market buildings in the United States."[47]

Besides a desire to improve the physical appearance of market houses, the driving force behind market reform during the Progressive Era was the high

FIGURE 8.11 City Market, Madison, Wisconsin, 1909. State Historical Society of Wisconsin, neg. (X3)36270.

FIGURE 8.12 West Side Market, Cleveland, 1915. National Archives, RG 83-G, neg. 3770.

cost of living. Don E. Mowry, a contributor to the *Municipal Journal and Engineer*, explained that "the market is, from the standpoint of economics and society, a necessity," because by bringing together producer and consumer it keeps down the cost of food. J. F. Carter, secretary of the chamber of commerce of San Antonio, also argued that markets owned and regulated by the municipality lowered the cost of living. Carter prayed that a "genius who will weld the producers of food into one great association, and who will then operate public markets in every city, will come some of these days; and with his coming will come the swan-song of the non-producing profit-taker, who will fall back where he ought to be—the great, God-blessed class of producers from the soil."[48]

Carter's radical proposal for total elimination of the intermediaries between producer and consumer was impractical, but some cities successfully implemented modest proposals. A quick and economical means of luring farmers into the city was the curb market, an informal market type that accommodated farmers and hucksters along a designated street or lot. The curb market was suitable for cities like Dubuque, Iowa, that did not need to finance or support an enclosed market building (fig. 8.13). Advocates of curb markets argued that farmers could charge reasonable prices if they did not have to pay for renting a fixed stall. Likewise, consumers would not have to pay the added costs for middlemen's services.

A New Market Type Is Born

The opposite of the curb market in terms of scale was the wholesale terminal market, a series of buildings designed for the large-scale storage and regional distribution of food. Linked to major transportation routes by rail, road, and waterways, the wholesale terminal market was a major step in the development of a comprehensive public system for food marketing and distribution. Advocates argued that such facilities, if properly organized, could move food in and out of cities quickly, protect goods against injury in transit, and lessen the chances of spoilage—factors that saved money in the long run. They also believed that wholesale terminal markets, by improving the storage and worldwide distribution of goods, could make the United States a world leader in food provisioning.

Raising awareness of the potential of wholesale terminal markets was a symposium sponsored by the American Academy of Political and Social Sci-

FIGURE 8.13 Curb Market, Dubuque, Iowa, 1916. National Archives,
RG 83-G, neg. 3228.

ences. Held in Philadelphia in 1913, the program gathered municipal leaders, academics, landscape architects, transportation officials, city planners, and consumer advocacy groups to discuss various ways to reduce the cost of food distribution. Also participating were national officials, including Charles J. Brand, chief of the newly established Office of Markets in the Department of Agriculture, and Stadtrat (Coucilman) D. Levin, Member of the Magistrate from Frankfurt, representing Germany.[49]

Two cities—Philadelphia and New York—again emerged as major players in public market reform, this time through improved wholesale facilities. Achsah Lippincott, clerk of the markets for the city of Philadelphia, presented her paper on the current state of the city's municipal markets, reporting that the North and South Second Street Markets were all that remained of "Philadelphia's once well-developed market system" (fig. 8.14). Philadelphia, she lamented, had not kept pace with the development of "modern industries," failing to build a waterfront terminal market and trolley freight depots at the municipal markets.[50] Wary of investing city expenditures in new retail markets in various sections of the city, Lippincott asked, "Can we, in this day of the telephone and the corner grocery store, bring back the old custom of marketing?" Her answer was no. "Since the corner grocer has come to stay, as he undoubtedly has in some sections of the city, it would seem that the city's next step should be to facilitate wholesale buying and distribution. Foreign cities have proved the advisability of such a system. Let Philadelphia be the first American city to adopt the improved market system, and to develop to the fullest extent the powerful agencies of local distribution at its immediate disposal."[51] Lippincott hoped that a well-organized wholesale municipal market would attract more farmers into the city. Existing wholesale facilities at the Dock Street Market, on the Delaware River waterfront, were outdated and caused frequent traffic jams. Her proposal called for a new wholesale municipal market away from the downtown.

Thomas J. Libbin, representing New York City at the symposium, reported the results of his extensive investigations of the city's food distribution. He claimed to have completed the "first statistical study ever made" of the profits and costs of handling grocery staples, from the time of receipt at city terminals through successive stages until final delivery to the consumer. Libbin reported that food was expensive because inadequate and outgrown terminals caused waste and excessive rehandling. Food was again mishandled in the stores by retailers, who suffered from "unplumbed depths of ignorance" re-

FIGURE 8.14 South Second Street Market, Philadelphia, 1913. An investigator for the USDA noted on the back of this photograph that the market was "extremely unsanitary, but serves a large number of poor people." National Archives, RG 83-G, neg. 4042.

garding the sanitary and economic aspects of food handling. Libbin proposed creating a municipal department of food supply that would run several types of experimental stores, much the same way as the agricultural colleges conducted experimental farms.[52]

Libbin's proposal did not stand up to New York's greater vision for market reform. Although other large cities faced similar difficulties with food distribution, New York presented a particular challenge. As the nation's largest metropolis and market for fresh food, the city fed a resident population of five million as well as thousands of daily commuters, it provisioned outgoing trains and transatlantic steamships, and it exported food to other cities and towns.[53] Aside from mere scale, New York's "food problem" was exacerbated by other factors, including nativism and fear of the foreign-born masses, as well as the recent advent of consumer protection. These factors generated popular support for municipal control over the food supply on a grand scale, beginning with the establishment of a wholesale terminal market in the Bronx.

Through the combined efforts of the boroughs of Manhattan and the Bronx, New York mayor William Gaynor appointed Cyrus C. Miller, president of the Bronx, as chairman of the mayor's market commission in 1912. The commission's task was to understand the present market system and to recommend improvements that would reduce the cost of food to consumers. Miller believed that marketing should be a government function, as it was in Europe, in order to keep people contented and prevent popular uprisings; to make people industrially efficient; and to prevent foreign aggression.[54] Using the popular principles of scientific management, the commission broke down New York's market system into its component parts to identify the exact causes of waste and inefficiency. Recognizing that some problems were out of the city's control, such as the rising cost of fertilizer, farm labor, and railroad rates, the commission began its study at the points where food arrived on the island. Most of the city's food supply arrived in lower Manhattan, where railroad and steamship terminals, warehouses, and icehouses lined the banks of the Hudson and East Rivers. Food sales and auctions were conducted directly at the piers and terminals of the nine railroad companies and twenty-three steamship lines that serviced the city. From there, food went by truck to major retail markets such as Washington Market on the West Side and Fulton Market on the East Side.[55]

New York retail markets were in a decrepit state at the time of the commission's study. Knowing that a new wholesale terminal market would be futile if food was contaminated or mishandled at the retail markets, the com-

FIGURE 8.15 Washington Market, New York City, under renovation, 1914. National Archives, RG 83-G, neg. 4275.

mission recommended a complete renovation of Washington Market. In 1913 the market received its first coat of paint since its construction in 1882, as well as a major interior overhaul that included a new concrete floor, terrazzo aisles, and white-tiled counter fronts. The white interior color scheme conformed to the contemporary notions of cleanliness and hygiene promoted by the City Beautiful movement. A sign over the entrance boasted that "when completed this market will be the best equipped model sanitary market in the world" (fig. 8.15).[56]

The commission also determined that most of the city's local food supply arrived by wagon from farms within forty miles of the city. Farmers preferred to unload at Gansevoort Market, on the West side at Little Twelfth Street, or the Wallabout Market in Brooklyn. According to the commission, the Wallabout was convenient to dealers and well situated along the Brooklyn waterfront, so it recommended improvements, such as adding railroad tracks and a refrigeration plant.[57]

The commission's most ambitious—not to mention controversial—recommendation was a wholesale terminal market in the Bronx. Chairman Miller believed that distributing food differed little from handling railroad passengers.

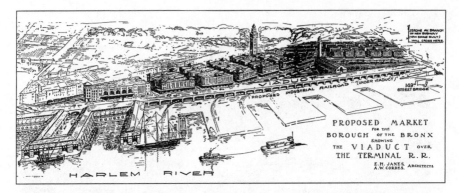

FIGURE 8.16 Proposed Bronx Terminal Market, 1912. From New York (City), Mayor's Market Commission, *Report of the Mayor's Market Commission of New York City* (New York: Little and Ives, 1913).

Just as New Yorkers would be better served if Pennsylvania Station and the Grand Central Station were united into one, he argued, a wholesale terminal market would more efficiently bring food to one place and then distribute it to various destinations. The commission's 1913 report unveiled a proposal for a comprehensively planned industrial complex on a twenty-eight-acre tract along the Harlem River between 149th Street and 152d Street (fig. 8.16).[58]

Accessibility to transportation was critical, and the proposal's highlight was the "industrial railroad" along the Harlem waterfront. This railroad would connect to the private lines that currently provisioned the city and would bring goods directly into the market buildings. Although New York City would own and manage the market, its function as a regional food distribution center would extend beyond the boroughs, to Mount Vernon, New Rochelle, and Yonkers. The design represented the shared interests of the commission's twenty-one-member advisory committee, which included municipal administrators, consumer groups, commission merchants, retailer associations, and boards of trade.[59]

Reformers considered the proposed Bronx Terminal Market the most progressive step the city of New York had ever taken toward a complete solution to the food problem. The market commission argued that municipally owned food depots near major rail and water routes were the way of the future. Furthermore, by investing in wholesale rather than retail markets, the city would gain control over the more lucrative aspect of food marketing and distribution, which was currently in the hands of steamship and railroad companies.[60]

Critics, however, saw the project as a boondoggle that would benefit only municipal officeholders and transportation officials. Speaking out against the work of the commission was J. W. Sullivan, assistant editor for Samuel Gompers, president of the American Federation of Labor (AFL). According to Sullivan, the enthusiasm for a municipal wholesale terminal market in the Bronx was based on the false assumption that it would produce substantial profits for the city. But Sullivan had collected his own data on the public markets of Boston, Baltimore, New Orleans, Buffalo, Cleveland, Washington, Nashville, Indianapolis, Rochester, and St. Paul and found that Miller's reports had exaggerated their profits. Besides, any market proposal claiming to produce profits was ludicrous, Sullivan argued, because "a public market has a two-fold character. First, it is a social institution; secondly, it is a financial undertaking." The promise of profits to the municipal treasury therefore should be "a minor consideration."[61]

Sullivan's opinions were informed by his tours of public markets in Europe, first with Gompers in 1909 and again, on his own, in 1912. As part of his work for the AFL, he was charged with identifying ways to reduce the cost of living for workers, particularly through lower food costs. During his visits, he collected official reports of market operations and ascertained popular views regarding them from representatives of the organized wage earners, centering his inquiries on the market systems of Paris, London, and Berlin. Over the years, Sullivan and Gompers also asked certain city officials in the United States questions about their market systems.[62]

After evaluating various domestic and European market systems, Sullivan concluded that a municipally owned wholesale terminal market, certainly on the scale proposed for the Bronx, was ridiculous, since pushcarts and open-air markets could just as easily provide fresh, affordable food for the masses at much less cost to the city. Influenced by the vibrant open-air markets of Europe, he demanded "streets for the people," by which he meant street selling free of excessive regulation.[63]

Several other factors formed Sullivan's negative opinion of large-scale municipal wholesale markets. First was the city's poor record at running a reasonably efficient public market system, which New York officials had allowed "to die" over the past fifty years. New York's reputation made him leery of any proposal that would increase government involvement in food distribution. Second, Sullivan had studied the universal "civic problem" of bringing together producer and consumer as it related specifically to New York, and he believed that different solutions should be designed around different foods. The distribution of meat, for example, was too embedded in the hands of large companies, such as Swift, that controlled private storage houses throughout the five boroughs. As Sullivan explained, "None but a dreamer could today propose confining wholesale meat selling to public markets in New York." But there was potential for improving the distribution of country produce. Highly perishable country produce would be better distributed by improved retail public markets, pushcarts, and open-air markets. He insisted that consumers had "a social and legal right to the uses, individually or through his purveyors, of public space for wholesale marketing purposes."[64]

Sullivan favored a conservative, low-cost proposal for market reform pending the immediate general transformation of the metropolis, by which he meant the changes expected to follow the new system of subways and tunnels. Accompanying these revolutionary systems in passenger transit, there could be "an epochal change in distribution of produce by freight; commercial transformation may follow in many districts, especially along the rivers and in the suburbs; wholesale markets advantageous at present to retailers might prove inconvenient to open-air marketmen; the transportation companies, with improved market yards and piers, might take away from public wholesale markets."[65] All these possible changes made Sullivan sure that "great public market ventures today would be uncertain city investments."

Ultimately, New York did not adopt Sullivan's "wait and see" attitude. Local officials wanted to do something grand, and they wanted to do it now. World War I only delayed the realization of the Bronx Terminal Market, and the market was begun in 1918 under the administration of Mayor John F. Hylan. It was completed in 1925 for a total cost of $22.5 million (fig. 8.17). The wholesale terminal market was conceived as a model public market for the twentieth century, and it remains the principal building type dedicated to wholesale food marketing and distribution in the United States.[66]

Municipal reformers pushed for wholesale terminal markets, curb markets, and modern retail market houses because they realized that not everyone would or could move to the suburbs. Unable to alter the shape of older neighborhoods and commercial centers, they promoted new market types or the modernization of existing markets, all with the aim of making urban markets work better for urban dwellers.[67]

FIGURE 8.17 Bronx Terminal Market, 1925. National Archives, RG 83-G, neg. 11903.

While resources, energy, and public investment went into the design and construction of new market facilities, many nineteenth-century public markets endured and remained vibrant places despite their poor physical condition. In 1918 the Bureau of the Census conducted a comprehensive survey of municipal markets in cities with populations over 30,000 and identified 237 markets reported by 128 of the 227 cities surveyed. Cities with multiple markets were not uncommon. New Orleans, for example, had 19, the largest number reported by one city, and Baltimore ranked second with 11, including the very successful and still extant Lexington Market. Longevity and continuity in physical form describe most of the markets at the turn of the century. Of the 96 enclosed market houses identified in the survey, 60 were established before 1900, as were most of the 180 open markets, whose dates of establishment ranged from 1785 to 1900. In Pittsburgh, for example, a small neighborhood market similar to one built in 1802 (see fig. 2.13) still stood in the middle of the street in its original location as late as 1914 (fig. 8.18).[68]

What impact, if any, did grocery stores have on the survival of public markets? In March 1917 a National Municipal League survey listed dozens of cities with several hundred grocery stores and at least seven cities with over a thousand: New York (25,000), Baltimore (3,197), Cleveland (2,575), Wash-

FIGURE 8.18 Market shed, Pittsburgh, 1914. National Archives,
RG 83-G, neg. 4150.

ington (2,557), Rochester (2,400), Denver (1,250), and Portland (1,100).[69] Additional results from the League's survey, however, showed that the two forms of urban food retailing—public markets and grocery stores—were not mutually exclusive. Despite the large number of grocery stores, thirty-five out of fifty cities reported at least an 80 percent occupancy rate in their public markets. Just nine cities out of forty-one declared that market expenses exceeded revenues, and then only by small amounts. In Duluth, Minnesota, for example, expenses exceeded revenues by only $200, and New York reported a net loss of $175,658—minor sums for a public service.[70]

Despite the hyperbole over railroads and their promise to transform urban food distribution, road improvements (and later motor trucks) did more than rails to encourage farmers to come into the cities. As a result, central markets were more crowded than ever before with farmers, many of whom had traveled great distances to sell their goods (fig. 8.19). Market gardeners on the western end of Long Island, for example, still hauled their produce twenty or thirty miles into New York City in 1,800-pound horse-drawn wagons. As late as 1917, the National Municipal League Survey discovered as "one of the striking facts" that sixteen cities reported farmers traveling over thirty miles by wagon or truck to their public markets.[71]

The League's 1917 survey also discovered, to the surprise of its analysts, that "if any evidence were needed to establish the large place that public markets are taking in the victualing of our urban places, that evidence will be found in the number of people that visit the markets during market days." Attendance ranged from 60 per day to 100,000 per week, depending on the city, and daily attendance of 10,000 was reported by Baltimore, Buffalo, Philadelphia, Rochester, Salem, Seattle, and St. Louis. Most cities also reported that attendance had increased over the past twenty-five to fifty years, for a number of reasons. Informants attributed it to the markets' variety, quality, low prices, direct buying, cleanliness, and cold storage. The invention of the telephone was another factor, since customers could place orders ahead of time.[72]

Market laws, too, remained an important component of the public market system and in some cases were strengthened at the state level. The public market law of Massachusetts, adopted in 1915, authorized cities with more than 10,000 inhabitants to maintain market buildings or to designate certain squares or streets for public markets. Likewise, under a law passed in New

FIGURE 8.19 City Market, Indianapolis, 1890s. Indiana State Library.

York in 1917, state aid was available to cities that wanted to establish new markets or repair and improve existing ones.[73]

So how *did* the public market system change over the course of a century? Engrossing and forestalling, which had once been illegal or severely restricted, were now routine practices in the food trade. At New York's Fly Market in 1797, a group of female hucksters had their licenses revoked when local officials caught them hoarding fruit—a violation of the city's engrossing laws. By the end of the nineteenth century, large-scale food storage was commonplace, particularly in cities with cold storage and wholesale markets. Entire wholesale districts, with seemingly endless rows of cast-iron-front warehouses, lined the waterfronts and railroad yards of cities coast to coast. Formerly feared and despised as middlemen, jobbers (who bought outright from shippers and then sold to retailers) and commission merchants (who received goods on consignment from shippers and disposed of them at a stipulated rate) had become legitimate and significant players in urban food marketing and distribution.

This revolution in the food trade affected the type of products sold in the public markets and, in turn, the type of food that reached the dinner table. Aided by rail and refrigeration technology, jobbers and commission mer-

FIGURE 8.20 Lexington Market, Baltimore. Postcard. Collection of David K. O'Neil.

chants found new markets for dressed beef, tropical fruit, and citrus fruit from California and Florida.[74] Low-cost truck farming in the post-Reconstruction South, where land and labor were cheap, extended the market in the North for beets, peas, onions, tomatoes, and strawberries.[75] The popularity of truck farming also persisted around Los Angeles, where Chinese Americans operated family farms growing a variety of fruits and vegetables for urban markets. These farmers either sold their produce directly at the city market or used brokers to sell for them.[76]

That grocery stores, and later supermarkets, replaced the public market obscures a larger, more complex history. Despite the mid-nineteenth-century collision between the ethos of the moral economy and the manifestations of a capitalist market economy (the legalization of meat shops, deregulation, the incorporation of market house companies, and the construction of grandiose market houses), ultimately public markets revealed both their resilience and their adaptability. As places of civic pride, they remained the focal point of neighborhoods and communities; they continued to foster direct contact between producer and consumer; and with the aid of the streetcar, they discovered ways to attract suburban and middle-class consumers (fig. 8.20). Cities and federal agencies fought hard to reclaim this urban civic space in the name of the common good. The public market, in short, was as much an idea (or ideal) as an architectural form. It remained the principal place where society could evaluate its success or failure at organizing urban life. The dynamic process by which markets were demolished, rebuilt, adapted, and reused reflected the active presence of the moral economy in nineteenth-century America. Government responsibility for guaranteeing an abundant supply of wholesome and affordable food could be met only by regulating the ethics of trade and by providing a common ground for producer and consumer. Thus these buildings and spaces continued, and will continue, to meet the needs of a civil society, despite the odds.

NOTES

Introduction

1. For distinctions between public and civic space, see Lynn Hollen Lees, "Urban Public Space and Imagined Communities in the 1980s and 1990s," *Journal of Urban History* 20 (August 1994): 443–465.

2. E. P. Thompson, "The Moral Economy of the English Crowd in the Eighteenth Century," *Past and Present,* no. 50 (February 1971): 76–136; E. P. Thompson, *Customs in Common* (New York: New Press, 1991), 336–351.

3. William J. Novak, *The People's Welfare: Law and Regulation in Nineteenth-Century America* (Chapel Hill: University of North Carolina Press, 1996), and William J. Novak, "Public Economy and the Well-Ordered Market: Law and Economic Regulation in Nineteenth-Century America," *Law and Social Inquiry* 18 (winter 1993): 1–32.

4. For the persistence of the moral economy in the countryside see Christopher Clark, *The Roots of Rural Capitalism: Western Massachusetts, 1780–1860* (Ithaca: Cornell University Press, 1991); James A. Henretta, *The Origins of American Capitalism: Collected Essays* (Boston: Northeastern University Press, 1991); Allan Kulikoff, *The Agrarian Origins of American Capitalism* (Charlottesville: University Press of Virginia, 1992); and Winifred Barr Rothenberg, *From Market-Places to a Market Economy: The Transformation of Rural Massachusetts, 1750–1850* (Chicago: University of Chicago Press, 1992).

5. Mary P. Ryan, *Civic Wars: Democracy and Public Life in the American City during the Nineteenth Century* (Berkeley: University of California Press, 1997).

6. For example, see Carole L. Crumley, "Periodic Markets in Contemporary Southern Burgundy," in *Regional Dynamics: Burgundian Landscapes in Historical Perspective,* ed. Carole L. Crumley and William H. Marquardt (San Diego: Academic Press, 1987), 335–359.

7. Jonathan Brown, *The English Market Town: A Social and Economic History, 1750–1914* (Ramsbury, Marlborough, Wiltshire: Crowood Press, 1986), and James Schmiechen and Kenneth Carls, *The British Market Hall: A Social and Architectural History* (New Haven: Yale University Press, 1999).

8. Donatella Calabi, ed., *Fabbriche, piazze, mercati: La città italiana nel Rinascimento* (Buildings, squares, markets: The Italian city in the Renaissance) (Rome: Officina Edizioni, 1997); Donatella Calabi, *Il mercato e la città: Piazze, strade, architet-*

tura d'Europea in età moderna (The market and the city: Squares, streets, and architecture in early modern Europe) (Venice: Marsilio Editori, 1993).

9. Città di Bra, *Le "agli" del mercato in provincia di Cuneo* (Market halls in the province of Cuneo) (Bra: Ministero Beni Culturali e Ambientali, Soprintendenza per i Beni Ambientali e Architettonici del Piemonte, Politecnico di Torino, 1992); Sergio Di Macco, *L'architettura dei mercati: Tecniche dell'edilizia annonaria* (The architecture of markets: Techniques for the buildings of provisions) (Rome: Edizioni Kappa, 1993); Anna Modigliani, *Mercati, botteghe e spazi di commercio a Roma tra medioevo ed età moderna* (Markets, shops and commercial spaces in Rome from the medieval to the modern age) (Rome: Roma nel Rinascimento, 1997); and Richard Vincent Moore, *L'architettura del mercato coperto: Dal mercato all'ipermercato* (The architecture of the covered market: From the market to the supermarket) (Rome: Officina Edizioni, 1997).

10. For a bibliography on Les Halles, see Bertrand Lemoine, *Les Halles de Paris* (Paris: Équerre, 1980). Studies of the social history of Les Halles include Steven Laurence Kaplan, *Provisioning Paris: Merchants and Millers in the Grain and Flour Trade during the Eighteenth Century* (Ithaca: Cornell University Press, 1984); Rene S. Marion, "The 'Dames de la Halle': Community and Authority in Early Modern Paris" (Ph.D. diss., Johns Hopkins University, 1994); and Victoria E. Thompson, "Urban Renovation, Moral Regeneration: Domesticating the *Halles* in Second-Empire Paris," *French Historical Studies* 20 (winter 1997): 87–109.

11. Jay R. Barshinger, "The Early Market Houses of Southeastern Pennsylvania: Forms and Precedents" (M.A. thesis, Pennsylvania State University, 1989); Jay R. Barshinger, "Provisions for Trade: The Market House in Southeastern Pennsylvania" (Ph.D. diss., Pennsylvania State University, 1995); James M. Mayo, *The American Grocery Store: The Business Evolution of an Architectural Space* (Westport, Conn.: Greenwood Press, 1993); and James M. Mayo, "The American Public Market," *Journal of Architectural Education* 45 (November 1991): 41–57.

12. Richard Longstreth, *City Center to Regional Mall: Architecture, the Automobile, and Retailing in Los Angeles, 1920–1950* (Cambridge: MIT Press, 1997), and Richard Longstreth, *The Drive-in, the Supermarket, and the Transformation of Commercial Space in Los Angeles, 1914–1941* (Cambridge: MIT Press, 1999).

13. For example, see Jon C. Teaford, *The Municipal Revolution in America: Origins of Modern Urban Government 1650–1825* (Chicago: University of Chicago Press, 1975), 98–100; and Jon C. Teaford, *The Unheralded Triumph: City Government in America, 1870–1900* (Baltimore: Johns Hopkins University Press, 1984), 217–250. Teaford was premature in claiming the victory of free trade in New York, Boston, and Philadelphia in the 1820s, when butchers protested the municipal monopoly by selling in their own shops. He was also premature in claiming that markets, docks, and livestock markets took second place to hospitals, reservoirs, and other public amenities in the late nineteenth-century city.

14. Sam Bass Warner Jr., *The Private City: Philadelphia in Three Periods of Its Growth* (1968; 2d ed., Philadelphia: University of Pennsylvania Press, 1987).

15. Mayo, "American Public Market," 56.

ONE Market Laws in the Early Republic

Epigraph: Thomas F. De Voe, *The Market Book: A History of the Public Markets of the City of New York* (1862; reprint, New York: Augustus M. Kelley, 1970), 390.

1. Unless otherwise stated, sources for this chapter can be found in the bibliography under "Government Documents."

2. Novak, *People's Welfare,* 94–95.

3. Ruth Bogin, "Petitioning and the New Moral Economy of Post-Revolutionary America," *William and Mary Quarterly* 45 (July 1988): 399–403.

4. Leonard P. Curry, *The Corporate City: The American City as a Political Entity, 1800–1850* (Westport, Conn.: Greenwood Press, 1997), 208–210.

5. Samuel Wilson Jr., *The Vieux Carré, New Orleans: Its Plan, Its Growth, Its Architecture* (New Orleans: Bureau of Governmental Research, 1968), 50.

6. Anne Newport Royall, *Sketches of History, Life, and Manners, in the United States* (New Haven, Conn., 1826), 88. On the close connection between municipal incorporation and the establishment of public markets in Virginia, see Bryan Clark Green, "The Structure of Civic Exchange: Market Houses in Early Virginia," in *Shaping Communities: Perspectives in Vernacular Architecture VI,* ed. Carter L. Hudgins and Elizabeth Collins Cromley (Knoxville: University of Tennessee Press, 1997), 190.

7. John Melish, *Travels in the United States of America, in the Years 1806 and 1807, and 1809, 1810, and 1811* (Philadelphia: Thomas and George Palmer, 1812), 1:57–59, and John Adams Paxton, *The Stranger's Guide: An Alphabetical List of All the Wards, Streets, Roads, Lanes, Alleys, Avenues, Courts, Wharves, Ship Yards, Public Buildings, etc. in the City and Suburbs of Philadelphia* (Philadelphia: Edward Parker, 1811), 15.

8. Louise E. Atherton, *The Southern Country Store, 1800–1860* (Baton Rouge: Louisiana State University Press, 1949); Gregory J. Brown, "Distributing Meat and Fish in Eighteenth-Century Virginia: The Documentary Evidence for the Existence of Markets in Early Tidewater Towns," typescript, Colonial Williamsburg Foundation, Department of Archaeological Research, July 1988, 5–6; J. R. Dolan, *The Yankee Peddlers of Early America* (New York: Bramhall House, 1964); Charles J. Farmer, *In the Absence of Towns: Settlement and Country Trade in Southside Virginia, 1730–1800* (Lanham, Md.: Rowman and Littlefield, 1993); and Mayo, *American Grocery Store,* 43–76.

9. New York (City), *Minutes of the Common Council of the City of New York, 1784–1831* (New York: City of New York, 1917), vol. 1, July 10, 1786, 293; De Voe, *Market Book,* 210–211.

10. "Philadelphia Markets," De Voe Papers, New-York Historical Society.

11. Samuel Latham Mitchill, *The Picture of New-York, and Stranger's Guide through the Commercial Emporium of the United States* (New York: A. T. Goodrich, 1818), 40–41.

12. De Voe, *Market Book,* 222–223.

13. David J. Rothman, *The Discovery of the Asylum: Social Order and Disorder in the New Republic* (Boston: Little, Brown, 1971), 152–154; Dell Upton, "Another City:

The Urban Cultural Landscape in the Early Republic," in *Everyday Life in the Early Republic*, ed. Catherine E. Hutchins (Winterthur, Del.: Henry Francis du Pont Winterthur Museum, 1994), 79.

14. J. P. Brissot de Warville, *New Travels in the United States of America, 1788*, trans. Mara Soceanu Vamos and Durand Echeverria (Cambridge: Belknap Press of Harvard University Press, 1964), 199–200.

15. Francis Baily, *Journal of a Tour in Unsettled Parts of North America in 1796 and 1797*, ed. Jack D. L. Holmes (Carbondale: Southern Illinois University Press, 1969), 28; Parker Cutler and Julia Perkins Cutler, eds., *Life Journals and Correspondence of Rev. Manasseh Cutler* (Athens: Ohio University Press, 1987), 271–272; Josiah Quincy Jr., "Journal of Josiah Quincy, Jr. 1773," in *Massachusetts Historical Society Proceedings*, June 1916, 475–478; Brissot de Warville, *New Travels in the United States*, 199–200.

16. De Voe, *Market Book*, 183–84.

17. Brown, "Distributing Meat and Fish," 13.

18. De Voe, *Market Book*, 151–152. For an example of public complaints against the lack of food inspection laws in colonial Williamsburg, see Brown, "Distributing Meat and Fish," 15–16.

19. Baily, *Journal of a Tour*, 28; William Newnham Blane, *An Excursion through the United States and Canada during the Years 1822–23* (London: Baldwin, Cradock, and Joy, 1824), 21; Brissot de Warville, *Travels in the United States*, 199–200; Cutler and Cutler, *Life of Manasseh Cutler*, 271; and Francisco de Miranda, *The New Democracy in America: Travels of Francisco Miranda in the United States, 1783–84*, trans. Judson P. Wood, ed. John S. Ezell (Norman: University of Oklahoma Press, 1963), 42.

20. Jeanne Boydston, "The Woman Who Wasn't There: Women's Market Labor and the Transition to Capitalism in the United States," *Journal of the Early Republic* 16 (summer 1996): 193; Seth Rockman, "Women's Labor, Gender Ideology, and Working-Class Households in Early Republic Baltimore," *Explorations in Early American Culture*, supplement to *Pennsylvania History* 66 (1999): 187–188; and Christine Stansell, *City of Women: Sex and Class in New York, 1789–1860* (New York: Alfred A. Knopf, 1986), 13–14.

21. "Petition to the Select and Common Councils of the City of Philadelphia," December 20, 1805, in Petitions to the Councils of Philadelphia, 1783–1868, Historical Society of Pennsylvania, 31. In 1816, four female hucksters in Baltimore sent a similar petition to the city council after a recent ordinance banned unlicensed peddling. See Rockman, "Women's Labor," 174.

22. Pittsburgh, Pa., Borough and Council Papers, 1789–1817, September 8, 1805; February 26, 1806; and n.d., 1810, microfilm, Pennsylvania State Archives, Harrisburg.

23. Ibid., September 21, 1816; October 12, 1816; n.d., 1816.

24. Benjamin Davies, *Some Account of the City of Philadelphia, the Capital of Pennsylvania* (Philadelphia: Richard Fowell, 1794), 25–26.

25. De Voe, *Market Book*, 203–204.

26. Melish, *Travels in the United States,* 57–59, 151.

27. *The Cries of New-York* (New York: Samuel Wood, 1808; reprint, New York: Harbor Press, 1931), and *The Cries of Philadelphia: Ornamented with Elegant Wood Cuts* (Philadelphia, Johnson and Warner, 1810). For similar street cries in London see Sean Shesgreen, "The Cries of London in the Seventeenth Century," *Papers of the Bibliographical Society of America* 86 (1992): 269–294.

28. Gary B. Nash, *Forging Freedom: The Formation of Philadelphia's Black Community, 1720–1840* (Cambridge: Harvard University Press, 1988), 72–75, 215.

29. New York (City), *Minutes of the Common Council of the City of New York,* vol. 2, February 20, 1797; June 18, 1798; October 28, 1799, 324, 450, 579; vol. 6, March 12, 1810; July 14, 1810, 106–107; and De Voe, *Market Book,* 325–326.

30. De Voe, *Market Book,* 347.

31. Mary Beth Corrigan, "'It's a Family Affair': Buying Freedom in the District of Columbia, 1850–1860," in *Working toward Freedom: Slave Society and Domestic Economy in the American South,* ed. Larry E. Hudson Jr. (Rochester, N.Y.: University of Rochester Press, 1994): 177–178, and Mary Beth Corrigan, "The Ties That Bind: The Pursuit of Community and Freedom among Slaves and Free Blacks in the District of Columbia, 1800–1860," in *Southern City, National Ambition: The Growth of Early Washington, D.C., 1800–1860,* ed. Howard Gillette Jr. (Washington, D.C.: George Washington University, Center for Washington Area Studies, 1995), 75.

32. Anneliese Harding, *John Lewis Krimmel: Genre Artist of the Early Republic* (Winterthur, Del.: Henry Francis du Pont Winterthur Museum, 1994), 16–18, 77.

TWO The Market House

Epigraph: Royall, *Sketches,* 321–322.

1. A similar effect, defined as "civic materialism," can be found in the architectural history of city halls. See Mary P. Ryan, "'A Laudable Pride in the Whole of Us': City Halls and Civic Materialism," *American Historical Review* 105 (October 2000): 1131–1170.

2. For more on the urban geography of markets in history see Spiro Kostof, *The City Assembled: The Elements of Urban Form through History* (Boston: Little, Brown, 1992), esp. 92–99, and Harold Carter, *An Introduction to Urban Historical Geography* (London: Edward Arnold, 1983), esp. 150–170.

3. Charleston, S.C., *Ordinances of the City Council of Charleston* (Charleston: W. P. Young, 1802–1804), 36.

4. Saul K. Padover, ed., *Thomas Jefferson and the National Capital,* vol. 6 (Washington, D.C.: Government Printing Office, 1946), 205–206. Jefferson approved their request the next day, and Center Market opened on December 15, 1801.

5. De Voe, *Market Book,* 125–126, 137.

6. Dell Upton, "The Master Street of the World: The Levee," in *Streets: Critical Perspectives on Urban Space,* ed. Zeynep Celik, Diane Favro, and Richard Ingersoll (Berkeley: University of California Press, 1994), 277–280, and Wilson, *Vieux Carré,* 50–54, 65–66.

7. Frederick, Md., *The By Laws and Ordinances of the Corporation of Frederick* (Frederick-Town: Hughes and Levely, 1836), November session 1785, chap. 54, 4.

8. David Chilcoat Osborn, "A History of Lexington Market in Baltimore, Maryland" (M.A. thesis, Pennsylvania State College, 1952), 5–9.

9. Daniel Byrne and Stuart Plattner, "Ethnicity at Soulard Farmers Market since 1930," *Bulletin of the Missouri Historical Society* 36 (April 1980): 175, and Philip Taylor, comp., "A Brief History of the Public Markets and Private Markets Referred to as Public Markets in the City of St. Louis, Missouri," typescript, January 1961, Missouri Historical Society Library, 44–45.

10. On the ancient precedent for market streets, see Spiro Kostof, *The City Shaped: Urban Patterns and Meanings through History* (Boston: Little, Brown, 1991), 142.

11. Jacob Duché, *Caspipina's Letters: Containing Observations on a Variety of Subjects, Literary, Moral, and Religious* (London: R. Cruttwell, 1777), 1: 8–9.

12. "The Petition of Sundry Owners and Tenants of the Houses and Lots on Both Sides of High Street between Delaware Third and Fourth Streets in the City of Philadelphia," November 10, 1785, Nead Papers, Historical Society of Pennsylvania.

13. Agnes Addison Gilchrist, "Market Houses in High Street," *Transactions of the American Philosophical Society* 43 (1953): 310.

14. Elizabeth Barrett Gould, *From Fort to Port: An Architectural History of Mobile, Alabama, 1711–1918* (Tuscaloosa: University of Alabama Press, 1988), 43, and Edward C. Carter II, ed., *The Virginia Journals of Benjamin Henry Latrobe, 1795–1798* (New Haven: Yale University Press, 1977), vol. 1, March 23, 1796, 75.

15. Logansport, Ind., Deed to Original Town of Logansport, 19 September 1828, 1983 facsimile, Cass County Historical Society, Logansport, Ind.; John W. Reps, *The Making of Urban America* (Princeton: Princeton University Press, 1965), 215, 226, 269.

16. "Records of the Norwich and Callowhill Markets, 1784–1845," May 29, 1789, Historical Society of Pennsylvania; Gould, *From Fort to Port*, 43.

17. De Voe, *Market Book*, 326–327; Barshinger, "Provisions for Trade," 92; William C. Dawson, *Compilation of the Laws of the State of Georgia* (Milledgeville, Ga.: Grantland and Orme, 1831), no. 1325.

18. John Hutchins Cady, "The Providence Market House and Its Neighborhood," *Rhode Island History* 11 (October 1952): 105; Lancaster, Pa., Minutes of Meetings of Burgesses and Assistants of the Borough of Lancaster, March 2, 1798, microfilm, Pennsylvania State Archives, Harrisburg; and Mary Gregory Powell, *The History of Old Alexandria, Virginia, from July 13, 1749 to May 24, 1861* (Richmond: William Byrd Press, 1928), 234–236.

19. Portsmouth, Va., Records of the Town and City of Portsmouth, vol. 1, 1796–1821, microfilm, Library of Virginia, April 20, 1796; June 24, 1798.

20. Jefferson County, Va., Deed Book, 1807–1808, microfilm, Library of Virginia, 4:153, 164.

21. Carl Lounsbury, ed., *An Illustrated Glossary of Early Southern Architecture and Landscape* (New York: Oxford University Press, 1994), 225–226, and Barshinger, "Provisions for Trade," 10–18; 42–43. Barshinger noted that the freestanding market

shed was more common than the combined town hall and market in southeastern Pennsylvania in the eighteenth and nineteenth centuries.

22. Walter Horn, "On the Origins of the Medieval Bay System," *Journal of the Society of Architectural Historians* 17 (1958): 15–20.

23. Douglas G. Bucher and W. Richard Wheeler, *A Neat Plain Modern Stile: Philip Hooker and His Contemporaries, 1796–1836*, exhibition catalog, Emerson Gallery, Hamilton College (Amherst: University of Massachusetts Press, 1993), 27.

24. Charles William Janson, *The Stranger in America: Containing Observations Made during a Long Residence in That Country of the Genius, Manners and Customs of the People of the United States* (London: James Cundee, 1807), 179; Luigi Castiglioni, *Luigi Castiglioni's Viaggio-Travels in the United States of North America, 1785–1787*, trans. and ed. Antonio Pace (Syracuse, N.Y.: Syracuse University Press, 1983), 206; and De Voe, *Market Book*, 223.

25. "Some Account of the Markets of Philadelphia," *Portfolio* (December 1809): 508–511.

26. Frederick L. Billon, *Annals of St. Louis in Its Territorial Days, from 1804 to 1821* (St. Louis: Author, 1888), 25.

27. Jehu Z. Powell, ed., *History of Cass County Indiana*, vol. 1 (Chicago: Lewis, 1913), 339–340.

28. Helen Tangires, "Contested Space: The Life and Death of Center Market," *Washington History* 7 (spring–summer 1995): 50–52; Michael E. Wilson, "Thomas Flintoff Visits Houston," *Houston Review: History and Culture of the Gulf Coast* 8 (1986): 138–139.

29. Bryan Clark Green, "The Market House in Virginia, 1736–ca. 1860" (M.A. thesis, University of Virginia, 1991), appendix 1, 42–52; Green, "Structure of Civic Exchange," 189–203.

30. Bucher and Wheeler, *Neat Plain Modern Stile*, 243–57.

31. Lawrence W. Kennedy, *Planning the City upon a Hill: Boston since 1630* (Amherst: University of Massachusetts Press, 1992), 48–50.

32. C. D. Arfwedson, *The United States and Canada, in 1832, 1833, and 1834*, vol. 1 (London: Richard Bentley, 1834), 136–137; G. M. Davison, *The Traveller's Guide through the Middle and Northern States, and the Provinces of Canada*, 7th ed. (Saratoga Springs, N.Y.: G. M. Davison; New York: S. S. and W. Wood, 1837), 384; and C. A. Goodrich, *The Family Tourist: A Visit to the Principal Cities of the Western Continent; Embracing an Account of Their Situation, Origin, Plan, Extent, Their Inhabitants, Manners, Customs, and Amusements, . . .* (Philadelphia: J. W. Bradley, 1848), 54–57.

33. Royall, *Sketches*, 321–322.

34. St. Francisville, La., "An Ordinance Providing for the Erection of a Market House and Establishing a Regular Market in and for the Town of St. Francisville," *Louisianian*, October 9, 1819, 1.

35. Jefferson County, Va., *Deed Book*, 153.

36. Pittsburgh, Pa., Borough and Council Papers, August 31, 1801; June 30, 1802.

37. De Voe, *Market Book,* 328–329, 518, 559, and 587.

38. Ibid., 325.

39. Ibid., 183.

40. West Chester, Pa., Borough Council Minutes, 1802–1885, microfilm, Pennsylvania State Archives, Harrisburg June 6, 1831.

41. Washington, D.C., *Acts of the Corporation of the City of Washington,* 11 vols. (Washington, D.C., 1805–1816), May 23, 1809.

42. Harrisburg, Pa., Harrisburg Borough Council Minutes, microfilm, Pennsylvania State Archives, Harrisburg, July 9, 1814; July 21, 1815.

43. Green, "Structure of Civic Exchange," 197–199, and Rebecca Zurier, *The American Firehouse: An Architectural and Social History* (New York: Abbeville Press, 1982), 16–22.

44. Trenton, N.J., *Acts and Ordinances of the City of Trenton,* 1799, Early American Imprints, 1st ser., no. 35896, and De Voe, *Market Book,* 324–325.

45. Kostof, *City Shaped,* 48.

46. Frederick, Md., *By Laws and Ordinances,* 5.

THREE Marketplace Culture

Epigraph: Theophilus Eaton, *Review of New-York, or Rambles through the City: Original Poems* (New York: John Low, 1814), 29–30.

1. Roger D. Abrahams, "The Discovery of Marketplace Culture," *Intellectual History Newsletter* 10 (April 1988): 24; Jean-Christophe Agnew, *Worlds Apart: The Market and the Theater in Anglo-American Thought, 1550–1750* (New York: Cambridge University Press, 1986), 40; Jean-Christophe Agnew, "The Threshold of Exchange: Speculations on the Market," *Radical History Review* 21 (fall 1979): 99–118; and Mikhail Mikhailovich Bakhtin, *Rabelais and His World,* trans. Helene Iswolsky (Cambridge: MIT Press, 1968), 154.

2. Natalie Zemon Davis, *Society and Culture in Early Modern France* (Stanford, Calif.: Stanford University Press, 1975), 97–123.

3. For a theory of public spectacle and its function in the commercial and cultural life in the early modern period, see Denis Cosgrove, "Spectacle and Society: Landscape as Theater in Premodern and Postmodern Cities," in *Understanding Ordinary Landscapes,* ed. Paul Groth and Todd W. Bressi (New Haven: Yale University Press, 1997), 99–110. See also Calabi, *Mercato e la città,* 25, and Jesús Roberto Escobar, "The Great Theater of the World," in his "The Plaza Mayor of Madrid: Architecture, Urbanism and the Imperial Capital, 1560–1640" (Ph.D. diss., Princeton University, 1996), 218–252.

4. Emily P. Burke, *Pleasure and Pain: Reminiscences of Georgia in the 1840's* (1850; reprint, Savannah, Ga.: Beehive Press, 1978), 18–25.

5. Washington Topham, "Centre Market and Vicinity," *Records of the Columbia Historical Society* 26 (1924): 28, 50.

6. Ibid., 57, 81.

7. Balthasar Henry Meyer, *History of Transportation in the United States before 1860* (Washington, D.C.: Carnegie Institution, 1917; reprint, New York: Peter Smith, 1948), 110.

8. *American Farmer* 10 (January 16, 1829): 352, and David C. Smith and Anne E. Bridges, "The Brighton Market: Feeding Nineteenth-Century Boston," *Agricultural History* 56 (January 1982): 9, 18.

9. Meyer, *History of Transportation,* 467–468.

10. Smith and Bridges, "Brighton Market," 5–9.

11. D. P. Fogle, "Baltimore's Butchers Hill: Preserving a Neighborhood," Seminar in Historic Preservation, University of Maryland at College Park, fall 1996, 7–8.

12. De Voe, *Market Book,* 345.

13. Philip Freneau, "A Midnight Soliloquy in the Market House of Philadelphia," *Freeman's Journal,* September 4, 1782; reprinted in *The Prose of Philip Freneau,* ed. Philip M. Marsh (New Brunswick, N.J.: Scarecrow Press, 1955), 72–73.

14. Thomas F. De Voe, *The Market Assistant: Containing a Brief Description of Every Article of Human Food Sold in the Public Markets of the Cities of New York, Boston, Philadelphia, and Brooklyn* (New York: Riverside Press, 1867), 21.

15. Arfwedson, *United States and Canada,* 138–139.

16. "Domestic Economy," *American Farmer* 1 (May 14, 1819): 54–55.

17. "Philadelphia Markets," May 11, 1819, De Voe Papers.

18. *Pennsylvania Magazine,* November 1775, 510–511.

19. Edward C. Carter II, John C. Van Horne, and Charles E. Brownell, eds., *Latrobe's View of America, 1795–1820* (New Haven: Yale University Press, 1985), 356.

20. Upton, "Master Street of the World," 286.

21. De Voe, *Market Book,* 335, 461.

22. Ibid., 322, 423, 461.

23. Joseph Pilmore, *The Journal of Joseph Pilmore, Methodist Itinerant: For the Years August 1, 1769 to January 2, 1774,* ed. Frederick E. Masur and Howard T. Maag (Philadelphia: Historical Society of the Philadelphia Annual Conference of the United Methodist Church, 1969), 61.

24. De Voe, *Market Book,* 180, 480.

25. De Voe, *Market Book,* 344–345; Shane White, "The Death of James Johnson," *American Quarterly* 51 (December 1999): 761–768; Shane White, "'It Was a Proud Day': African Americans, Festivals, and Parades in the North, 1741–1834," *Journal of American History* 81 (June 1994): 47–48; and W. T. Lhamon Jr., "Dancing for Eels at Catherine [*sic*] Market," in *Raising Cain: Blackface Performance from Jim Crow to Hip Hop* (Cambridge: Harvard University Press, 1998).

26. *Alexandria Advertiser and Commercial Intelligencer,* February 22, 1804; *Baltimore Evening Post,* June 20, 1809; and *Georgetown Gazette and Commercial Advertiser,* July 6, 1808.

27. Edward Hazen, *The Panorama of Professions and Trades, or Every Man's Book* (Philadelphia: Uriah Hunt, 1837), 37. See also Edward Hazen, *Popular Technology, or Professions and Trades* (New York: Harper, 1841), 1:57.

28. C. Turner Thackrah, *The Effects of the Principal Arts, Trades, and Professions, and of Civic States and Habits of Living, on Health and Longevity* (Philadelphia: Literary Rooms, 1831), 15–16.

29. "List of Butchers in New York City, 1656–1844," De Voe Papers; De Voe, *Market Book*, 430.

30. Eaton, *Review of New-York*, 52–56.

31. Thomas David Beal, "Selling Gotham: The Retail Trade in New York City from the Public Market to Alexander T. Stewart's Marble Palace, 1625–1860" (Ph.D. diss., State University of New York at Stony Brook, December 1998), 371–441.

32. De Voe, *Market Book*, 392.

33. Susan G. Davis, *Parades and Power: Street Theater in Nineteenth-Century Philadelphia* (Philadelphia: Temple University Press, 1986), 117–125; Mary P. Ryan, *Women in Public: Between Banners and Ballots, 1825–1880* (Baltimore: Johns Hopkins University Press, 1990), 22–23; and Helen Tangires, "Celebrating Nature's Bounty: Butcher Parades in Nineteenth-Century New York and Philadelphia," in *Food and Celebration: From Fasting to Feasting*, ed. Patricia Lysaght (Ljubljana: Zalozba, 2002), 393–400.

34. De Voe, *Market Book*, 316; Brooks McNamara, *Day of Jubilee: The Great Age of Public Celebrations in New York, 1788–1909* (New Brunswick, N.J.: Rutgers University Press, 1997), 17–22.

35. De Voe, *Market Book*, 213–216; William Spence Robertson, *The Life of Miranda*, vol. 1 (New York: Cooper Square, 1969), 293–327.

36. De Voe, *Market Book*, 413, 431–433.

37. Ibid., 421, 477.

38. Ibid., 322.

39. Ibid., 237, 419–420.

40. The engraving is described in *Philadelphia: Three Centuries of American Art*, bicentennial exhibition, April 11-October 10, 1976 (Philadelphia: Philadelphia Museum of Art, 1976), 253–254.

41. James Mease, "Remarks on the Late Cattle Procession in Philadelphia, with Directions How to Effectually Promote the Breed of Cattle," paper read March 20, 1821; reprinted in *Philadelphia Society for Promoting Agriculture: Memoirs* (Philadelphia: Robert H. Small, 1826), 5:158–160.

42. "Unrivaled Show Beef," *Pennsylvanian*, March 1, 1845. In Wilmington, Delaware, show beef parades traditionally were held on Washington's Birthday and lasted until the 1920s. See Constance J. Cooper, *To Market, to Market, in Wilmington: King Street and Beyond* (Wilmington, Del.: Cedar Tree Press, 1992), 23–24.

43. De Voe, *Market Book*, 506–507.

44. Ibid., 467–468. The butchers were undoubtedly referring to the infamous "Peggy Eaton affair." See John F. Marszalek, *The Petticoat Affair: Manners, Mutiny, and Sex in Andrew Jackson's White House* (New York: Free Press, 1997).

45. On the democratic element in New York see especially Howard B. Rock, *Artisans of the New Republic; The Tradesmen of New York City in the Age of Jefferson*

(New York: New York University Press, 1979), and Sean Wilentz, *Chants Democratic: New York City and the Rise of the American Working Class, 1788–1850* (New York: Oxford University Press, 1984). On the eastern origins of laissez-faire radicalism in the United States see Arthur M. Schlesinger Jr., *The Age of Jackson* (Boston: Little, Brown, 1945), 283.

46. Graham Russell Hodges, *New York City Cartmen, 1667–1850* (New York: New York University Press, 1986), 146–147.

47. De Voe, *Market Book,* 532.

FOUR The Legalizing of Private Meat Shops
in Antebellum New York

1. De Voe, *Market Book,* 226–227.

2. Ibid., 241, 343, and Hendrik Hartog, *Public Property and Private Power: The Corporation of the City of New York in American Law, 1730–1870* (Chapel Hill: University of North Carolina Press, 1983), 152–153.

3. De Voe, *Market Book,* 412.

4. Ibid., 421–422, 471.

5. New York (City), *Minutes of the Common Council,* vol. 2, October 29, 1798; November 5, 1798; March 11, 1799; 476, 477, 524; De Voe Papers, "Extracts of Minutes," April 20, 1812.

6. William Bridges, *Map of the City of New-York and Island of Manhattan: With Explanatory Remarks and References* (New York: T and J. Swords, 1811), 26–29; Hartog, *Public Property and Private Power,* 165; and Reps, *Making of Urban America,* 297–299.

7. De Voe, *Market Book,* 393–395.

8. Ibid., 395.

9. Ibid., 528–529, 383.

10. Ibid., 484.

11. Unless otherwise stated, all quotations in this section can be found in De Voe, *Market Book,* 533–545.

12. New York (City), Board of Aldermen, Special Committee on the New York City Market Laws, Report of the Special Committee, on the Subject of Repealing the Market Laws, and Refunding to the Butchers the Premiums Paid by Them, Document no. 43, January 11, 1841, 599–600.

13. *New York Evening Post,* February 24, 1841.

14. Peter Cooper is better known as the inventor of the "Tom Thumb," one of the earliest locomotives in the United States, and as founder of the Cooper-Union.

15. Letter from W. F. Piatt [Platt?], M.D., [to the Common Council], March 3, 1834, N.Y., in "Ground Plans of Public Markets in New York City, and the Names of Butchers, 1694–1866," De Voe Papers.

16. New York (City), Board of Aldermen, Joint Committee on Markets. "The Joint Committee on Markets, to Whom Was Referred the Petition Asking for the Repeal of the Ordinance Authorizing the Establishment of Meat-Shops throughout the

City, . . . ," in Food Supply, document no. 52, February 10, 1845, VTE p.v.3, New York Public Library, 523.

17. *Evening Star,* January 8 and 18, 1839; De Voe, *Market Book,* 472–473.

18. Edward K. Spann, *The New Metropolis: New York City, 1840–1857* (New York: Columbia University Press, 1981), 447 n.17.

19. "The Market Laws," *New World* 4 (June 25, 1842): 413.

20. New York (City), Board of Aldermen, *Proceedings of the Boards of Aldermen, Approved by the Mayor, from May 31, 1842 to May 3, 1843, Inclusive,* vol. 10 (New York: Thomas Snowden, 1843), 63.

21. Spann, *New Metropolis,* 126–127.

22. Amy Bridges, *A City in the Republic: Antebellum New York and the Origins of Machine Politics* (1984; reprint, Ithaca: Cornell University Press, 1987), 182 n. 26, and Ira M. Leonard, "The Rise and Fall of the American Republican Party in New York City, 1843–1845," *New-York Historical Society Quarterly* 50 (April 1966): 163–164.

23. Spann, *New Metropolis,* 36, 447 n. 17.

24. "Abattoirs—Pure and Healthy Meats," *Weekly Herald,* December 31, 1842.

25. New York (City), Board of Aldermen, *Proceedings,* 1843, 145–149.

26. Beal, "Selling Gotham," 348–349.

27. "The Parisian Abattoirs," *Weekly Herald,* December 31, 1842.

28. "Reform of the City Government," *Weekly Herald,* December 31, 1842.

29. New York (City), Board of Aldermen, Joint Committee on Markets, 518–528.

30. Leonard, "American Republican Party," 173–175; Spann, *New Metropolis,* 38.

31. William G. Bishop and William H. Attree, *Report of the Debates and Proceedings of the Convention for the Revision of the Constitution of the State of New York* (Albany: Evening Atlas, 1846), 7–16. See also James Henretta, "The Strange Birth of Liberal America: Michael Hoffman and the New York Constitution of 1846," *New York History* 77 (April 1996): 151–176.

32. New York (City), Convention in relation to the Charter . . . , *Amendments to the Charter of the City of New York* (New York: Jared W. Bell, 1846), 9.

33. New York (City), Common Council, *The Charter of the City of New York, with Notes Thereon:. Also, a Treatise on the Powers and Duties of the Mayor, Aldermen and Assistant Aldermen, Prepared at the Request of the Common Council, by Chancellor Kent* (New York: McSpedon and Baker, 1851), 100–101, 238–239.

34. For the opinions of Robert J. Dillon and Richard Busteed, counsel to the corporation, on the subject of public markets see New York (City), Board of Councilmen, *Compilation of the Opinions of the Counsels of the City of New York, from the Year 1849 to the Year 1860,* document no. 13 (New York: Jones, 1859), 140, 275–276, 602–603, 615–616, 645–650.

35. *New-York Daily Tribune,* September 4, 1855.

36. New York (City), Board of Alderman, Comptroller's Office [A. C. Flagg], Communication in Reply to Resolution relative to the Market Property of the City, document no. 41, May 15, 1854, 647–649.

37. Spann, *New Metropolis,* 127–128.

38. Thomas F. De Voe, "The Public Markets: True Value of the Markets to the City," *New-York Daily Times,* January 23, 1855.

39. Thomas F. De Voe, "Petition to the Honorable the Market Committees of the Boards of Aldermen and Councilmen of the City of New-York," in New York (City), Board of Aldermen, Report of the Committee on Markets, Stated Session, April 14, 1854.

40. New York (City), Board of Aldermen, Report of the Commissioner of Streets and Lamps [Heman W. Childs], Document no. 9, January 9, 1851.

41. New York (City), Mayor, 1854–1857 [Fernando Wood], *Communication from His Honor the Mayor, Fernando Wood: Transmitted to the Common Council of New-York, February 4th, 1856* (New York, 1856), 43–44.

42. The best account of the meat shops in this period can be found in Beal, "Selling Gotham," 342–357. See also Spann, *New Metropolis,* 127–129.

43. E. A. Hutchinson, *A Model Mayor: Early Life, Congressional Career, and Triumphant Municipal Administration of Honorable Fernando Wood, Mayor of the City of New York* (New York: Family Publication Establishment, 1855), 47; Jerome Mushkat, *Fernando Wood: A Political Biography* (Kent, Ohio: Kent State University Press, 1990), 46–47. On the city's financial crisis in the 1840s and 1850s see Spann, *New Metropolis,* 45–53.

44. New York (City), *Communication from Mayor Fernando Wood,* 50–51.

45. Eric Homberger, *Scenes from the Life of a City: Corruption and Conscience in Old New York* (New Haven: Yale University Press, 1994), 57.

46. New York (City), *Communication from Mayor Fernando Wood,* 51.

47. Roy Rosenzweig and Elizabeth Blackmar, *The Park and the People: A History of Central Park* (Ithaca: Cornell University Press, 1992).

48. Population figures from Kenneth T. Jackson, ed., *The Encyclopedia of New York City* (New Haven: Yale University Press; New York: New-York Historical Society, 1995), 923.

49. De Voe, *Market Book,* 554, 563. Roger Scola measured the impact of meat shops on occupancy rates in the public markets in Manchester, England. He found that the number of occupied market stalls declined from 264 in 1848, when restrictions against selling anywhere but in the public markets were lifted, to only 29 by 1871. See Roger Scola, *Feeding the Victorian City: The Food Supply of Manchester, 1770–1870* (Manchester: Manchester University Press, 1992), 179–190.

50. Theodore and Cynthia Corbett also suggested that the legalization of shops in 1843 signaled the victory of free trade and the decline of public markets as instruments of public welfare. See Theodore Corbett and Cynthia Corbett, "New York's Public Markets, 1680–1850," in *Foodways in the Northeast,* ed. Peter Benes, Dublin Seminar for New England Folklife, Annual Proceedings, 1982 (Boston: Boston University, 1984), 142–143.

51. Spann, *New Metropolis,* 122.

52. De Voe, *Market Assistant,* 9.

FIVE Market House Company Mania in Philadelphia

1. Barshinger, "Provisions for Trade," 69–73; Michael Feldberg, *The Philadelphia Riots of 1844: A Study of Ethnic Conflict* (Westport, Conn.: Greenwood Press, 1975), 104; and *A Full and Complete Account of the Late Awful Riots in Philadelphia* (Philadelphia: John B. Perry, 1844), 18–21.

2. Washington Topham, "Northern Liberty Market," *Records of the Columbia Historical Society* 24 (1920): 49–50.

3. Howard Gillette Jr., "The Emergence of the Modern Metropolis: Philadelphia in the Age of Its Consolidation," in *The Divided Metropolis: Social and Spatial Dimensions of Philadelphia, 1800–1975,* ed. William M. Cutler III and Howard Gillette Jr. (Westport, Conn.: Greenwood Press, 1980), 3–25; Michael McCarthy, "The Philadelphia Consolidation of 1854: A Reappraisal," *Pennsylvania Magazine of History and Biography* 110 (October 1986): 531–548; and Warner, *Private City,* 49–51, 99–123, 152–157.

4. Gilchrist, "Market Houses in High Street," 304. Henceforth in this chapter, High Street will be referred to as Market Street.

5. James F. O'Gorman, Jeffrey A. Cohen, George E. Thomas, and G. Holmes Perkins, *Drawing toward Building: Philadelphia Architectural Graphics, 1732–1986* (Philadelphia: University of Pennsylvania Press for the Pennsylvania Academy of the Fine Arts, 1986), 100.

6. "Market Street Improvements," *Public Ledger,* January 17, 1853.

7. Gilchrist, "Market Houses in High Street," 304–312. On the architecture of cast-iron markets in England, see Jeremy Taylor, "Charles Fowler: Master of Markets," *Architectural Review* 135 (1964): 174–182; and in France, see Frances H. Steiner, *French Iron Architecture,* Studies in the Fine Arts: Architecture 3 (Ann Arbor: UMI Research Press, 1984), 46–53.

8. Barshinger, "Provisions for Trade," 55–56.

9. Ibid., 57–58.

10. *Wartman v. The City of Philadelphia* and *Pratt v. The Same,* in Pennsylvania, *State Reports, Comprising Cases Adjudged in the Supreme Court of Pennsylvania,* vol. 33 (Philadelphia: Kay, 1859) 202–212. Quotations from the plaintiffs, defendants, and witnesses in these cases can be found in RG 33, Pennsylvania Supreme Court, *Equity Dockets, Eastern District,* 1836–1860, and *Equity Papers, Eastern District,* 1848–1853; 1853–1854, Pennsylvania State Archives, Harrisburg. See also Helen Tangires, "The Country Connection: Farmers Markets in the Public Eye," *Pennsylvania Heritage* 24 (fall 1998): 4–11.

11. Pennsylvania, *Laws of the General Assembly of the Commonwealth of Pennsylvania, Passed at the Session of 1853* (Harrisburg: Theo. Fenn, 1853), 730–731.

12. Although Black's decision does not appear in the court reporter until 1859, it was made on April 3, 1854, and announced in the "The Market House Question," *Public Ledger,* on April 4, 1854. See also Novak, *People's Welfare,* 99, and Barshinger, "Provisions for Trade," 59.

13. Philadelphia, Pa., Mayor, 1855 [Robert T. Conrad], *Message of Robert T. Conrad, Mayor of the City of Philadelphia, with Accompanying Documents* (Philadelphia: Crissy and Markley, 1855), 94–95.

14. Philadelphia, Pa., Common Council, *Journal of the Common Council of the City of Philadelphia, Beginning June 12, Ending December 2, 1854* (Philadelphia: W. H. Sickels, 1854), 619.

15. Philadelphia, Pa., Common Council, *Journal of the Common Council of the City of Philadephia Beginning December 7, 1854, Ending May 7, 1855* (Philadelphia: W. H. Sickels, 1855), 433.

16. Philadelphia, Pa., Common Council, *Journal of the Common Council of the Consolidated City of Philadelphia, Begining November 1, 1855, Ending May 8, 1856* (Philadelphia: W. H. Sickels, 1856, 607–617. Some three hundred memorialists in favor of removing the sheds are listed by name on pages 612–617.

17. Philadelphia, Pa., Common Council, *Journal of the Common Council of the Consolidated City of Philadelphia, Beginning November 13, 1856, Ending May 7, 1857* (Philadelphia: W. H. Sickels, 1847), 229–231.

18. "Market Wagons in the Streets," [1857?], in Charles A. Poulson, *Scrap-Books Consisting of Engravings, etc. and Newspaper Clippings of Philadelphia* (Philadelphia: Library Company of Philadelphia, ca. 1828–1864), 9:49.

19. Philadelphia, Pa., Common Council, *Journal of the Common Council of the Consolidated City of Philadelphia, Beginning November 19, 1957, Ending May 6, 1858* (Philadelphia: Town, 1858), 466–468.

20. Roger Miller and Joseph Siry, "The Emerging Suburb: West Philadelphia, 1850–1880," *Pennsylvania History* 46 (April 1980): 99–114.

21. Philadelphia, Pa., Select Council, *Journal of the Select Council of the City of Philadelphia* (Philadelphia: Crissy and Markley, 1858), appendix 1, 1–7.

22. "Proceedings of Councils," *Public Ledger,* November 26, 1858.

23. "Monopoly and Bribery Triumphant," *Sunday Dispatch,* November 28, 1858.

24. "The Removal of the Market Houses," *Public Ledger,* April 23, 1859. See also "In Common Council," *Public Ledger,* April 26, 1859; "About to Be Settled," *Public Ledger,* April 27, 1859; "Local Affairs," *Public Ledger,* April 29, 1859; and "Sale of Market Sheds in Market Street, *Public Ledger,* November 2, 1859.

25. Philadelphia, Pa., Mayor, *First Annual Message of Alexander Henry, Mayor of the City of Philadelphia, with Accompanying Documents, January 27, 1859* (Philadelphia: Inquirer Printing Office, 1859), 24, and "Markets," *Public Ledger,* March 24, 1859.

26. *Twitchell v. The City of Philadelphia,* in Pennsylvania, *State Reports,* 212–221.

27. Alan Trachtenberg, *The Incorporation of America: Culture and Society in the Gilded Age* (New York: Hill and Wang, 1982), 4–7.

28. The transfer of economic power from the public domain to private enterprise through the legal system is best described in Morton J. Horwitz, *The Transformation of American Law, 1780–1860* (Cambridge: Harvard University Press, 1977).

29. "Act to Incorporate the Monument Cemetery of Philadelphia," in Pennsylvania, *Laws of the General Assembly of the Commonwealth of Pennsylvania, Passed at the Session of 1837–38* (Harrisburg: Theo. Fenn, 1838), 127–131. This charter was accompanied in the act by another charter for the Smithfield Market Company. Both charters were anomalous for their time, and no more market company charters appear in the Pennsylvania laws until 1853, when the Broad Street Market House Company was incorporated.

30. "Act to Incorporate the Western Market Company," in Pennsylvania, *Laws of the General Assembly of the State of Pennsylvania, Passed at the Session of 1859* (Harrisburg: A. Boyd Hamilton, 1859), 23–25.

31. On the rise of the "business man" see Charles Sellers, *The Market Revolution: Jacksonian America, 1815–1846* (New York: Oxford University Press, 1991), 237–238.

32. Sentiments in favor of privatizing markets also smoldered in England and France at midcentury. The debate is summarized in James Newlands, *A Short Description of the Markets and Market System of Paris: With Notes on the Markets of London* (Liverpool: George M'Corquodale, 1865).

33. Mrs. L. C. Tuthill, *Success in Life: The Merchant* (New York: George P. Putnam, 1850).

34. On Freedley as a secondary source see Warner, *Private City*, 69–71.

35. Edwin T. Freedley, *A Practical Treatise on Business, or How to Get, Save, Spend, Give, Lend, and Bequeath Money* . . . (Philadelphia: Lippincott, Grambo, 1852), 85.

36. Edwin T. Freedley, *Opportunities for Industry and the Safe Investment of Capital, or A Thousand Chances to Make Money, by a Retired Merchant* (Philadelphia: J. B. Lippincott, 1859), 76–77, 220–224.

37. "Markets," *Public Ledger*, March 24, 1859.

38. *Fresh Fruits and Vegetables, All the Year, at Summer Prices* (Philadelphia: Arthur, Burnham, 1855).

39. Details of the demolition can be found in Barshinger, "Provisions for Trade," 59–62.

40. John M. Gries was a promising Philadelphia architect, noted for his design of the Farmers' and Mechanics' Bank, Bank of Pennsylvania, and Christ Church Hospital. He interrupted his career to volunteer in the Civil War and subsequently died of wounds. Sandra L. Tatman and Roger W. Moss, *Biographical Dictionary of Philadelphia Architects: 1700–1930* (Boston: G. K. Hall, 1985), 317.

41. "Laying of the Corner Stone of the New Market House," n.d., in Poulson, *Scrap-Books*, 10:66, and "The New Market House," November 17, 1858, in Poulson, *Scrap-Books*, 10:87.

42. "Laying of the Corner Stone"; Poulson, *Scrap-Books*, 10:66.

43. "The Western Market House," April 16, 1859, in Poulson, *Scrap-Books*, 1:54.

44. "The New Market House," April 11, 1859, in Poulson, *Scrap-Books*, 1:60; "The Dedication of the Western Market House," April [?], 1859, in Poulson, *Scrap-Books*, 1:67; and Barshinger, "Provisions for Trade," 351.

45. "Meeting of Butchers," December 16, 1858, in Poulson, *Scrap-Books,* 1:36.

46. "The Old Market Shed Sites," *Public Ledger,* April 2, 1860.

47. "An Act to Incorporate the Eastern Market Company of the city of Philadelphia," in Pennsylvania, *Laws of the General Assembly* (1859), 65–68.

48. Barshinger, "Provisions for Trade," 114–121, 355; Harold N. Cooledge Jr., *Samuel Sloan: Architect of Philadelphia, 1815–1884* (Philadelphia: University of Pennsylvania Press, 1986), 208; and O'Gorman et al., *Drawing toward Building,* 100.

49. Barshinger, "Provisions for Trade," 115.

50. Pennsylvania, *Laws of the General Assembly* (1859–1861).

51. "The Market Companies," in Philadelphia Box, De Voe Papers. See also Letter from Thomas De Voe to John A. McAllister, Philadelphia, March 1, 1865, in "Copies of Old Letters," De Voe Papers.

52. "The Market Companies," in Philadelphia Box, De Voe Papers.

six The Landscape of Deregulation

Epigraph: Paul Armour, "A Plea for Manhattan Market," *New York Times,* March 26, 1873.

1. Hartog, *Public Property and Private Power,* 237–239.

2. Calvin G. Beitel, *A Digest of Titles of Corporations Chartered by the Legislature of Pennsylvania between the Years 1700 and 1873* (Philadelphia: John Campbell, 1874); Pennsylvania, *Laws of the General Assembly* (1859–1800); and Tangires, "Country Connection," 9–10.

3. Edward Strahan [pseud. Earl Shinn], *A Century After: Picturesque Glimpses of Philadelphia and Pennsylvania* (Philadelphia: Allen, Lane, and Scott and J. W. Lauderbach, 1875), 149–165.

4. "The New Market Houses," [1860?], in Poulson, *Scrap-Books,* 8:54.

5. Primitive Market Houses," April 16, 1857, in Poulson, *Scrap-Books,* 9:37; "A Move in the Right Quarter," November 17, 1858, in Poulson, *Scrap-Books,* 10:85; "The New Market House—the Sheds Once More," November 28, 1858, in Poulson, *Scrap-Books,* 10:62.

6. "The Market Houses—Their Doom Sealed," November 26, 1858, in Poulson, *Scrap-Books,* 10:68.

7. "An Act to Incorporate the West Harrisburg Market House Company," in Pennsylvania, *Laws of the General Assembly of the State of Pennsylvania* (Harrisburg: A. Boyd Hamilton, 1860), 777–778; A. S. Hamman, "Broad St. Market to Celebrate One Hundredth Year of Founding April 20," *Evening News,* January 20, 1960; Catherine McCurdy Zimmerman, "Market Houses of Harrisburg," paper presented at meeting of the Dauphin County Historical Society, February 17, 1964, typescript, 11–15, Dauphin County Historical Society, Harrisburg.

8. Barshinger, "Provisions for Trade," 299; Stockholders Minute Book, November 17, 1864–October 8, 1901, and Stocks, 1864–1875, West Harrisburg Market House Company, MG-248, Pennsylvania State Archives, Harrisburg.

9. "Kinnard to Quit as Market Head," *Evening News,* December 7, 1958. John N. Kinnard retired after fifty-eight years of service, having succeeded his father, Leonard Kinnard, who was superintendent from 1883 to 1900.

10. Harrisburg, Pa., Borough Council Minutes, January 30, 1860.

11. George H. Morgan, *Annals, Comprising Memoirs, Incidents and Statistics of Harrisburg* (Harrisburg, Pa.: George A. Brooks, 1858), 91.

12. Charles E. Walmer, "Farmers Markets of Harrisburg, Pennsylvania: Their Origin and History," *Dauphin County Historical Review* 5 (December 1956): 31–36.

13. Barshinger, "Provisions for Trade," 79–80.

14. "Against the Sheds," January 8, 1888, newspaper clipping in Photographs and Newspapers file, West Harrisburg Market House Company, MG-248, Pennsylvania State Archives, Harrisburg; "Market Sheds Must Go," *Daily Patriot,* January 22, 1889; "Tearing Them Down," *Daily Patriot,* February 7, 1889; Barshinger, "Provisions for Trade," 65–67.

15. Barshinger, "Provisions for Trade," 64, 142–144, 363–366; George R. Prowell, *History of York County Pennsylvania,* vol. 1 (Chicago: J. H. Beers, 1907), 794–797. City Market House was demolished in 1963.

16. Henry L. Fischer, *'S Alt Marik-Haus Mittes In D'r Schtadt, un Die Alte' Zeite* (The old market house in the middle of the city, and the olden days) (York: York Republican, 1879).

17. Ibid., ix.

18. York, Pa., Borough Council Journal, 1883–1887, microfilm, Pennsylvania State Archives, Harrisburg.

19. Barshinger, "Provisions for Trade," 64–65.

20. Ibid., 62–67.

21. Lancaster, Pa., City Select Council Minutes, Pennsylvania State Archives, Harrisburg.

22. "Mayor's Message, August 11, 1873," in Lancaster, Pa., City Select Council Minutes, Pennsylvania State Archives, Harrisburg.

23. Barshinger, "Provisions for Trade," 320; John J. Snyder Jr., *Lancaster Architecture, 1719–1927* (Lancaster, Pa.: Historical Preservation Trust of Lancaster County, 1979), 28. The Lancaster Central Market House is still a municipal market.

24. Barshinger, "Provisions for Trade," 160; Beitel, *Digest of Titles of Corporations; Pennsylvania, Laws of the General Assembly* (for the years 1863 through 1895).

25. Frank M. Eastman, *A Treatise on the Law relating to Private Corporations in Pennsylvania,* 2 vols. (Philadelphia: George T. Bisel, 1903), 1:52; 2:1006–1007.

26. Board of Directors Minute Book, West Harrisburg Market House Company, MG-248, Pennsylvania State Archives, Harrisburg.

27. Junius Henri Browne, *The Great Metropolis: A Mirror of New York* (1869; reprint, New York: Arno Press, 1975), 408.

28. *New York Times,* December 16, 1871.

29. Homberger, *Scenes from the Life of a City,* 198–209.

30. De Voe, *Market Book,* 574.

31. Letter from John C. Wandell to Thomas De Voe, December 19, 1871, "New York City Markets—Official Transactions, 1871–1876," BV, De Voe Papers.

32. "How Our Markets Were Managed under Tammany Rule—the Case of Mr. Robert Gow [Clinton Market]," *New York Times*, January 17, 1872; "Washington Market Frauds: The Old Regime and the New—a Record of Blackmailing and Robbery—How Tammany Politicians Worked a Rich Placer," *New York Times*, December 15, 1871.

33. Citizens' Association of New York, *The Public Markets: the Citizens' Association to Comptroller Connolly—the Present Meagre Revenue of the Public Markets and Their Capacity to Yield Seven Per Cent.—the True Remedy, the Sale of the Entire Market Property* (New York: Citizens' Association of New York, 1867).

34. Homberger, *Scenes from the Life of a City*, 180–211, 260, 335 n. 130. Another historian of the Tweed ring described New York's public markets as the most profitable source of graft, with Croker as "the black brain and bully" behind the market corruption. See Alexander B. Callow Jr., *The Tweed Ring* (New York: Oxford University Press, 1966), 190–192.

35. "Market Reform. Important Movement of the Occupants of Stalls. A Change for the Better in the Public Markets—Action of a Committee from the Various Markets—Indorsing Mr. Green and Mr. De Voe," *New York Times*, February 3, 1872. See also "The True Ideal of Reform," *New York Times*, March 22, 1872.

36. Thomas F. De Voe, *Report upon the Present Condition of the Public Markets of the City and County of New York* (New York: Evening Post Steam Presses, 1873), 5.

37. Letter from "Take the Hint" to De Voe, June 9, 1873, "Official Transactions, 1871–1876," De Voe Papers.

38. De Voe, *Present Condition of the Public Markets*, 9.

39. "Washington Market," *Gleason's Pictorial Drawing-Room Companion* 4 (March 5, 1853): 160; "A Municipal Mouth at Daybreak," *Appleton's Journal*, February 18, 1871, 192–194.

40. De Voe, *Present Condition of the Public Markets*, 8–9.

41. New York (City), Board of Assistant Aldermen, Common Council, *Majority and Minority Reports of the Committee on Repairs and Supplies, in relation to Rebuilding Washington Market* (New York: McSpedon and Baker, 1851). See also De Voe, *Market Book*, 453.

42. "A Municipal Mouth at Daybreak," *Appleton's Journal*, February 18, 1871, 192–194.

43. Richard B. Stott, *Workers in the Metropolis: Class, Ethnicity, and Youth in Antebellum New York City* (Ithaca: Cornell University Press, 1990), 176–178.

44. J. C. Hutcheson, "The Markets of New York," *Harper's New Monthly Magazine* 35 (July 1867): 230–231; Browne, *Great Metropolis*, 408.

45. Solon Robinson, "Economy in Food—What Shall We Eat," *New York Tribune*, November 14, 1855; reprinted in Solon Robinson, *How to Live: Saving and Wasting, and Domestic Economy Illustrated* (New York: Samuel R. Wells, 1874), 301–315.

46. De Voe, *Present Condition of the Public Markets*, 6.

47. De Voe, *Market Book,* 555; Robert M. Fogelson, *America's Armories: Architecture, Society, and Public Order* (Cambridge: Harvard University Press, 1989), 9, 118.

48. De Voe, *Present Condition of the Public Markets,* 16; Fogelson, *America's Armories,* 16, 48–50, 85–87.

49. De Voe, *Present Condition of the Public Markets,* 11.

50. New York (State), *Laws of the State of New York, Passed at the Ninety-fourth Session of the Legislature,* vol. 2 (Albany: Argus, 1871), 1866–1892.

51. New York (State), "An Act to Incorporate the 'Manhattan Market Company of the City of New York,'" in *Laws of the State of New York, Passed at the Ninety-third Session of the Legislature,* vol. 1 (Albany: Weed, Parsons, 1870), 317–319; "The Manhattan Market: A Description of the Market Building in Thirty-fourth-Street—Its Management and Promises to the People," *New York Times,* November 13, 1871; "The New Manhattan Market," *New York Times,* January 23, 1872.

52. De Voe, *Market Book,* 576.

53. New York (State), "An Act to Incorporate the East River Market Association of the City of New York, and to Authorize the Building of a Public Market on the East River, Near Thirty-fourth Street, in the City of New York," *Laws of the State of New York,* 1:1081–1084.

54. De Voe, *Present Condition of the Public Markets,* 21–22.

55. Armour, "Plea for Manhattan Market."

56. Theodor Risch, *Bericht über Markthallen in Deutschland, Belgien, Frankreich, England und Italien* (Report on the market halls of Germany, Belgium, France, England and Italy) (Berlin: Wolf Peiser, 1867), 454–463.

57. "The New Manhattan Market," *New York Times,* January 23, 1872; William H. Riding, "How New York Is Fed," *Scribner's Monthly* 14 (October 1877): 729–743.

58. De Voe, *Present Condition of the Public Markets,* 22.

59. *Frank Leslie's,* December 27, 1884; "Washington Market," *Carpentry and Building* 7 (May 1885): 81.

60. "Reorganizing a City Bureau: Mr. Tomes to Collect Revenues and Col. De Voe Given Charge of the Markets," *New York Times,* October 21, 1883, and various letters in De Voe Papers, New York City Markets—Copies of Old Letters, 1855–1871; Official Transactions, 1881–1885; and Miscellaneous.

61. "Outside of Fulton Market: The City to Obstruct the Sidewalks with Outside Stalls," *New York Times,* February 9, 1884.

62. "Events in the Metropolis: Demolishing an Old Landmark. Beginning the Tearing down of Washington Market," *New York Times,* July 25, 1883; "Lands for a New Market: Opposition of the Dock Commissioners to the Project," *New York Times,* March 8, 1884; "Dissatisfied Market Men," *New York Times,* December 30, 1888; "West Washington Market Scandal," *New York Times,* December 30, 1888; *New York Times,* March 29, 1889.

63. U.S. Department of Interior, Census Office, *Report on the Social Statistics of Cities,* comp. George E. Waring Jr. (Washington, D.C.: Government Printing Office, 1886), 588–589.

64. Jackson, *Encyclopedia of New York City,* 1200.

65. De Voe, *Market Book,* 454, 516.

66. Ibid., 831.

SEVEN Consumer Protection and the New Moral Economy

Epigraph: Boston, Mass., Joint Special Committee on Free Markets, *Report of the Joint Special Committee on Free Markets,* City Document no. 91 (Boston, 1870), 33. The committee members were George O. Carpenter, Francis W. Jacobs, Eugene C. Donnelly, Sewall B. Bond, and William Pope.

1. U.S. Department of Agriculture, Commissioner of Agriculture [Horace Capron], *Report of the Commissioner of Agriculture in the Year 1870* (Washington, D.C.: Government Printing Office, 1871), 243.

2. Letter from William F. Channing to Senator Charles Sumner, August 4, 1869, RG 46, Records of the U.S. Senate, 41st Cong., Committee on Agriculture, Sen 41A–E1, box 13, National Archives.

3. Letter [from W. C. Gould?] to Senator Charles Sumner, April 13, 1870, RG 46, Records of the U.S. Senate, 41st Cong., Committee on Agriculture, Sen 41A–E1, box 13, National Archives.

4. U.S. Department of Agriculture, *Report of the Commissioner in the Year 1870,* 251.

5. William Cronon, *Nature's Metropolis: Chicago and the Great West* (1991; reprint, New York: W. W. Norton, 1992), 218.

6. Smith and Bridges, "Brighton Market," 13.

7. U.S. Department of Agriculture, *Report of the Commissioner in the Year 1870,* 252–253.

8. Horace Capron, "Memoirs of Horace Capron," 2 vols., typescript, National Agricultural Library, 2:1–4.

9. U.S. Department of Agriculture, Commissioner of Agriculture [Frederick Watts], *Report of the Commissioner of Agriculture for the Year 1871* (Washington, D.C.: Government Printing Office, 1872), 1; U.S. Department of Agriculture, Commissioner of Agriculture [Frederick Watts], *Report of the Commissioner of Agriculture for the Year 1872* (Washington, D.C.: Government Printing Office, 1874), 438.

10. James R. Cameron, *The Public Service of Josiah Quincy, Jr., 1802–1882* (Quincy, Mass.: Quincy Co-operative Bank, 1964), 1–2.

11. Josiah Quincy, *Cheap Food Dependent on Cheap Transportation: An Address Delivered before the Boston Social Science Association, January 14th, 1869* (Boston: Boston Social Science Association, 1869).

12. Josiah Quincy, *Public Interest and Private Monopoly: An Address Delivered before the Boston Board of Trade, October 16, 1867* (Boston: J. H. Eastburn, 1867), 5, 11.

13. Cameron, *Public Service of Josiah Quincy,* 13–14.

14. Boston, Mass., *Committee on Free Markets.*

15. Ibid., 29.

16. Boston, Mass., Common Council, *Report on the Sale of Bad Meat in Boston,* City Document no. 74 (Boston, 1871), 6.

17. Ibid., 27.

18. Ibid., 47–56.

19. Ibid., 20–23.

20. Smith and Bridges, "Brighton Market," 6–7.

21. William M. Wheildon, *Semi-centennial Celebration of the Opening of Faneuil Hall Market, August 26, 1876* (Boston: L. F. Lawrence, 1877).

22. Abram English Brown, *Faneuil Hall and Faneuil Hall Market* (Boston: Lee and Shepard, 1900), 203–206; quotations from Wheildon, *Semi-centennial Celebration.*

23. Brown, *Faneuil Hall and Faneuil Hall Market,* 187–188.

24. Ibid., 197–199.

25. U.S. Department of the Interior, Census Office, *Report on the Social Statistics of Cities.* In the Far West, where urban development was just beginning, markets were virtually nonexistent.

26. Novak, *People's Welfare,* 103.

27. "An Ordinance in relation to Markets," March 29, 1870, St. Louis Ordinances, Missouri Historical Society.

28. Philip Taylor [market master, city of St. Louis], comp., "A Brief History of the Public Markets and Private Markets Referred to as Public Markets in the City of St. Louis, Missouri, from the Time of Their Inception in 1764 through the Present Day," typescript, January 1961, Missouri Historical Society Library, 22–23.

29. U.S. Department of Commerce, Bureau of the Census [Samuel L. Rogers, director], *Municipal Markets in Cities Having a Population of Over 30,000* (Washington, D.C.: Government Printing Office, 1919), tables 3 and 5.

30. Richard C. Wade, *The Urban Frontier: Pioneer Life in Early Pittsburgh, Cincinnati, Lexington, Louisville, and St. Louis* (Chicago: University of Chicago Press, 1959), 280–282. A strong defense of the municipal market system among local elites can be found in Canada. See Sean Gouglas, "Produce and Protection: Covent Garden Market, the Socioeconomic Elite, and the Downtown Core in London, Ontario, 1843–1915," *Urban History Review/Revue d'Histoire Urbaine* 25 (October 1996): 3–18, and William Thomas Matthews, "By and for the Large Propertied Interests: The Dynamics of Local Government in Six Upper Canadian Towns during the Era of Commercial Capitalism, 1832–1860" (Ph.D. diss., McMaster University, 1985), 132–176.

31. Harold L. Platt, "The Stillbirth of Urban Politics in the Reconstruction South: Houston, Texas as a Test Case," *Houston Review: History and Culture of the Gulf Coast* 4 (summer 1982): 61–67.

32. Barrie Scardino, "A Legacy of City Halls for Houston," *Houston Review: History and Culture of the Gulf Coast* 4 (fall 1982): 155–156.

33. The following summary of Mobile is based on George Herman Ewert, "Old Times Will Come Again: The Municipal Market System of Mobile, Alabama, 1888–1901" (M.A. thesis, University of South Alabama, 1993).

EIGHT Rebirth of the Municipal Market

Epigraph: J. W. Sullivan, *Markets for the People: The Consumer's Part* (New York: Macmillan, 1913), 299.

1. U.S. Senate Committee on the District of Columbia, *Papers relating to the Washington Market Company,* 60th Cong., 1st sess., S. Doc. 495 (Washington, D.C., 1908), 31–33.

2. U.S. Department of Commerce, Bureau of the Census, *Municipal Markets,* table 5.

3. Robert A. Sauder, "Municipal Markets in New Orleans," *Journal of Cultural Geography* 2 (fall–winter 1981): 86; Robert A. Sauder, "The Origin and Spread of the Public Market System in New Orleans," *Louisiana History* 22 (summer 1981): 287.

4. Stanley Buder, *Pullman: An Experiment in Industrial Order and Community Planning, 1880–1930* (New York: Oxford University Press, 1967), 68.

5. Thomas A. Markus, *Buildings and Power: Freedom and Control in the Origin of Modern Building Types* (London: Routledge, 1993), 300–316.

6. Center Market was on the present site of the National Archives.

7. Washington, D.C., *Journal of the Council of the City of Washington* (Washington, D.C., Gideon and Pearson, 1864–1870), November 7, 1866.

8. Western Market, at Twenty-first and K Streets, Northwest, was demolished in the 1960s. Eastern Market, on Capitol Hill at Seventh Street and South Carolina Avenue, Southeast, is still a thriving market.

9. Howard Gillette Jr., *Between Justice and Beauty: Race, Planning, and the Failure of Urban Policy in Washington, D.C.* (Baltimore: Johns Hopkins University Press, 1995), 62–68; Constance McLaughlin Green, *Washington: A History of the Capital, 1800–1950* (1962; reprint, Princeton: Princeton University Press, 1976), 344–362.

10. Tangires, "Contested Space," 55.

11. Washington Market Company, Copy of Statement Made to the Senate Committee on Public Buildings and Grounds, ca. 1869, Records of the House of Representatives, RG 233, National Archives.

12. Pamela Scott and Antoinette J. Lee, *Buildings of the District of Columbia* (New York: Oxford University Press, 1993), 40–41, 73.

13. U.S. Senate Committee on Public Buildings and Grounds, *Report of Justin Morrill on the Washington Market Company,* 43d Cong., 1st sess., S. Rept. 449 (Washington, D.C., 1874), 34–35.

14. U.S. Senate Committee on the District of Columbia, *Papers relating to the Washington Market Company,* 50–51.

15. Topham, "Centre Market and Its Vicinity," 77–79.

16. U.S. Senate Committee on the District of Columbia, *Papers relating to the Washington Market Company,* 50, 70.

17. Washington, D.C., *Report of the Commissioners of the District of Columbia* (Washington, D.C.: Government Printing Office, 1891), 215; Washington, D.C., *Re-*

port of the Commissioners of the District of Columbia (Washington, D.C.: Government Printing Office, 1902), 588.

18. "Public Market Houses: Their Legitimate Uses and Their Abuses," *Bee,* December 23, 1882, 1. I thank Nancy Schwartz for this citation.

19. On similar social motives in the new market halls of Victorian England, see Schmiechen and Carls, *British Market Hall,* 165–166.

20. Donald Hoffmann, *The Architecture of John Wellborn Root* (Baltimore: Johns Hopkins University Press, 1973), 55 n. 23, 217–218.

21. Mary L. Lincoln et al., "A Symposium—the Markets of Some Great Cities," *Chautauquan* 24 (December 1896): 332–335.

22. "Are the Markets Doomed?" *Cook* 1 (August 24, 1885): 3.

23. Ibid.

24. "Talk of Selling Markets," *Brooklyn Daily Eagle* 59 (December 21, 1899): 1.

25. Royal Commission on Market Rights and Tolls, *Final Report of the Commissioners. Presented to Both Houses of Parliament by Command of Her Majesty,* vol. 11 (London: Eyre and Spottiswoode, 1891), 17; New York (City), Mayor's Market Commission [Cyrus C. Miller, chairman]. *Report of the Mayor's Market Commission New York City* (New York: Little and Ives, 1913), 20.

26. Charles Tilly, "Food Supply and the Public Order in Modern Europe," in *The Formation of National States in Western Europe,* ed. Charles Tilly (Princeton: Princeton University Press, 1975), 380–455.

27. Schmiechen and Carls, *British Market Hall,* 146–153.

28. Lemoine, *Les Halles de Paris;* Newlands, *Short Description of the Markets and Market System of Paris;* Steiner, *French Iron Architecture,* 48–50. The last two pavilions were not completed until the 1930s. See David H. Pinkney, *Napoleon III and the Rebuilding of Paris* (1958; reprint, Princeton: Princeton University Press, 1972), 78–79.

29. The most complete account of market houses constructed in Europe in the nineteenth century, including plans, elevations, details, and a bibliography of projects, is Georg Osthoff and Eduard Schmitt, "Markthallen und Marktplätze," in *Handbuch der Architektur,* ed. Josef Durm (Darmstadt: Arnold Bergsträsser, 1888–1923), vol. 4, pt. 3, 2, 194–273.

30. Gilbert Herbert, *Pioneers of Prefabrication: The British Contribution in the Nineteenth Century* (Baltimore: Johns Hopkins University Press, 1978), 40–45, 71, 139, 170–172; Malcolm Higgs, "The Exported Iron Buildings of Andrew Handyside and Co. of Derby," *Journal of the Society of Architectural Historians* 29 (May 1970): 175–180; Ewing Matheson, *Works in Iron: Bridge and Roof Structures* (London: E. and F. N. Spon, 1877), 252–254, 264–265; Steiner, *French Iron Architecture,* 64.

31. Judith Ettinger Marti, "Subsistence and the State: Municipal Government Policies and Urban Markets in Developing Nations, the Case of Mexico City and Guadalajara, 1877–1910" (Ph.D. diss., University of California, Los Angeles, 1990), 97–136; Geraldo Gomes, "Artistic Intentions in Iron Architecture," *Journal of Decorative and Propaganda Arts, 1875–1945* 21 (1995): 87–106; and Sonia Berjman and José Fiszelew,

El Abasto: Un barrio y un mercado (El Abasto: A neighborhood and a market) (Buenos Aires: Corregidor, 1999), 25–59, 109–134.

32. For example, see Alexandre Friedmann, *Nouvelles dispositions pour la construction de halles, marchés et entrepôts* (New designs for the construction of halls, markets and warehouses) (Paris: J. Boudry, 1877), 18–19. Friedmann was a civil engineer for the city of Vienna.

33. Risch, *Bericht über Markthallen.*

34. Wolfgang Herrmann, ed., *In What Style Should We Build? The German Debate on Architectural Style* (Santa Monica, Calif.: Getty Center for the History of Art and the Humanities, 1992).

35. Ostoff and Schmitt, "Markthallen und Marktplätze," 249–250; Andrew Lohmeier, "'Bürgerliche Gesellschaft' and Consumer Interests: The Berlin Public Market Reform, 1867–1891," *Business History Review* 73 (spring 1999): 99.

36. Arthur Drexler, ed., *The Architecture of the École des Beaux-Arts* (New York: Museum of Modern Art; Cambridge: MIT Press, 1977), 422.

37. Edgar Lange, *Die Versorgung der grosstädtischen Bevölkerung mit frischen Nahrungsmitteln unter besonderer Berücksichtigung des Marktwesens der Stadt Berlin* (Provisioning large cities with fresh food with particular regard to the market system of Berlin) (Leipzig: Duncker und Humblot, 1911); Lohmeier, "'Bürgerliche Gesellschaft' and Consumer Interests," 91–113.

38. *Builder,* December 29, 1866, 955; Osthoff and Schmitt, "Markthallen und Marktplätze," 214–218.

39. David Alexander, *Retailing in England during the Industrial Revolution* (London: University of London, Athlone Press, 1970), 40–41.

40. Carol M. Highsmith and James L. Holton, *Reading Terminal and Market: Philadelphia's Historic Gateway and Grand Convention Center* (Washington, D.C.: Chelsea, 1994), 40–42, and David K. O'Neil, *An Illustrated History of Reading Terminal Market* (Philadelphia: Camino Books, in press).

41. New York (City), Mayor's Market Commission, *Report,* 30.

42. Helen Tangires, "Feeding the Cities: Public Markets and Municipal Reform in the Progressive Era," *Prologue: Quarterly of the National Archives and Records Administration* 29 (spring 1997): 16–26.

43. George E. Waring Jr., "The Waring Market Play-Grounds: How We Are to Treat the New York Push-Carts," *Harper's Weekly* 39 (December 28, 1895): 1237. For more on Waring see Martin V. Melosi, *Garbage in the Cities: Refuse, Reform, and the Environment, 1880–1980* (College Station: Texas A&M University Press, 1981), 51–78.

44. Hollis Godfrey, "The Food of the City Worker," *Atlantic Monthly* 103 (February 1909): 272; William H. Wilson, *The City Beautiful Movement* (Baltimore: Johns Hopkins University Press, 1989).

45. See U.S. Department of Commerce, Bureau of the Census *Municipal Markets,* table 3.

46. "Work Progresses on New Market Building," *Wisconsin State Journal,* December 27, 1909. The market has been converted into an apartment building.

47. Eric Johannesen, *Cleveland Architecture, 1876–1976* (Cleveland, Ohio: Western Reserve Historical Society, 1979), 116, 122–12. U.S. Department of Commerce, Bureau of the Census, *Municipal Markets,* 19. This market house is still in operation.

48. Don E. Mowry, "Municipal Markets: An Economic Necessity," *Municipal Journal and Engineer,* October 23, 1907, 462; J. F. Carter, "Public Markets and Marketing Methods," *American City* 8, 2 (1913): 124.

49. Clyde Lyndon King, ed., *Reducing the Cost of Food Distribution,* Annals, vol. 50 (Philadelphia: American Academy of Political and Social Science, 1913).

50. Achsah Lippincott, "Municipal Markets in Philadelphia," in King, *Reducing the Cost of Food Distribution,* 134–135.

51. Ibid., 136.

52. Thomas J. Libbin, "Constructive Program for Reduction of Cost of Food Distribution in Large Cities," in King, *Reducing the Cost of Food Distribution,* 247–251.

53. New York (City), Mayor's Market Commission, *Report,* 10.

54. Cyrus Chace Miller, "What the City Can Do to Reduce the Cost of Living," address delivered at Binghamton, N.Y., June 6, 1913, before the Conference of Mayors and other city officials of the State of New York, in SER p.v.41, New York Public Library, 1–14. See also Cyrus C. Miller, *Terminal Markets in the United States: A Plan to Bring about the Systematic and Economical Distribution of Food in Our Cities* [reprinted from the *Housewives League Magazine,* January 1913], in SER p.v.37, Pamphlets, no. 19, New York Public Library.

55. New York (City), Mayor's Market Commission, *Report,* 16.

56. Ibid., 19–20. For a description of the remodeling of Washington Market, see Jennie Wells Wentworth, "Public Markets," American Association for Promoting Hygiene and Public Baths, Fifth Annual Congress, Baltimore, Md., May 9, 1916, VTB p.v.22, no. 11, New York Public Library, 4–5.

57. New York (City), Mayor's Market Commission, *Report,*20–21.

58. Miller, *What the City Can Do to Reduce the Cost of Living,* 7.

59. New York (City), Mayor's Market Commission, *Report,* 49–54. The planning process and design principles for the wholesale terminal market are reminiscent of the development of planned shopping centers in Los Angeles in the 1920s. See Longstreth, *City Center to Regional Mall,* 145–175.

60. Cyrus C. Miller, *Municipal Market Policy* (New York: City Club of New York, 1912), 3–5.

61. Sullivan, *Markets for the People,* 269–286; quotation on 247.

62. Ibid., 1–3. On Sullivan's background and labor activities, see John R. Commons, *History of Labor in the United States, 1896–1932* (New York: MacMillan, 1935), 3:378.

63. Sullivan, *Markets for the People,* 13. Sullivan was alluding to the current debate over pushcarts in New York City. See Daniel M. Bluestone, "'The Pushcart Evil': Peddlers, Merchants, and New York City's Streets, 1890–1940," *Journal of Urban History* 18 (November 1991): 68–92, and Daniel Burnstein, "The Vegetable Man Cometh: Political and Moral Choices in Pushcart Policy in Progressive Era New York City," *New York History* 77 (January 1996): 47–84.

64. Sullivan, *Markets for the People*, 270, 296–299, 312.

65. Ibid., 10–11.

66. Arthur E. Goodwin, *Markets: Public and Private* (Seattle: Montgomery, 1929), 303.

67. A similar conclusion about the Progressives and their ultimate effect on urban form is argued in David Schuyler, *The New Urban Landscape: The Redefinition of City Form in Nineteenth-Century America* (Baltimore: Johns Hopkins University Press, 1986).

68. U.S. Department of Commerce, Bureau of the Census, *Municipal Markets;* see esp. tables 3 and 5.

69. Clyde Lyndon King, *Public Markets in the United States* (Philadelphia: National Municipal League, 1917), 31.

70. Ibid., 3, 15–16, 28.

71. Ibid., 21; Marc Linder and Lawrence Z. Zacharias, *Of Cabbages and Kings County: Agriculture and the Formation of Modern Brooklyn* (Iowa City: University of Iowa Press, 1999), 58.

72. King, *Public Markets in the United States*, 23–25.

73. U.S. Department of Commerce, Bureau of the Census, *Municipal Markets,* 9.

74. Cronon, *Nature's Metropolis*, 206–259; Steven Stoll, *The Fruits of Natural Advantage: Making the Industrial Countryside in California* (Berkeley: University of California Press, 1998).

75. Linder and Zacharias, *Of Cabbages and Kings County*, 63.

76. Dolores Hayden, *The Power of Place: Urban Landscapes as Public History* (Cambridge: MIT Press, 1995), 112–119.

SELECTED BIBLIOGRAPHY

PRIMARY SOURCES
Books, Articles, and Treatises

Bridges, William. *Map of the City of New-York and Island of Manhattan; With Explanatory Remarks and References.* New York: T and J. Swords, 1811.

Browne, Junius Henri. *The Great Metropolis: A Mirror of New York.* 1869. Reprint, New York: Arno Press, 1975.

Capron, Horace. "Memoirs of Horace Capron." 2 vols. Typescript. National Agricultural Library.

Citizens' Association of New York. *The Public Markets: The Citizens' Association to Comptroller Connolly—the Present Meagre Revenue of the Public Markets and Their Capacity to Yield Seven Per Cent.—the True Remedy, the Sale of the Entire Market Property.* New York: Citizens' Association of New York, 1867.

The Cries of New-York. New York: Samuel Wood, 1808; reprint, New York: Harbor Press, 1931.

The Cries of Philadelphia: Ornamented with Elegant Wood Cuts. Philadelphia: Johnson and Warner, 1810.

De Voe, Thomas F. *Abattoirs. A Paper Read before the Polytechnic Branch of the American Institute, June 8, 1865.* Albany, N.Y.: Charles Van Benthuysen, 1866.

———. *The Market Assistant: Containing a Brief Description of Every Article of Human Food Sold in the Public Markets of the Cities of New York, Boston, Philadelphia, and Brooklyn.* New York: Riverside Press, 1867.

———. *The Market Book: A History of the Public Markets of the City of New York.* 1862. Reprint, New York: Augustus M. Kelley, 1970.

———. "The Public Markets. True Value of the Markets to the City." *New-York Daily Times,* January 23, 1855.

———. *Report upon the Present Condition of the Public Markets of the City and County of New York.* New York: Evening Post Steam Presses, 1873.

Eaton, Theophilus. *Review of New-York, or Rambles through the City: Original Poems.* New York: John Low, 1814.

Farmers' Market Company of Philadelphia. *Thirty-second and Final Report of the Board of Directors, Treasurer and Superintendent of the Farmers' Market Company of Philadelphia.* West Chester, Pa.: F. S. Hickman, 1892.

Field, Marriott. *City Architecture, or Designs for Dwelling Houses, Stores, Hotels, Etc.* New York: G. P. Putnam, 1853.

Fischer, Henry L. *S Alt Marik-Haus Mittes In D'r Schtadt, un Die Alte' Zeite* (The old market house in the middle of the city, and the olden days). York, Pa.: York Republican, 1879.

Freedley, Edwin T. *Opportunities for Industry and the Safe Investment of Capital, or A Thousand Chances to Make Money, by a Retired Merchant.* Philadelphia: J. B. Lippincott, 1859.

———. *A Practical Treatise on Business, or How to Get, Save, Spend, Give, Lend, and Bequeath Money. . . .* Philadelphia: Lippincott, Grambo, 1852.

Freneau, Philip. "A Midnight Soliloquy in the Market House of Philadelphia." 1782. In *The Prose of Philip Freneau,* edited by Philip M. Marsh, 72–73. New Brunswick, N.J.: Scarecrow Press, 1955.

Fresh Fruits and Vegetables, All the Year, at Summer Prices. Philadelphia: Arthur, Burnham, 1855.

Friedmann, Alexandre. *Nouvelles dispositions pour la construction de halles, marchés et entrepôts* (New designs for the construction of halls, markets, and warehouses). Paris: J. Boudry, 1877.

A Full and Complete Account of the Late Awful Riots in Philadelphia. Philadelphia: John B. Perry, 1844.

Hazard, Willis P. *Annals of Philadelphia and Pennsylvania in the Olden Times.* Philadelphia: Edwin S. Stuart, 1877.

Hazen, Edward. *The Panorama of Professions and Trades, or Every Man's Book.* Philadelphia: Uriah Hunt, 1837.

———. *Popular Technology, or Professions and Trades.* Vol. 1. New York: Harper, 1841.

Hutcheson, J. C. "The Markets of New York." *Harper's New Monthly Magazine* 35 (July 1867): 230–231.

Hutchinson, E. A. *A Model Mayor: Early Life, Congressional Career, and Triumphant Municipal Administration of Honorable Fernando Wood, Mayor of the City of New York.* New York: Family Publication Establishment, 1855.

King, Clyde Lyndon. *Public Markets in the United States.* Philadelphia: National Municipal League, 1917.

———, ed. *Reducing the Cost of Food Distribution.* Annals, vol. 50. American Academy of Political and Social Science, 1913.

Lange, Edgar. *Die Versorgung der grosstädtischen Bevölkerung mit frischen Nahrungsmitteln unter besonderer Berücksichtigung des Marktwesens der Stadt Berlin* (Provisioning large cities with fresh food with particular regard to the market system of Berlin). Leipzig: Duncker und Humblot, 1911.

Marvell, Andrew [William Goddard?]. *Second Address to the Inhabitants of Philadelphia.* Philadelphia, 1773.

———. *To My Fellow Citizens, Friends to Liberty and Enemies to Despotism.* June 10. Small Broadsides. Philadelphia: Library Company of Philadelphia, 1773.

Matheson, Ewing. *Works in Iron: Bridge and Roof Structures.* London: E. and F. N. Spon, 1877.

Mease, James. "Remarks on the Late Cattle Procession in Philadelphia, with Directions How to Effectually Promote the Breed of Cattle." Paper read March 20, 1821. Reprinted in *Philadelphia Society for Promoting Agriculture. Memoirs,* 5:158–159. Philadelphia: Robert H. Small, 1826.

Miller, Cyrus Chace. *Municipal Market Policy.* New York: City Club of New York, 1912.

———. *Terminal Markets in the United States: A Plan to Bring about the Systematic and Economical Distribution of Food in Our Cities* (reprinted from the *Housewives League Magazine,* January 1913). In SER p.v.37, Pamphlets, no. 19, New York Public Library.

———. "What the City Can Do to Reduce the Cost of Living." Address delivered at Binghamton, N.Y., on June 6, 1913, before the Conference of Mayors and other city officials of the State of New York. In SER p.v.41, New York Public Library.

"A Municipal Mouth at Daybreak." *Appleton's Journal,* February 18, 1871, 192–194.

Newlands, James [engineer, Borough of Liverpool]. *A Short Description of the Markets and Market System of Paris: With Notes on the Markets of London. In the Form of a Report to the Markets Committee of Liverpool.* Liverpool: George M'Corquodale, 1865.

Osthoff, Georg, and Eduard Schmitt, "Markthallen und Marktplätze." In *Handbuch der Architektur,* edited by Josef Durm, vol. 4, pt. 3, 2, 194–273. Darmstadt: Arnold Bergsträsser, 1888–1923.

Poulson, Charles A. *Scrap-Books Consisting of Engravings, etc. and Newspaper Clippings Illustrative of Philadelphia.* 11 vols. Philadelphia: Library Company of Philadelphia, ca. 1828–1864.

"Public Market Houses: Their Legitimate Uses and Their Abuses." *Bee,* December 23, 1882, 1.

Quincy, Josiah. *Cheap Food Dependent on Cheap Transportation: An Address Delivered before the Boston Social Science Association, January 14th, 1869.* Boston: Boston Social Science Association, 1869.

———. *Public Interest and Private Monopoly: An Address Delivered before the Boston Board of Trade, October 16, 1867.* Boston: J. H. Eastburn, 1867.

Riding, William H. "How New York Is Fed." *Scribner's Monthly* 14 (October 1877): 729–743.

Risch, Theodor. *Bericht über Markthallen in Deutschland, Belgien, Frankreich, England und Italien* (Report on the market halls of Germany, Belgium, France, England and Italy). Berlin: Wolf Peiser, 1867.

Robinson, Solon. "Economy in Food—What Shall We Eat." *New York Tribune,* November 14, 1855. Reprinted in *How to Live: Saving and Wasting, and Domestic Economy Illustrated,* by Solon Robinson, 301–315. New York: Samuel R. Wells, 1874.

Sullivan, J. W. *Markets for the People: The Consumer's Part.* New York: Macmillan, 1913.

Selected Bibliography

Thackrah, C. Turner. *The Effects of the Principal Arts, Trades, and Professions, and of Civic States and Habits of Living, on Health and Longevity*. Philadelphia: Literary Rooms, 1831.

Tuthill, Mrs. L. C. *Success in Life: The Merchant*. New York: George P. Putnam, 1850.

Wentworth, Jennie Wells. *Public Markets*. Baltimore: American Association for Promoting Hygiene and Public Baths, May 9, 1916. VTB p.v.22, no. 11. New York Public Library.

Wheildon, William M. *Semi-centennial Celebration of the Opening of Faneuil Hall Market, August 26, 1876*. Boston: L. F. Lawrence, 1877.

Archives and Manuscript Records

Broad Street Market, Harrisburg (Dauphin County). National Register Nomination Files, Bureau for Historic Preservation, Pennsylvania Historical and Museum Commission, Harrisburg.

Central Market House Company, Bangor, Maine. No. 61, Stetson Family Interests (1822–1880). Baker Library, Harvard University, Cambridge, Mass.

De Voe, Thomas Farrington. Papers. New-York Historical Society.

Farmers' Market Company of Harrisburg, Pa. Record Group 246. Historical Society of Dauphin County, Harrisburg.

Nead Papers, Historical Society of Pennsylvania.

Norwich and Callowhill Markets, 1784–1845. Records. Historical Society of Pennsylvania.

Pennsylvania Supreme Court. Equity Dockets, Eastern District, 1836–1860; Equity Papers, Eastern District, 1848–1853; 1853–1854. Record Group 33. Pennsylvania State Archives.

Petitions to the Councils of Philadelphia, 1783–1868. Historical Society of Pennsylvania.

Ridge Avenue Farmers' Market Company. Records. Collection of David K. O'Neil.

Small Broadsides, 1778–1779, Pennsylvania Supreme Executive Council. Library Company of Philadelphia.

U.S. Department of Agriculture, Bureau of Agricultural Economics. Record Group 83. National Archives.

U.S. House of Representatives. Record Group 233. National Archives.

U.S. Senate, 41st Congress, Committee on Agriculture. Record Group 46. National Archives.

West Harrisburg Market House Company. Manuscript Group 248. Pennsylvania State Archives, Harrisburg.

Government Documents

Baltimore, Md. *Ordinances of the Corporation of the City of Baltimore*. 1797. Early American Imprints, 1st ser., no. 48044.

———. *Ordinances of the Corporation of the City of Baltimore*. 1805. Early American Imprints, 2d ser., no. 7914.

Beitel, Calvin G. *A Digest of Titles of Corporations Chartered by the Legislature of Pennsylvania between the Years 1700 and 1873.* Philadelphia: John Campbell, 1874.

Bishop, William G., and William H. Attree. *Report of the Debates and Proceedings of the Convention for the Revision of the Constitution of the State of New York.* Albany: Evening Atlas, 1846.

Boston, Mass., Common Council, *Report on the Sale of Bad Meat in Boston,* City Document no. 74. Boston, 1871.

Boston, Mass., Joint Special Committee on Free Markets. *Report of the Joint Special Committee on Free Markets.* City Document no. 91. Boston, 1870.

Bridges, William. *Map of the City of New-York and Island of Manhattan: With Explanatory Remarks and References.* New York: T and J. Swords, 1811.

Charleston, S.C. *Ordinances of the City Council of Charleston.* Charleston: W. P. Young, 1802–1804.

Dawson, William C. *Compilation of the Laws of the State of Georgia.* Milledgeville, Ga.: Grantland and Orme, 1831.

Frederick, Md. *The By Laws and Ordinances of the Corporation of Frederick Together with the Acts of Incorporation and Other Acts of the Legislature of Maryland, relating to Frederick.* Frederick-Town: Hughes and Lively, 1836.

———. "An Ordinance for the Regulation of the Markets in the Town of Frederick." *Fredericktown Herald,* April 5, 1817.

Fredericksburg, Va. City of Fredericksburg Council Minutes, 1801–1829. Microfilm. Library of Virginia.

Harrisburg, Pa. Harrisburg Borough Council Minutes. Microfilm. Pennsylvania State Archives, Harrisburg.

Hartford, Conn. *By-Laws of the City of Hartford.* 1788. Early American Imprints, 1st ser., no. 21134.

Lancaster, Pa. Minutes of Meetings of Burgesses and Assistants of the Borough of Lancaster; City Select Council Minutes. Microfilm. Pennsylvania State Archives, Harrisburg.

Logansport, Ind. Deed to Original Town of Logansport, 19 Sept. 1828. 1983 facsimile. Cass County Historical Society, Logansport, Ind.

New Orleans, La. *City Council Ordinances,* New Council Series. Ordinance no. 312, October 24, 1900.

———. *Police Code, or Collection of the Ordinances of Police Made by the City Council of New-Orleans.* 1808. Early American Imprints, 2d ser., no. 15741.

New York (City). *Laws and Ordinances: Ordained and Established by the Mayor, Aldermen, and Commonality of the City of New York.* 1805. Early American Imprints, 2d ser., no. 9011.

———. *Minutes of the Common Council of the City of New York, 1784–1831.* New York: City of New York, 1917.

New York (City), Board of Aldermen. *Proceedings of the Boards of Aldermen, Approved by the Mayor, from May 31, 1842, to May 3, 1843, Inclusive.* Vol. 10. New York: Thomas Snowden, 1843.

————. Report of the Commissioner of Streets and Lamps [Heman W. Childs], Document no. 9, January 9, 1851.

New York (City), Board of Alderman, Comptroller's Office [A. C. Flagg]. Communication in Reply to Resolution relative to the Market Property of the City. Document no. 41, May 15, 1854.

New York (City), Board of Aldermen, Joint Committee on Markets. The Joint Committee on Markets, to Whom Was Referred the Petition Asking for the Repeal of the Ordinance Authorizing the Establishment of Meat-Shops throughout the City. . . . . In Food Supply, document no. 52, February 10, 1845, VTE p.v.3. New York Public Library.

New York (City), Board of Aldermen, Special Committee on the New York City Market Laws. Report of the Special Committee, on the Subject of Repealing the Market Laws, and Refunding to the Butchers the Premiums Paid by Them. Document no. 43, January 11, 1841.

New York (City), Board of Assistant Alderman, Common Council. *Majority and Minority Reports of the Committee on Repairs and Supplies, in relation to Rebuilding Washington Market.* New York: McSpedon and Baker, 1851.

New York (City), Board of Councilmen. *Compilation of the Opinions of the Counsels of the City of New York, from the Year 1849 to the Year 1860,* Document no. 13. New York: Jones, 1859.

New York (City), Common Council. *The Charter of the City of New York, with Notes Thereon: Also, a Treatise on the Powers and Duties of the Mayor, Aldermen and Assistant Aldermen, Prepared at the Request of the Common Council, by Chancellor Kent.* New York: McSpedon and Baker, 1851.

New York (City), Convention in relation to the Charter. . . . *Amendments to the Charter of the City of New York.* New York: Jared W. Bell, 1846.

New York (City), Mayor, 1854–1857 [Fernando Wood]. *Communication from His Honor the Mayor, Fernando Wood: Transmitted to the Common Council of New-York, February 4th, 1856.* New York, 1856.

New York (City), Mayor's Market Commission [Cyrus C. Miller, chairman]. *Report of the Mayor's Market Commission of New York City.* New York: Little and Ives, 1913.

New York (State). *Laws of the State of New York, Passed at the Ninety-third Session of the Legislature.* Vol. 1. Albany: Weed, Parsons, 1870.

————. *Laws of the State of New York, Passed at the Ninety-fourth Session of the Legislature.* Vol. 2. Albany: Argus, 1871.

Norfolk, Va. Minutes of the Common Council of the Borough of Norfolk. Microfilm. Virginia State Library and Archives, Richmond.

Pennsylvania. [Thomas McKean Thompson]. *Laws of the Commonwealth of Pennsylvania.* Vol. 5. Lancaster: George Helmbold, 1803.

————. *Laws of the General Assembly of the Commonwealth of Pennsylvania, Passed at the Session of 1837–38.* Harrisburg: Theo. Fenn, 1838.

————. *Laws of the General Assembly of the Commonwealth of Pennsylvania, Passed at the Session of 1853.* Harrisburg: Theo. Fenn, 1853.

———. *Laws of the General Assembly of the State of Pennsylvania*. Harrisburg: Commonwealth, 1859–1899.

———. *State Reports, Comprising Cases Adjudged in the Supreme Court of Pennsylvania,* Vol. 33. Philadelphia: Kay, 1859.

Petersburg, Va. City Council Minute Book, 1784–1811. Microfilm. Virginia State Library and Archives, Richmond.

Philadelphia, Pa. *Ordinances of the Corporation of the City of Philadelphia*. 1812. Early American Imprints, 2d ser., no. 26440.

Philadelphia, Pa., Common Council. *Journal of the Common Council of the City of Philadelphia*. Philadelphia: W. H. Sickels, 1854–1858.

Philadelphia, Pa., Mayor, 1855 [Robert T. Conrad]. *Message of Robert T. Conrad, Mayor of the City of Philadelphia, with Accompanying Documents*. Philadelphia: Crissy and Markley, 1855.

Philadelphia, Pa., Mayor, 1859 [Alexander Henry]. *First Annual Message of Alexander Henry, Mayor of the City of Philadelphia, with Accompanying Documents, January 27, 1859*. Philadelphia: Inquirer Printing Office, 1859.

Philadelphia, Pa., People's Executive Committee. *The Municipal Government Examined by Its Own Records*. Philadelphia, 1858.

Philadelphia, Pa., Select Council. *Journal of the Select Council of the City of Philadelphia*. Philadelphia: Crissy and Markley, 1858.

Pittsburgh, Pa., Borough and Council Papers, 1789–1817. Microfilm. Pennsylvania State Archives, Harrisburg.

Portland, Me. *Additional By-Laws of the Town of Portland*. 1818. Early American Imprints, 2d ser., no. 45391.

Portsmouth, Va. Records of the Town and City of Portsmouth. Vol. 1, 1796–1821. Microfilm, Virginia State Library and Archives.

Royal Commission on Market Rights and Tolls. *Final Report of the Commissioners. Presented to Both Houses of Parliament by Command of Her Majesty*. Vol. 11. London: Eyre and Spottiswoode, 1891.

St. Francisville, La. "An Ordinance, Providing for the Erection of a Market House and Establishing a Regular Market in and for the Town of St. Francisville." *Louisianian* (1:15), October 9, 1819.

St. Louis, Mo. St. Louis Ordinances, etc., 1823–1903. Scrapbook. Missouri Historical Society Library.

Trenton, N.J. *Acts and Ordinances of the City of Trenton*. 1799. Early American Imprints, 1st ser., no. 35896.

U.S. Department of Agriculture, Commissioner of Agriculture [Horace Capron]. "The Market Systems of the Country, Their Usages and Abuses." In *Report of the Commissioner of Agriculture in the Year 1870*, 241–254. Washington, D.C.: Government Printing Office, 1871.

U.S. Department of Agriculture, Commissioner of Agriculture [Frederick Watts]. *Report of the Commissioner of Agriculture for the Year 1871*. Washington, D.C.: Government Printing Office, 1872.

Selected Bibliography

———. *Report of the Commissioner of Agriculture for the Year 1872*. Washington, D.C.: Government Printing Office, 1874.

U.S. Department of Commerce, Bureau of the Census [Samuel L. Rogers, director]. *Municipal Markets in Cities Having a Population of Over 30,000*. Washington, D.C.: Government Printing Office, 1919.

U.S. Department of Commerce and Labor, Bureau of Manufactures. *Municipal Markets and Slaughterhouses in Europe*, Special Consular Reports, vol. 42, pt. 3. Washington, D.C.,: Government Printing Office, 1910.

U.S. Department of Interior, Census Office. *Report on the Social Statistics of Cities*. Comp. George E. Waring Jr. Washington, D.C.: Government Printing Office, 1886.

U.S. Senate Committee on the District of Columbia. *Papers relating to the Washington Market Company*. 60th Cong., 1st sess., S. Doc. 495. Washington, D.C., 1908.

U.S. Senate Committee on Public Buildings and Grounds. *Report of Justin Morrill on the Washington Market Company*. 43d Cong., 1st sess., June 13, 1874, S. Rept. 449. Washington, D.C., 1874.

Washington, D.C. *Acts of the Corporation of the City of Washington*, 11 vols. Washington, D.C., 1805–1816. Continued as *Laws of the Corporation of the City of Washington*, 45 vols., Washington, D.C., 1817–1862.

———. *Journal of the Council of the City of Washington*. Washington, D.C.: Gideon and Pearson, 1864–1871.

———. *Report of the Commissioners of the District of Columbia*. Washington, D.C.: Government Printing Office, 1891, 1902.

West Chester, Pa. Borough Council Minutes, 1802–1885. Microfilm. Pennsylvania State Archives, Harrisburg.

Wilmington, Del. *The Ordinances of the City of Wilmington*. Wilmington: Johnson and Chandler, 1849.

York, Pa. Borough Council Journal, 1883–1887. Microfilm. Pennsylvania State Archives, Harrisburg.

Journals and Travelers' Accounts

Arfwedson, C. D. *The United States and Canada, in 1832, 1833, and 1834.*, Vol. 1. London: Richard Bentley, 1834.

Baily, Francis. *Journal of a Tour in Unsettled Parts of North America in 1796 and 1797*. Ed. Jack D. L. Holmes. Carbondale: Southern Illinois University Press, 1969.

Birkbeck, Morris. *Notes on a Journey in America, from the Coast of Virginia to the Territory of Illinois*. London: Ridgway, 1818.

Blane, William Newnham. *An Excursion through the United States and Canada during the Years 1822–23*. London: Baldwin, Cradock, and Joy, 1824.

Brissot de Warville, J. P. *New Travels in the United States of America, 1788*. Translated by Mara Soceanu Vamos and Durand Echeverria. Cambridge: Belknap Press of Harvard University Press, 1964.

Selected Bibliography

Burke, Emily P. *Pleasure and Pain: Reminiscences of Georgia in the 1840's.* 1850. Reprint, Savannah, Ga.: Beehive Press, 1978.

Carter, Edward C., II, ed. *The Virginia Journals of Benjamin Henry Latrobe, 1795–1798.* Vol. 1. New Haven: Yale University Press, 1977.

Carter, Edward C., II, John C. Van Horne, and Charles E. Brownell, eds. *Latrobe's View of America, 1795–1820.* New Haven: Yale University Press, 1985.

Castiglioni, Luigi. *Luigi Castiglioni's Viaggio-Travels in the United States of North America, 1785–1787.* Translated and edited by Antonio Pace. Syracuse, N.Y.: Syracuse University Press, 1983.

Cutler, Parker, and Julia Perkins Cutler, eds. *Life Journals and Correspondence of Rev. Manasseh Cutler.* Athens: Ohio University Press, 1987.

Davies, Benjamin. *Some Account of the City of Philadelphia, the Capital of Pennsylvania.* Philadelphia: Richard Fowell, 1794.

Davison, G. M. *The Traveller's Guide through the Middle and Northern States, and the Provinces of Canada.* 7th ed. Saratoga Springs, N.Y.: G. M. Davison; New York: S. S. and W. Wood, 1837.

Duché, Jacob. *Caspipina's Letters: Containing Observations on a Variety of Subjects, Literary, Moral, and Religious.* Vol. 1. London: R. Cruttwell, 1777.

Goodrich, C. A. *The Family Tourist: A Visit to the Principal Cities of the Western Continent; Embracing an Account of Their Situation, Origin, Plan, Extent, Their Inhabitants, Manners, Customs, and Amusements, ...* Philadelphia: J. W. Bradley, 1848.

Janson, Charles William. *The Stranger in America: Containing Observations Made during a Long Residence in That Country of the Genius, Manners and Customs of the People of the United States.* London: James Cundee, 1807.

Melish, John. *Travels in the United States of America, in the Years 1806 and 1807, and 1809, 1810, and 1811.* Vol. 1. Philadelphia: Thomas and George Palmer, 1812.

Miranda, Francisco de. *The New Democracy in America: Travels of Francisco Miranda in the United States, 1783–84.* Translated by Judson P. Wood, edited by John S. Ezell. Norman: University of Oklahoma Press, 1963.

Mitchill, Samuel Latham. *The Picture of New-York, and Stranger's Guide through the Commercial Emporium of the United States.* New York: A. T. Goodrich, 1818.

Paxton, John Adams. *The Stranger's Guide: An Alphabetical List of All the Wards, Streets, Roads, Lanes, Alleys, Avenues, Courts, Wharves, Ship Yards, Public Buildings, etc. in the City and Suburbs of Philadelphia.* Philadelphia: Edward Parker, 1811.

Pilmore, Joseph. *The Journal of Joseph Pilmore, Methodist Itinerant: For the Years August 1, 1769 to January 2, 1774.* Edited by Frederick E. Masur and Howard T. Maag. Philadelphia: Historical Society of the Philadelphia Annual Conference of the United Methodist Church, 1969.

Quincy, Josiah, Jr. "Journal of Josiah Quincy, Jr. 1773." In *Massachusetts Historical Society Proceedings,* June 1916, 475–478.

Royall, Anne Newport. *Sketches of History, Life, and Manners in the United States.* New Haven, Conn., 1826.

Selected Bibliography

Strahan, Edward [pseud. Earl Shinn]. *A Century After: Picturesque Glimpses of Philadelphia and Pennsylvania*. Philadelphia: Allen, Lane, and Scott and J. W. Lauderbach, 1875.

Newspapers and Periodicals

Alexandria Advertiser and Commercial Intelligencer
American Farmer
Baltimore Evening Post
The Bee, Washington, D.C.
The Brooklyn Daily Eagle Almanac
The Cook, New York
Daily Patriot, Harrisburg
The Evening News, Harrisburg
Evening Star, New York
Frank Leslie's
Georgetown Gazette and Commercial Advertiser
Gleason's Pictorial Drawing-Room Companion
The Graphic, Chicago
The Louisianian, St. Francisville
The New World
New York Times
Niles' Weekly Register
Patriot, Boston
Patriot Union, Harrisburg
The Pennsylvania Magazine
The Pennsylvanian
Portfolio, Philadelphia
Public Ledger, Philadelphia
St. Francisville Democrat, Louisiana
Sunday Dispatch, Philadelphia
The Weekly Herald, New York

SECONDARY SOURCES
Books

Agnew, Jean-Christophe. *Worlds Apart: The Market and the Theater in Anglo-American Thought, 1550–1750*. New York: Cambridge University Press, 1986.
Albion, Robert G. *The Rise of New York Port*. New York: Charles Scribner's Sons, 1939.
Alexander, David. *Retailing in England during the Industrial Revolution*. London: University of London, Athlone Press, 1970.
Anderson, B. L., and A. J. H. Latham, eds. *The Market in History*. London: Croom Helm, 1986.

Selected Bibliography

Atherton, Louise E. *The Southern Country Store, 1800–1860.* Baton Rouge: Louisiana State University Press, 1949.

Bakhtin, Mikhail Mikhailovich. *Rabelais and His World.* Translated by Helene Iswolsky. Cambridge: MIT Press, 1968.

Beall, Karen. *Kaufrufe und Strassenhändler: Cries and Itinerant Trades.* Hamburg: Hauswedell, 1975.

Benes, Peter, ed. *Foodways in the Northeast.* Annual Proceedings, Dublin Seminar for New England Folklife, 1982. Boston: Boston University, 1984.

Berjman, Sonia, and José Fiszelew. *El Abasto: Un barrio y un mercado.* (El Abasto: A neighborhood and a market). Buenos Aires: Corregidor, 1999.

Biesenthal, Linda. *To Market, to Market: The Public Market Tradition in Canada.* Toronto: Peter Martin, 1980.

Billon, Frederick L. *Annals of St. Louis in Its Territorial Days, from 1804 to 1821.* St. Louis: Author, 1888.

Black, Mary. *Old New York in Early Photographs, 1853–1901.* New York: Dover, 1973.

Bowser, Barbara. "'Flies in the Market House': The Fresh Meat Market in Salem, North Carolina." In *Common Frontiers,* edited by Donna R. Braden and Susan Gangwere McCabe, 154–159. Proceedings, vol. 19. North Bloomfield, Ohio: Association for Living Historical Farms and Agricultural Museums, 1997.

Bridenbaugh, Carl. *Cities in Revolt: Urban Life in America, 1743–1776.* New York: Alfred A. Knopf, 1955.

———. *Cities in the Wilderness: The First Century of Urban Life in America, 1625–1742.* London: Oxford University Press, 1938.

———. *Peter Harrison: First American Architect.* Chapel Hill: University of North Carolina Press, 1949.

Bridges, Amy. *A City in the Republic: Antebellum New York and the Origins of Machine Politics.* 1984. Reprint, Ithaca: Cornell University Press, 1987.

Brown, Abram English. *Faneuil Hall and Faneuil Hall Market.* Boston: Lee and Shepard, 1900.

Brown, Gregory J. "Distributing Meat and Fish in Eighteenth-Century Virginia: The Documentary Evidence for the Existence of Markets in Early Tidewater Towns." Typescript. Colonial Williamsburg Foundation, Department of Archaeological Research, July 1988.

Brown, Jonathan. *The English Market Town: A Social and Economic History, 1750–1914.* Ramsbury, Marlborough, Wiltshire: Crowood Press, 1986.

Bucher, Douglas G., and W. Richard Wheeler, *A Neat Plain Modern Stile: Philip Hooker and His Contemporaries, 1796–1836.* Exhibition catalog, Emerson Gallery, Hamilton College. Amherst: University of Massachusetts Press, 1993.

Buder, Stanley. *Pullman: An Experiment in Industrial Order and Community Planning, 1880–1930.* New York: Oxford University Press, 1967.

Calabi, Donatella, ed. *Fabbriche, piazze, mercati: La città italiana nel Rinascimento* (Buildings, squares, markets: The Italian city in the Renaissance). Rome: Officina Edizioni, 1997.

Selected Bibliography

———. *Il mercato e la città: Piazze, strade, architettura d'Europea in età moderna* (The market and the city: Squares, streets, and architecture in early modern Europe). Venice: Marsilio Editori, 1993.

Calhoun, Jeanne A., et al. *Meat in Due Season: Preliminary Investigations of Marketing Practices in Colonial Charleston.* Archaeological Contributions 9. Charleston, S.C.: Charleston Museum, 1984.

Cameron, James R. *The Public Service of Josiah Quincy, Jr., 1802–1882.* Quincy, Mass.: Quincy Co-operative Bank, 1964.

Carter, Harold. *An Introduction to Urban Historical Geography.* London: Edward Arnold, 1983.

Città di Bra. *Le "agli" del mercato in provincia di Cuneo* (Market halls in the province of Cuneo). Bra: Ministero Beni Culturali e Ambientali, Soprintendenza per i Beni Ambientali e Architettonici del Piemonte, Politecnico di Torino, 1992.

Clark, Christopher. *The Roots of Rural Capitalism: Western Massachusetts, 1780–1860.* Ithaca: Cornell University Press, 1991.

Cohen, William B. *Urban Government and the Rise of the French City: Five Municipalities in the Nineteenth Century.* New York: St. Martin's Press, 1998.

Cooledge, Harold N., Jr. *Samuel Sloan: Architect of Philadelphia, 1815–1884.* Philadelphia: University of Pennsylvania Press, 1986.

Cooper, Constance J. *To Market, to Market, in Wilmington: King Street and Beyond.* Wilmington, Del.: Cedar Tree Press, 1992.

Corbett, Theodore, and Cynthia Corbett. "New York's Public Markets, 1680–1850." In *Foodways in the Northeast,* edited by Peter Benes, 142–43. Dublin Seminar for New England Folklife, Annual Proceedings, 1982. Boston: Boston University, 1984.

Corrigan, Mary Beth. "'It's a Family Affair': Buying Freedom in the District of Columbia, 1850–1860." In *Working toward Freedom: Slave Society and Domestic Economy in the American South,* edited by Larry E. Hudson Jr., 163–191. Rochester, N.Y.: University of Rochester Press, 1994.

———. "The Ties That Bind: The Pursuit of Community and Freedom among Slaves and Free Blacks in the District of Columbia, 1800–1860." In *Southern City, National Ambition: The Growth of Early Washington, D.C., 1800–1860,* edited by Howard Gillette Jr., 69–90. Washington, D.C.: George Washington University, Center for Washington Area Studies, 1995.

Cosgrove, Denis. "Spectacle and Society: Landscape as Theater in Premodern and Postmodern Cities." In *Understanding Ordinary Landscapes,* edited by Paul Groth and Todd W. Bressi, 99–110. New Haven: Yale University Press, 1997.

Cotter, John L., Daniel G. Roberts, and Michael Parrington. *The Buried Past: An Archaeological History of Philadelphia.* Philadelphia: University of Pennsylvania Press, 1992.

Cronon, William. *Nature's Metropolis: Chicago and the Great West.* 1991. Reprint, New York: W. W. Norton, 1992.

Cunningham, Noble E., Jr., ed. *The Early Republic, 1789–1828.* New York: Harper Torchbooks, 1968.

Selected Bibliography

Curry, Leonard P. *The Corporate City: The American City as a Political Entity, 1800–1850.* Westport, Conn.: Greenwood Press, 1997.

Cutler, William M., III, and Howard Gillette Jr., eds. *The Divided Metropolis: Social and Spatial Dimensions of Philadelphia, 1800–1975.* Westport, Conn.: Greenwood Press, 1980.

Davis, Natalie Zemon. *Society and Culture in Early Modern France.* Stanford, Calif.: Stanford University Press, 1975.

Davis, Susan G. *Parades and Power: Street Theater in Nineteenth-Century Philadelphia.* Philadelphia: Temple University Press, 1986.

De Ligt, L. *Fairs and Markets in the Roman Empire: Economic and Social Aspects of Periodic Trade in a Pre-industrial Society.* Dutch Monographs on Ancient History and Archaeology, vol. 11. Amsterdam: J. C. Geiben, 1993.

Di Macco, Sergio. *L'architettura dei mercati: Tecniche dell'edilizia annonaria* (The architecture of markets: Techniques for the buildings of provisions). Rome: Edizioni Kappa, 1993.

Dolan, J. R. *The Yankee Peddlers of Early America.* New York: Bramhall House, 1964.

Downing, Antoinette F., and Vincent J. Scully Jr. *The Architectural Heritage of Newport, Rhode Island, 1640–1915.* 1952. 2d ed. rev. New York: Clarkson N. Potter, 1967.

Eastman, Frank M. *A Treatise on the Law relating to Private Corporations in Pennsylvania,* 2 vols. Philadelphia: George T. Bisel, 1903.

Farmer, Charles J. *In the Absence of Towns: Settlement and Country Trade in Southside Virginia, 1730–1800.* Lanham, Md.: Rowman and Littlefield, 1993.

Fogelson, Robert M. *America's Armories: Architecture, Society, and Public Order.* Cambridge: Harvard University Press, 1989.

Gilje, Paul A. *The Road to Mobocracy: Popular Disorder in New York City, 1763–1834.* Chapel Hill: University of North Carolina Press for the Institute of Early American Culture, 1987.

Gillette, Howard, Jr. *Between Justice and Beauty: Race, Planning, and the Failure of Urban Policy in Washington, D.C.* Baltimore: Johns Hopkins University Press, 1995.

———. "The Emergence of the Modern Metropolis: Philadelphia in the Age of Its Consolidation." In *The Divided Metropolis: Social and Spatial Dimensions of Philadelphia, 1800–1975,* edited by William M. Cutler III and Howard Gillette Jr., 3–25. Westport, Conn.: Greenwood Press, 1980.

———, ed. *Southern City, National Ambition: The Growth of Early Washington, D.C., 1800–1860.* Washington, D.C.: George Washington University, Center for Washington Area Studies, 1995.

Goodwin, Arthur E. *Markets: Public and Private.* Seattle: Montgomery, 1929.

Gould, Elizabeth Barrett. *From Fort to Port: An Architectural History of Mobile, Alabama, 1711–1918.* Tuscaloosa: University of Alabama Press, 1988.

Green, Bryan Clark. "The Structure of Civic Exchange: Market Houses in Early Virginia." In *Shaping Communities: Perspectives in Vernacular Architecture, VI,* edited by Carter L. Hudgins and Elizabeth Collins Cromley, 189–203. Knoxville: University of Tennessee Press, 1997.

Selected Bibliography

Green, Constance McLaughlin. *Washington: A History of the Capital, 1800–1950.* 1962. Reprint, Princeton: Princeton University Press, 1976.

Harding, Anneliese. *John Lewis Krimmel: Genre Artist of the Early Republic.* Winterthur, Del.: Henry Francis du Pont Winterthur Museum, 1994.

Hartog, Hendrik. *Public Property and Private Power: The Corporation of the City of New York in American Law, 1730–1870.* Chapel Hill: University of North Carolina Press, 1983.

Hayden, Dolores. *The Power of Place: Urban Landscapes as Public History.* Cambridge: MIT Press, 1995.

Henretta, James. *The Origins of American Capitalism: Collected Essays.* Boston: Northeastern University Press, 1991.

Herbert, Gilbert. *Pioneers of Prefabrication: The British Contribution in the Nineteenth Century.* Baltimore: Johns Hopkins University Press, 1978.

Herrmann, Wolfgang, ed. *In What Style Should We Build? The German Debate on Architectural Style.* Santa Monica, Calif.: Getty Center for the History of Art and the Humanities, 1992.

Highsmith, Carol M., and James L. Holton, *Reading Terminal and Market: Philadelphia's Historic Gateway and Grand Convention Center.* Washington, D.C.: Chelsea, 1994.

Hilliard, Sam Bowers. *Hog Meat and Hoecake: Food Supply in the Old South, 1840–1860.* Carbondale: Southern Illinois University Press, 1972.

Hines, Mary Anne, Gordon Marshall, and William Woys Weaver. *The Larder Invaded: Reflections on Three Centuries of Philadelphia Food and Drink.* Philadelphia: Library Company of Philadelphia and Historical Society of Pennsylvania, 1987.

Hodges, Graham Russell. *New York City Cartmen, 1667–1850.* New York: New York University Press, 1986.

Hoffmann, Donald. *The Architecture of John Wellborn Root.* Baltimore: Johns Hopkins University Press, 1973.

Homberger, Eric. *Scenes from the Life of a City: Corruption and Conscience in Old New York.* New Haven: Yale University Press, 1994.

Horwitz, Morton J. *The Transformation of American Law, 1780–1860.* Cambridge: Harvard University Press, 1977.

Jackson, Kenneth T., ed. *The Encyclopedia of New York City.* New Haven: Yale University Press; New York: New-York Historical Society, 1995.

Johannesen, Eric. *Cleveland Architecture, 1876–1976.* Cleveland, Ohio: Western Reserve Historical Society, 1979.

Kaplan, Steven Laurence. *Provisioning Paris: Merchants and Millers in the Grain and Flour Trade during the Eighteenth Century.* Ithaca: Cornell University Press, 1984.

Kennedy, Lawrence W. *Planning the City upon a Hill: Boston since 1630.* Amherst: University of Massachusetts Press, 1992.

Kostof, Spiro. *The City Assembled: The Elements of Urban Form through History.* Boston: Little, Brown, 1992.

———. *The City Shaped: Urban Patterns and Meanings through History.* Boston: Little, Brown, 1991.

Kulikoff, Allan. *The Agrarian Origins of American Capitalism.* Charlottesville: University Press of Virginia, 1992.

Lemoine, Bertrand. *Les Halles de Paris.* Paris: Équerre, 1980.

Lhamon, W. T., Jr. "Dancing for Eels at Catherine [*sic*] Market." In *Raising Cain: Blackface Performance from Jim Crow to Hip Hop.* Cambridge: Harvard University Press, 1998.

Linder, Marc, and Lawrence Z. Zacharias. *Of Cabbages and Kings County: Agriculture and the Formation of Modern Brooklyn.* Iowa City: University of Iowa Press, 1999.

Longstreth, Richard. *City Center to Regional Mall: Architecture, the Automobile, and Retailing in Los Angeles, 1920–1950.* Cambridge: MIT Press, 1997.

———. *The Drive-in, the Supermarket, and the Transformation of Commercial Space in Los Angeles, 1914–1941.* Cambridge: MIT Press, 1999.

———. "Innovation without Paradigm: The Many Creators of the Drive-in Market." In *Images of an American Land,* edited by Thomas Carter, 231–264. Albuquerque: University of New Mexico Press, 1997.

———. "The Perils of a Parkless Town." In *The Car and the City: The Automobile, the Built Environment, and Daily Urban Life,* edited by Martin Wachs and Margaret Crawford, 141–153. Ann Arbor: University of Michigan Press, 1992.

Lounsbury, Carl, ed. *An Illustrated Glossary of Early Southern Architecture and Landscape.* New York: Oxford University Press, 1994.

Loyd, William H. *The Early Courts of Pennsylvania.* Boston: Boston Book Company, 1910.

Markus, Thomas A. *Buildings and Power: Freedom and Control in the Origin of Modern Building Types.* London: Routledge, 1993.

Masters, Betty R. *The Public Markets of the City of London Surveyed by William Leybourn in 1677.* Publication 117. London: London Topographical Society, 1974.

Mayo, James M. *The American Grocery Store: The Business Evolution of an Architectural Space.* Westport, Conn.: Greenwood Press, 1993.

Meyer, Balthasar Henry. *History of Transportation in the United States before 1860.* 1917. Reprint, New York: Peter Smith, 1948.

McNamara, Brooks. *Day of Jubilee: The Great Age of Public Celebrations in New York, 1788–1909.* New Brunswick, N.J.: Rutgers University Press, 1997.

Modigliani, Anna. *Mercati, botteghe e spazi di commercio a Roma tra medioevo ed età moderna* (Markets, shops and commercial spaces in Rome from the medieval to the modern era). Rome: Roma nel Rinascimento, 1997.

Moore, Richard Vincent. *L'architettura del mercato coperto: Dal mercato all'ipermercato* (The architecture of the covered market: From the market to the supermarket). Rome: Officina Edizioni, 1997.

Morgan, George H. *Annals, Comprising Memoirs, Incidents and Statistics of Harrisburg.* Harrisburg: George A. Brooks, 1858.

Mund, Vernon A. *Open Markets: An Essential of Free Enterprise.* New York: Harper, 1948.

Mushkat, Jerome. *Fernando Wood: A Political Biography.* Kent, Ohio: Kent State University Press, 1990.

Selected Bibliography

Nash, Gary B. *Forging Freedom: The Formation of Philadelphia's Black Community, 1720–1840.* Cambridge: Harvard University Press, 1988.

Nevins, Allan. *Abram S. Hewitt: With Some Account of Peter Cooper.* New York: Octagon Books, 1967.

Novak, William J. *The People's Welfare: Law and Regulation in Nineteenth-Century America.* Chapel Hill: University of North Carolina Press, 1996.

O'Gorman, James F., Jeffrey A. Cohen, George E. Thomas, and G. Holmes Perkins. *Drawing toward Building: Philadelphia Architectural Graphics, 1732–1986.* Philadelphia: University of Pennsylvania Press for the Pennsylvania Academy of the Fine Arts, 1986.

O'Neil, David K. *An Illustrated History of Reading Terminal Maarket.* Philadelphia: Camino Books, in press.

Pevsner, Nikolaus. *A History of Building Types.* Bollingen Series. Princeton: Princeton University Press, 1976.

Pinkney, David H. *Napoleon III and the Rebuilding of Paris.* 1958, Reprint, Princeton: Princeton University Press, 1972.

Powell, Jehu Z., ed. *History of Cass County Indiana.* Vol. 1. Chicago: Lewis, 1913.

Powell, Mary Gregory. *The History of Old Alexandria, Virginia, from July 13, 1749 to May 24, 1861.* Richmond: William Byrd Press, 1928.

Prowell, George R. *History of York County Pennsylvania,* vol. 1. Chicago: J. H. Beers, 1907.

Reps, John W. *The Making of Urban America.* Princeton: Princeton University Press, 1965.

Rock, Howard B. *Artisans of the New Republic; The Tradesmen of New York City in the Age of Jefferson.* New York: New York University Press, 1979.

Root, Edward W. *Philip Hooker: A Contribution to the Study of the Renaissance in America.* New York: Charles Scribners' Sons, 1929.

Rosenzweig, Roy, and Elizabeth Blackmar. *The Park and the People: A History of Central Park.* Ithaca: Cornell University Press, 1992.

Rothenberg, Winifred Barr. *From Market-Places to a Market Economy: The Transformation of Rural Massachusetts, 1750–1850.* Chicago: University of Chicago Press, 1992.

Rothman, David J. *The Discovery of the Asylum: Social Order and Disorder in the New Republic.* Boston: Little, Brown, 1971.

Ryan, Mary P. *Civic Wars: Democracy and Public Life in the American City during the Nineteenth Century.* Berkeley: University of California Press, 1997.

———. *Women in Public: Between Banners and Ballots, 1825–1880.* Baltimore: Johns Hopkins University Press, 1990.

Schmiechen, James, and Kenneth Carls. *The British Market Hall: A Social and Architectural History.* New Haven: Yale University Press, 1999.

Schuyler, David. *The New Urban Landscape: The Redefinition of City Form in Nineteenth-Century America.* Baltimore: Johns Hopkins University Press, 1986.

Scola, Roger. *Feeding the Victorian City: The Food Supply of Manchester, 1770–1870.* Manchester: Manchester University Press, 1992.

Scott, Pamela, and Antionette J. Lee. *Buildings of the District of Columbia.* New York: Oxford University Press, 1993.

Selected Bibliography

Sellers, Charles. *The Market Revolution: Jacksonian America, 1815–1846*. New York: Oxford University Press, 1991.

Smith, Barbara Clark. "Markets, Streets, and Stores: Contested Terrain in Pre-industrial Boston." In *Autre temps autre espace*, edited by Elise Marienstras and Barbara Karsky, 181–197. Nancy: Presses Universitaires de Nancy, 1986.

Snyder, John J., Jr. *Lancaster Architecture, 1719–1927*. Lancaster, Pa.: Historical Preservation Trust of Lancaster County, 1979.

Spann, Edward K. *The New Metropolis: New York City, 1840–1857*. New York: Columbia University Press, 1981.

Stansell, Christine. *City of Women: Sex and Class in New York, 1789–1860*. New York: Alfred A. Knopf, 1986.

Steiner, Frances H. *French Iron Architecture*. Studies in the Fine Arts: Architecture 3. Ann Arbor: UMI Research Press, 1984.

Stoll, Steven. *The Fruits of Natural Advantage: Making the Industrial Countryside in California*. Berkeley: University of California Press, 1998.

Stott, Richard B. *Workers in the Metropolis: Class, Ethnicity, and Youth in Antebellum New York City*. Ithaca: Cornell University Press, 1990.

Tangires, Helen. "Celebrating Nature's Bounty: Butcher Parades in Nineteenth-Century New York and Philadelphia." In *Food and Celebration: From Fasting to Feasting*, ed. Patricia Lysaght, 393–400. Ljubljana: Zalozba, 2002.

Tatman, Sandra L., and Roger W. Moss, *Biographical Dictionary of Philadelphia Architects: 1700–1930*. Boston: G. K. Hall, 1985.

Taylor, Philip [market master, city of St. Louis], comp. "A Brief History of the Public Markets and Private Markets Referred to as Public Markets in the City of St. Louis, Missouri, from the Time of Their Inception in 1764 through the Present Day." Typescript, January 1961. Missouri Historical Society Library.

Teaford, Jon C. *The Municipal Revolution in America: Origins of Modern Urban Government, 1650–1825*. Chicago: University of Chicago Press, 1975.

———. *The Unheralded Triumph: City Government in America, 1870–1900*. Baltimore: Johns Hopkins University Press, 1984.

Thompson, E. P. *Customs in Common*. New York: New Press. 1991.

Tilly, Charles. "Food Supply and the Public Order in Modern Europe." In *The Formation of National States in Western Europe*, edited by Charles Tilly, 380–455. Princeton: Princeton University Press, 1975.

Trachtenberg, Alan. *The Incorporation of America: Culture and Society in the Gilded Age*. New York: Hill and Wang, 1982.

Upton, Dell. "Another City: The Urban Cultural Landscape in the Early Republic." In *Everyday Life in the Early Republic*, edited by Catherine E. Hutchins, 61–117. Winterthur, Del.: Henry Francis du Pont Winterthur Museum, 1994.

———. "The Master Street of the World: The Levee." In *Streets: Critical Perspectives on Urban Space*, edited by Zeynep Celik, Diane Favro, and Richard Ingersoll, 277–288. Berkeley: University of California Press, 1994.

Selected Bibliography

Wade, Richard C. *The Urban Frontier: Pioneer Life in Early Pittsburgh, Cincinnati, Lexington, Louisville, and St. Louis.* Chicago: University of Chicago Press, 1959.

Warner, Sam Bass, Jr. *The Private City: Philadelphia in Three Periods of Its Growth.* 1968. 2d ed. Philadelphia: University of Pennsylvania Press, 1989.

Wilentz, Sean. *Chants Democratic: New York City and the Rise of the American Working Class, 1788–1850.* New York: Oxford University Press, 1984.

Wilson, Samuel, Jr. *The Vieux Carré, New Orleans: Its Plan, Its Growth, Its Architecture.* New Orleans: Bureau of Governmental Research, 1968.

Wilson, William H. *The City Beautiful Movement.* Baltimore: Johns Hopkins University Press, 1989.

Zimmerman, Catherine McCurdy. "Market Houses of Harrisburg." Typescript, Dauphin County Historical Society, February 17, 1964.

Zurier, Rebecca. *The American Firehouse: An Architectural and Social History.* New York: Abbeville Press, 1982.

Articles

Abrahams, Roger D. "The Discovery of Marketplace Culture." *Intellectual History Newsletter* 10 (April 1988): 23–32.

Agnew, Jean-Christophe. "The Threshold of Exchange: Speculations on the Market." *Radical History Review* 21 (fall 1979): 99–118.

Bluestone, Daniel M. "'The Pushcart Evil': Peddlers, Merchants, and New York City's Streets, 1890–1940." *Journal of Urban History* 18 (November 1991): 68–92.

Bogin, Ruth. "Petitioning and the New Moral Economy of Post-Revolutionary America." *William and Mary Quarterly* 45 (July 1988): 391–425.

Boydston, Jeanne. "The Woman Who Wasn't There: Women's Market Labor and the Transition to Capitalism in the United States." *Journal of the Early Republic* 16 (summer 1996): 183–206.

Byrne, Daniel, and Stuart Plattner. "Ethnicity at Soulard Farmers Market since 1930." *Bulletin of the Missouri Historical Society* 36 (April 1980): 174–181.

Burnstein, Daniel. "The Vegetable Man Cometh: Political and Moral Choices in Pushcart Policy in Progressive Era New York City." *New York History* 77 (January 1996): 47–84.

Cady, John Hutchins. "The Providence Market House and Its Neighborhood." *Rhode Island History* 11 (October 1952): 97–116.

Evenson, Norma. "The Assassination of Les Halles." *Journal of the Society of Architectural Historians* 32 (December 1973): 308–315.

Friedmann, Karen. "Victualling Colonial Boston." *Agricultural History* 47 (July 1973): 189–205.

Gilchrist, Agnes Addison. "Market Houses in High Street." *Transactions of the American Philosophical Society* 43 (1953): 304–312.

Gomes, Geraldo. "Artistic Intentions in Iron Architecture." *Journal of Decorative and Propaganda Arts, 1875–1945* 21 (1995): 87–106.

Selected Bibliography

Gouglas, Sean. "Produce and Protection: Covent Garden Market, the Socioeconomic Elite, and the Downtown Core in London, Ontario, 1843–1915." *Urban History Review/Revue d'Histoire Urbaine* 25 (October 1996): 3–18.

Heisey, M. Luther. "The Famed Markets of Lancaster." *Papers Read before the Lancaster County Historical Society* 53, no. 1 (1949): 1–31.

Henretta, James. "The Strange Birth of Liberal America: Michael Hoffman and the New York Constitution of 1846." *New York History* 77 (April 1996): 151–176.

Higgs, Malcolm. "The Exported Iron Buildings of Andrew Handyside and Co. of Derby." *Journal of the Society of Architectural Historians* 29 (May 1970): 175–180.

Hild, Theodore. "The Galena Market House." *Material Culture* 32 (fall 2000): 1–26.

Horn, Walter. "On the Origins of the Medieval Bay System." *Journal of the Society of Architectural Historians* 17 (1958): 2–23.

Lees, Lynn Hollen. "Urban Public Space and Imagined Communities in the 1980s and 1990s." *Journal of Urban History* 20 (August 1994): 443–465.

Leonard, Ira M. "The Rise and Fall of the American Republican Party in New York City, 1843–1845." *New-York Historical Society Quarterly* 50 (April 1966): 150–192.

Lohmeier, Andrew. "'Bürgerliche Gesellschaft' and Consumer Interests: The Berlin Public Market Hall Reform, 1867–1891." *Business History Review* 73 (spring 1999): 91–113.

Mayo, James M. "The American Public Market." *Journal of Architectural Education* 45 (November 1991): 41–57.

McCarthy, Michael. "The Philadelphia Consolidation of 1854: A Reappraisal." *Pennsylvania Magazine of History and Biography* 110 (October 1986): 531–548.

Miller, Roger, and Joseph Siry. "The Emerging Suburb: West Philadelphia, 1850–1880." *Pennsylvania History* 46 (April 1980): 99–114.

Novak, William J. "Public Economy and the Well-Ordered Market: Law and Economic Regulation in Nineteenth-Century America." *Law and Social Inquiry* 18 (winter 1993): 1–32.

Platt, Harold L. "The Stillbirth of Urban Politics in the Reconstruction South: Houston, Texas as a Test Case." *Houston Review: History and Culture of the Gulf Coast* 4 (summer 1982): 54–74.

Rockman, Seth. "Women's Labor, Gender Ideology, and Working-Class Households in Early Republic Baltimore." *Explorations in Early American Culture.* Supplement to *Pennsylvania History* 66 (1999): 174–200.

Ryan, Mary P. "'A Laudable Pride in the Whole of Us': City Halls and Civic Materialism." *American Historical Review* 105 (October 2000): 1131–1170.

Sauder, Robert A. "Municipal Markets in New Orleans." *Journal of Cultural Geography* 2 (fall–winter 1981): 82–95.

———. "The Origin and Spread of the Public Market System in New Orleans." *Louisiana History* 22 (summer 1981): 281–297.

Scardino, Barrie. "A Legacy of City Halls for Houston." *Houston Review: History and Culture of the Gulf Coast* 4 (fall 1982): 154–164.

Selected Bibliography

Schweitzer, Mary M. "The Spatial Organization of Federalist Philadelphia." *Journal of Interdisciplinary History* 24 (summer 1993): 31–57.

Shesgreen, Sean. "The Cries of London in the Seventeenth Century." *Papers of the Bibliographical Society of America* 86 (1992): 269–294.

Smith, Barbara Clark. "Food Rioters and the American Revolution." *William and Mary Quarterly* 51 (January 1994): 3–38.

Smith, David C., and Anne E. Bridges. "The Brighton Market: Feeding Nineteenth-Century Boston." *Agricultural History* 56 (January 1982): 3–21.

Tangires, Helen. "Contested Space: The Life and Death of Center Market." *Washington History* 7 (spring–summer 1995): 46–67.

———. "The Country Connection: Farmers Markets in the Public Eye." *Pennsylvania Heritage* 24 (fall 1998): 4–11.

———. "Feeding the Cities: Public Markets and Municipal Reform in the Progressive Era." *Prologue: Quarterly of the National Archives and Records Administration* 29 (spring 1997): 16–26.

Taylor, Jeremy. "Charles Fowler: Master of Markets." *Architectural Review* 135 (1964): 174–182.

Thompson, E. P. "The Moral Economy of the English Crowd in the Eighteenth Century." *Past and Present,* no. 50 (February 1971): 76–136.

Thompson, Victoria E. "Urban Renovation, Moral Regeneration: Domesticating the Halles in Second-Empire Paris." *French Historical Studies* 20 (winter 1997): 87–109.

Tinkcom, Margaret B. "The New Market in Second Street." *Pennsylvania Magazine of History and Biography* 82 (1955): 879–896.

Topham, Washington. "Centre Market and Vicinity." *Records of the Columbia Historical Society* 26 (1924): 1–87.

———. "Northern Liberty Market." *Records of the Columbia Historical Society* 24 (1920): 43–66.

Walmer, Charles E. "Farmers Markets of Harrisburg, Pennsylvania: Their Origin and History." *Dauphin County Historical Review* 5 (December 1956): 29–36.

White, Shane. "The Death of James Johnson." *American Quarterly* 51 (December 1999): 753–795.

———. "'It was a Proud Day': African Americans, Festivals, and Parades in the North, 1741–1834." *Journal of American History* 81 (June 1994): 13–50.

Theses and Dissertations

Andrews, Robert James. "A Survey of Forty-nine Pennsylvania Public Produce Markets." M.S. thesis, Pennsylvania State College, 1947.

Barshinger, Jay R. "The Early Market Houses of Southeastern Pennsylvania: Forms and Precedents." M.A. thesis, Pennsylvania State University, 1989.

———. "Provisions for Trade: The Market House in Southeastern Pennsylvania." Ph.D. diss., Pennsylvania State University, 1995.

Selected Bibliography

Beal, Thomas David. "Selling Gotham: The Retail Trade in New York City from the Public Market to Alexander T. Stewart's Marble Palace, 1625–1860." Ph.D. diss., State University of New York at Stony Brook, December 1998.

Escobar, Jesús Roberto. "The Great Theater of the World." In "The Plaza Mayor of Madrid: Architecture, Urbanism and the Imperial Capital, 1560–1640." Ph.D. diss., Princeton University, 1996.

Ewert, George Herman. "Old Times Will Come Again: The Municipal Market System of Mobile, Alabama, 1888–1901." M. A. thesis. University of South Alabama, 1993.

Green, Bryan Clark. "The Market House in Virginia, 1736–ca. 1860." M.A. thesis, University of Virginia, 1991.

Marion, Rene S. "The 'Dames de la Halle': Community and Authority in Early Modern Paris." Ph.D. diss., Johns Hopkins University, 1994.

Marti, Judith Ettinger. "Subsistence and the State: Municipal Government Policies and Urban Markets in Developing Nations, the Case of Mexico City and Guadalajara, 1877–1910." Ph.D. diss., University of California, Los Angeles, 1990.

Matthews, William Thomas. "By and for the Large Propertied Interests: The Dynamics of Local Government in Six Upper Canadian Towns during the Era of Commercial Capitalism, 1832–1860." Ph.D. diss., McMaster University, 1985.

Osborn, David Chilcoat. "A History of Lexington Market in Baltimore, Maryland." M.A. thesis, Pennsylvania State College, 1952.

Pyle, Jane. "The Public Markets of Mexico City." Ph.D. diss., University of Oregon, 1968.

Reinberger, Mark. "The Baltimore Exchange and Its Place in the Career of Henry Benjamin Latrobe." Ph.D. diss., Cornell University, 1988.

Thompson, Victoria E. "Gender, Class, and the Marketplace: Women's Work and the Transformation of the Public Sphere in Paris, 1825–1870." Ph.D. diss., University of Pennsylvania, 1993.

INDEX

Numbers in *italics* denote illustrations.

Index

Index

Index

market hours, 11, 12–14, 103, 175

market house, xvii, 26; construction, 42–43; financing, 31–34; floor plans, 43–46, 92, 136–37, 177–79, *178;* furnishings, 43–47; siting, xvii, 27–30, *28, 32,* 103; size, 45, 79–80, 81, 173–74; typology, xviii–xix, 34–42, 102, 130–32, 174–75, 193–200. *See also* brick; iron construction.

market house companies, xvii–xviii, 172, 205; in Chicago, 181; in New York City, 117, 140–44; in Pennsylvania, xix–xx, 117, 118–19, 122–32, 147–48; in Philadelphia, xix, 94, 95, 103, 108–10, 112–17, 119–22; in Washington, D.C., 176–79

marketing, direct, 152–53, 155, 193, 203

market laws, xvii, xix, 162; dissemination of, 23–24; and duties of clerk, 14–15; on forestalling, regrating, engrossing, 5–8; historic precedent for, 3–4, 103–4; for limits of market, 14; for maintaining peace and order, 11–12, 65, 186; for market days and hours, 12–13; and municipal corporation, 4–5; for protection of trades, 9–10; for public health, 15–17; and the state, 4–5, 203–204; for street vendors, 17–23; for weights and measures, 8–9

market peace (order), 11–12, 65, 186

marketplace culture, xix; in Europe, 48–49; features of, 48–68

market revenue, importance of to municipality, 5, 14–15, 78, 88–89, 151–52, 130, 162, 166, 170–72

market square, 27, 27, 119, 122–30, 176

market stall: assignment of, 45; auctioning of, 45, 71, 73–75, 81, 115; description of, 43–47, 114, 116–17, 178, 181, 182, 191; images of, *46, 179, 180*

market street, 29–31, 47, 98, 99

market town, xviii

Maryland, 4–5. *See also* Baltimore; Frederick

masonic halls, combined with markets, 34, 40

Massachusetts, 159–60; 203. *See also* Boston; Salem

Mayo, James, xviii

McKay, George E., 166–67

meat, 81, 89, 91, 107, 115, 121–22, 137–38, 151–55, 160, 188–89; bad, 17, 85, 153–54, 156, 162–64; dressed, 93, 157, 205; inspection of, 82, 84; wholesale trade in, 200. *See also* butchers; game, wild; livestock; slaughterhouses

meat shops, xvii, xix, 172, 205; in New York, 71–73, 75–93, 134, 153; in Newark, 154; in St. Louis, 168

Mechanicsburg, Pa., 130

Melish, John, 5

Mexico, 187

middlemen (commission and wholesale merchants), xvi, 102, 110–12, 134, 136, 141, 153–57, 161, 172, 174, 185, 204–5

Milan, 187

Miller, Cyrus C., 196–98

Miller, Lewis, *10, 16, 50, 59*

Milton, Pa., 130

Minnesota, 133; Duluth, 202; St. Paul, 167, 199

Miranda, Francisco de, 17, 64–65

Missouri, 133. *See also* St. Louis

Mitchill, Samuel Latham, 8, 53

Mobile, 30, 155–56, 170–72

Monroe, James, 43

Montreal, 133

moral economy: and butcher trade, 71, 78–81, 85, 93; challenges to, 110; history and features of, xvii, xx, 9–11, 23–25; persistence of, xvii, 3–4, 144, 151–52, 172, 205

municipal corporation, and rights to regulate markets: xvii, xix–xx, 4–5, 87, 88, 103–4, 151–52, 167–72

municipal market reform: in Boston, 158–67; in Europe, 185–189; in Midwest and South, 167–72; nationwide, xx, 151–58, 173–74, 180–85, 189–94, 203–4; in New York, 191, 194–200; in Philadelphia, 194–95; in Washington, D.C., 173–80

Nashville, 199

National Guard. *See* armories/National Guard

Index

National Municipal League, 174, 189,
201–3
nativism, 82, 83, 86, 96, 196
New Castle, Pa., 130
New Haven, 133
New Jersey, 27, 77, 114, 142, 143, 154;
Newark, 154; Trenton, 8, 46
New Orleans, 5, 27–28, 55–56, 56, 199;
market laws, 14, 17, 133; unique market
system, 88, 91, 174, 199, 201
New York City, xviii, xix; in antebellum
period, 86, 92; Central Park, 93; city
charter, 87; city hall, 22; Commissioners'
Map of 1811, 75–77, 76; Croton Aque-
duct, 71, 79; in early republic, 3, 5, 7, 8,
19–22, 43, 46–47; in 1880s and 90s, 182–
85; Five Points, 63–64; and municipal
reform movement, 191, 195–200; in
post–Civil War era, 117, 119, 132–48,
153–54, 175; Tweed ring, 119, 132, 134;
in 20th century, 201, 202. See also meat
shops
New York City markets: Bear Market, 31,
57, 58, 65; Catharine Market, 53, 58, 60,
146; Centre Market, 46, 57, 68, 75, 80–
81, 139, 146; Clinton Market, 77, 78, 81,
133, 146; Crown Market, 43; Essex
Market, 57, 139, 146; Fly Market, 7, 15,
19–20, 27, 37, 45, 54, 57, 58, 65, 73–74,
204; Franklin Market, 43, 82; Fulton
Fish Market, 140; Fulton Market, 146,
153, 182–84, 191, 196; Gansevoort
Market, 197; Jefferson Market, xviii,
43, 72, 73, 88–89, 89, 133, 139, 140,
146; Lafayette Market, 43; Liberty
Market, 43; Manhattan Market, 118,
140–43, 142; Monroe Market, 43, 82;
Old Slip Market, 43; Oswego Market,
57; Spring Street Market, 77; Tompkins
Market, 139, 139, 146; Union Market,
82, 146; Wallabout Market, 197; Weehawken Market, 82; West Washington Market, 147. See also Bronx
Terminal Market; Washington Market,
New York
New York City mayors: Franklin Edson,
145–46; William Gaynor, 196; James

Harper, 84–86; John F. Hylan, 200;
Robert H. Morris, 82; Fernando Wood,
89–93, 90, 110, 137
New York State, 160; Assembly, 140, 159;
Constitution, 86–87. See also Albany;
Brooklyn; Buffalo; Long Island; New
York City; Rochester
Newark, N.J., 154
Norfolk, 5, 15, 30, 153

Ohio, 51, 133. See also Cincinnati; Cleveland; Columbus; Dayton; Petersburg
Omaha, 157
O'Neil, David K., xii
opera houses, combined with markets, 40,
131–32
Oregon, 166, 202

parades, xvii, 49, 50, 60–61, 61, 64–68,
66, 67
Paris, 84, 91, 134, 143, 176, 181. See also
Les Halles
parking. See market peace (order); traffic;
wagons/carts
Parris, Alexander, 41
patriotism, 60–61, 64–68, 126, 133, 164
Paxton, John Adams, 5
peddlers, 5, 8, 31. See also hawkers;
hucksters; street vendors
Pennsylvania, xviii, xix–xx; Assembly, 131,
159; Supreme Court, 102–4, 108–10,
124. See also specific cities
pepperpot, 20, 21
Petersburg, Ohio, 51
Petersen, Frederick A., 136–37
petitioning, 3, 4, 7, 18–20, 29–30, 32–34,
49, 68, 74–81, 84–85, 124, 128, 160
Philadelphia, xix; in antebellum period,
94–117, 99, 119–22; in early republic
5, 7–8, 11, 18–23, 24, 51, 67; market
attendance in 1917, 203; and municipal
reform movement, 194–95; in post–
Civil War era, 130–33, 147, 155, 162,
175
Philadelphia markets, 6, 21, 121; Delaware
Avenue Fish Market, 96, 97; Dock
Street Market, 195; Eastern Market,

Index

114–15, 117; Farmers' Market, 115–17, *116, 120;* Hubbell Market, 96; Jersey Market, 12, *30, 97,* 99, *101;* New (South Second Street) Market, 5, *66,* 120, 194, *195;* Northern Liberties Market, 5; Norwich Market, 31; Reading Terminal Market, xii, 189; Washington (Nanny Goat) Market, 96, *96;* Western Market, 109–10, 112–14, *113, 114,* 117. *See also* High Street Market, Philadelphia

Philadelphia mayors: Robert T. Conrad, 104; Charles Gilpin, 103; Alexander Henry, 106, 108, 112–13; Richard Vaux, 105–6, 115

pigs, *52, 55,* 97

Pilmore, Joseph, 57

Pike Place Market, xvi

Pittsburgh, 18, 35, *36,* 43, *44,* 201, 202

politics. *See* American Republican Party; Democrats; Whigs

population, 93, 95–96, 143, 160, 201

Portland, Ore., 202

Portsmouth, Va., 14, 34

poultry, 7, 51, 52, 153, 189

preachers, 57

privatizing markets, xviii, xix; in New York, 118, 119, 140–44, 146; in Pennsylvania, 119, 122–32, 147; in Philadelphia, 95–122, 147; in Washington, D.C., 176–79. *See also* deregulation; market house companies; meat shops

produce. *See* fruits/vegetables (produce)

Project for Public Spaces, xvi

prostitutes, 96, 179–80

Providence, R.I., 34, 133

public good (welfare), xvii, xx, 3, 4, 23, 25, 71, 79. *See also* market laws; moral economy

public health, xv, xvii, xix, 15–17, 78–91, 144, 148, 156–57, 162–64, 172. *See also* hygiene; sanitation

public order, 138, 186. *See also* market peace (order); traffic

public works, xvii, xix, 3, 71, 98, 109, 172

Pullman, Ill., 174

pushcarts, 199, 200

Quakers, 11–12, 53

Quincy, Josiah, Jr. (1772–1864), 12, 40–42, *40,* 158

Quincy, Josiah (son, 1802–1882), 158–60, 165

railroad: and food transportation, 51, 151, 156–60, 200, 202; use of streets for, 95–108; with direct connection to markets, 172, 187–89, 196–200. *See also* streetcars, train stations

railroad companies: Boston and Albany, 160; New York Central and Hudson, 143, 185; Pennsylvania, 105, 189, 198; Philadelphia and Columbia, 99; Philadelphia and Reading, 189

Raleigh, 133

Read, John Meredith, 108–9

Reading, Pa., 129, 131

Reading Terminal Market, Philadelphia, xii, 189

Reconstruction, 168–71

refrigeration, 178, 197, 204. *See also* cold storage; ice/icehouses

reform, of market laws, 71–94, 203–4. *See also* municipal market reform

regrating, 5, 8

republicanism, and market regulations, xix, 4, 7, 8, 11, 22, 23

Rhode Island: Providence, 34, 133; Society for the Encouragement of Domestic Industry, 156

Rice, John, 101, 103, 105, 108, 112

riots, 86, 96, *96*

Risch, Theodor, 188

Roanoke, Va., 174

Robinson, Solon, 138

Rochester, N.Y., 199, 202, 203

Root, John Wellborn, 181

Royall, Anne Newport, 5, 26, 41–42

St. Francisville, La., 7, 42

St. Louis, 38, *38,* 155, 157, 162, 167, 203; market laws, 11, 13, 17, 23; meat shops, 168

St. Louis markets: Soulard Market, 29, 168; Union Market, 133, 168, *169*

Index

ABOUT THE AUTHOR

Helen Tangires is administrator at the Center for Advanced Study in the Visual Arts, National Gallery of Art, Washington, D.C. She received a B.A. in art history from the Johns Hopkins University, an M.B.A. in management from Lamar University in Beaumont, Texas, and a Ph.D. in American studies from George Washington University. She is a frequent contributor to books and journals on urban foodways and is an active member of the Society of Architectural Historians. A native of Baltimore, she has traveled widely throughout Europe, Latin America, and the Middle East.

RELATED BOOKS IN THE SERIES

Apostle of Taste: Andrew Jackson Downing, 1815–1852
David Schuyler

Boston's "Changeful Times": Origins of Preservation and Planning in America
Michael Holleran

Cities and Buildings: Skyscrapers, Skid Rows, and Suburbs
Larry R. Ford

The City Beautiful Movement
William H. Wilson

Entrepreneurial Vernacular: Developers' Subdivisions in the 1920s
Carolyn S. Loeb

Greenbelt, Maryland: A Living Legacy of the New Deal
Cathy D. Knepper

Historic American Towns along the Atlantic Coast
Warren Boeschenstein

Invisible New York: The Hidden Infrastructure of the City
Stanley Greenberg

The Last Great Necessity: Cemeteries in American History
David Charles Sloan

Local Attachments: The Making of an American Urban Neighborhood, 1850 to 1920
Alexander von Hoffman

John Nolen and Mariemont: Building a New Town in Ohio
Millard F. Rogers

Manufacturing Montreal: The Making of an Industrial Landscape, 1850 to 1930
Robert Lewis

The New England Village
Joseph S. Wood

The Sanitary City: Urban Infrastructure in America from Colonial Times to the Present
Martin V. Melosi